D1046949

MY PRISON, MY HOME

Also by Haleh Esfandiari

Reconstructed Lives: Women and Iran's Islamic Revolution

MY PRISON, MY HOME

One Woman's Story of Captivity in Iran

HALEH ESFANDIARI

An Imprint of HarperCollins*Publishers*

HarperCollins books may be purchased for educational, business, or sales promotional use. For information, please write: Special Markets Department, HarperCollins Publishers, 10 East 53rd Street, New York, NY 10022.

FIRST EDITION

Designed by Mary Austin Speaker

Library of Congress Cataloging-in-Publication Data is available upon request.

ISBN: 978-0-06-158327-8

09 10 11 12 13 ID/QWF 10 9 8 7 6 5 4 3 2 1

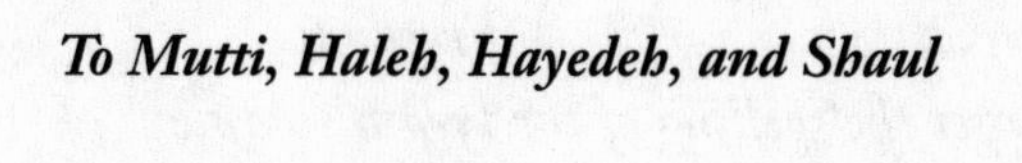

To Mutti, Haleh, Hayedeh, and Shaul

Freedom
is when you forget the spelling of the tyrant's name
and your mouth's saliva is sweeter than Persian pie,
and though your brain is wrung tight as the horn of a ram
nothing drops from your pale-blue eyes.

—Joseph Brodsky, "A Part of Speech"

CONTENTS

1 The "Robbery" 1

2 An Iranian Childhood 17

3 A Career Interrupted 34

4 The Interrogation 52

5 "Things Will Get Worse" 71

6 The Lull 89

7 The Arrest 122

8 Evin Prison 155

9 The Release 185

10 Freedom 208

Epilogue 219

Acknowledgments 225

MY PRISON, MY HOME

1.

THE "ROBBERY"

THE EARLY HOURS OF DECEMBER 30, 2006, began for me like any day when I would depart Tehran for the United States. I had come back to Iran, as I did two or three times a year, to visit my ninety-three-year-old mother. The doorbell rang at one a.m. It was Mr. Modarress, the taxi driver I used whenever I was in Iran, to take me to the airport. My mother held up a Quran for me to kiss and walk under for blessing and good luck; from a jug, she poured water on the hallway floor outside the apartment, as is customary in Iran to ensure a voyager a safe, prosperous journey.

Mother had stopped coming to visit us in the States after suffering a stroke two years earlier, although she could manage the shorter trip to Vienna, where my sister, Hayedeh, lived. Hayedeh came to Tehran once a year, on my mother's birthday. I came more often, and always made it a point to spend Christmas with Mother in Tehran, returning to Washington, D.C., to be with my family for New Year's Day. On this night, Mother and I sat up together, waiting for the driver. We talked about my childhood in Tehran; as well as my daughter, Haleh; my grandchildren, Ariana and Karenna, ages six and four; and my husband, Shaul. Mother was very fond of her grandchildren and great-grandchildren. I always saved these stories for the last few hours, to keep her mind away from my leaving.

Mother—"Mutti" as we called her in the German tradition—had come to Iran as a twenty-three-year-old bride in the late 1930s. She had met and fallen in love with my father while at the University of Vienna, where he was studying for his doctorate in botany. In more than fifty-five years of marriage, she had never fallen out of love. When my father died in 1995, she chose to remain in Iran, wishing to be buried next to him.

On this night, Mutti was on edge. "If you were only in Austria already!" she said. "I will feel better when you call me from Vienna Airport." I tried to sound upbeat. "I will see you in three months," I replied. I never prolonged our good-byes. They were too difficult for her. I kissed her face one last time, smoothed her gray hair, and walked down the stairs.

As I got into Mr. Modarress's beat-up Peykan, the most common passenger car in Iran, I saw my mother looking down at me and waving from an upstairs window. She had removed her shawl, and I could see the beige cashmere sweater I had given her. Her last words to the driver had been "Call me when *Khanum Doktor* [Madame Doctor] is gone." Ever since I had received my Ph.D. in 1964, my proud mother always referred to me as "Frau Doktor" when she spoke of me to Europeans, and "Khanum Doktor" when she spoke to Iranians.

It was a cold, clear Tehran night. The haze from factory smokestacks and car exhaust pipes that shrouds the city by day had dissipated. The street was quiet. No one else was out—not even at the revolutionary magistrate's court at the end of the street, where I often saw people escorted in wearing handcuffs. My mother's street was usually packed with parked cars and shoppers by eight a.m. Residents blocked their small driveways with huge flowerpots to stop nonresidents from stealing their parking spaces. Only when evening fell did Street No. 18 revert back to its residents.

I checked again that I had my passport, plane ticket, and other documents, and settled into the backseat, only mildly apprehensive, as I always was when leaving Iran. Under President Ahmadinejad, who had been elected a little over a year before, the security services had cracked down on writers and academics. We all knew of newspaper closures and arrests. The well-known intellectual and political philosopher Ramin Jahanbegloo had been arrested at the airport on his way to Europe, and spent four months at Evin Prison, where he was coerced into saying he had unknowingly acted against the interests of state security. But Jahanbegloo was interested in politically charged ideas, such as democratic transitions. My work as the director of the Middle East Program at the Woodrow Wilson Center in Washington, D.C., on the other hand, merely involved organizing talks and conferences on Middle Eastern issues, and hardly merited the attention of the Iranian authorities.

In the car, Modarress was not his usual talkative self. He drove in silence. He was also going slowly. Usually, he acted like everyone else in Tehran's frantic, everything-goes traffic, weaving in and out of the lanes as if he were on a racetrack. Now he seemed preoccupied—with monetary or family problems, I assumed. He is getting old, I thought. He doesn't like driving at night anymore. The day before, he had made all sorts of excuses not to drive me to the airport. His mother-in-law was sick, he said; he might have to go to the provinces, to Tabriz. But my mother insisted. "You are the only driver I trust to take *Khanum Doktor* to the airport," she told him and in the end he came.

We were almost at the exit ramp to Yadegar-e Imam Highway, the road that would take us to the airport, when I first noticed the dark green Peugeot sedan that had pulled alongside us. The driver was motioning for us to stop. When we didn't, the Peugeot began to force us off the road. I had called my mother earlier to wish her good night; we had hung up, but I was still holding the cell phone in my hand, unsure what was happening, thinking that perhaps we had a flat tire. I had barely made out the Peugeot's four occupants before our car was pushed onto the shoulder, blocked off by the Peugeot, its doors inches away from the hood of our car.

Three men, large knives strapped to their hips, jumped out of the car. They all seemed to be wearing identical, olive drab outfits. One, a tall, burly man with a crude Persian accent, ordered Modarress to switch off the motor, open the trunk, and hand him the car keys. Even in the dark, I could make out an ugly, pockmarked, unshaven face. He took my suitcase. Another disheveled man snatched my carry-on bag from the front passenger seat. The third got into the backseat beside me. In the semidarkness he looked sinister. Slivers of light glinted on his rimless eyeglasses and bald head. Astonishingly, he was grinning as he examined the contents of my handbag. "Take everything, but leave my passport and plane ticket," I managed to say. "I am traveling tonight."

He paid no heed. Still grinning, he took both my American and Iranian passports, my plane ticket, and my purse. He inched his way closer to me and thrust his hand into my coat pockets. The ridiculous thought crossed my mind that, in the Islamic Republic, strange men were not allowed to sit next to or look at women they did not know, let alone search their coat pockets. I pleaded again for my passport and plane ticket but to no avail. I kept praying for a passing car to stop. None did.

I heard Modarress's voice outside the car, followed by the trunk being slammed shut. The burly man, who clearly was in charge, reappeared at my window. "Did you find everything?" he asked the man sitting beside me. The man nodded. "Okay. Let's move." I heard him order Modarress to sit behind the wheel and put his head down, then change his mind and order him to lie down on the front seat. Modarress meekly complied. "If you raise your head, I will break your neck; I will beat you to death. I will kill you," he told him. He ordered me to get on the floor. "There is no room," I said, eyeing the narrow space between the front and the back seats. "Get down, you bitch," he said, "or I will smash your skull; I will kill you. Do as you are told." In minute, they were gone. As I raised my head, I noticed that the license plate on the Peugeot was splattered with mud—I couldn't read a single number.

Modarress raised his head from the seat. "We were robbed," he said. His voice was shaky. "We have to report this to the highway police."

"We don't have a phone," I said. My cell phone had been taken, along with my purse and baggage. Modarress said they hadn't taken his cell phone—a much-prized possession in Tehran. They hadn't taken his wallet, either. Or my Cartier wristwatch. Or the necklace I was wearing.

The highway police told Modarress that we should stay put and wait for them. I used Modarress's cell phone to call my mother. "How quickly you got to the airport," she said. I told her what had happened and quickly added, "But I'm not harmed, nor is Modarress." All her life, my mother had experienced severe coughing attacks when she was upset. As I held the phone to my ear, I could hear her hard, uneven breathing and the inevitable coughing fit that followed. I tried to reassure her. "Who cares about the lost bags?" I said. "I am alive and they didn't harm me."

☙ Like a Refugee

Although I was frightened and disconcerted, my mind was also focused on practical matters. I asked my mother to phone my sister, Hayedeh, in Vienna and my husband, Shaul, in Potomac, Maryland, outside Washington, to tell them what had happened. I also asked her to call my travel agent and have him cancel my ticket.

I got out of the car and stood by the side of the road, staring down the dark, empty highway. I was buffeted by conflicting emotions. I was grateful I hadn't been kidnapped, injured, or killed. Like every other visitor to Tehran, I had heard of people being abducted from their cars or homes and held for ransom; I had heard of the armed robberies, which had increased in recent years. I had also read of Iranians being beaten up and thrown, half-dead, into alleys—the ugly handiwork, it was thought, of the secret police. But I was still in one piece. I had not been knifed by my assailants. They had not hit me, broken my jaw. I was grateful to be alive.

But I had lost all of my belongings and money. Worse, I had lost my Iranian identification cards and my Iranian and American passports. I dreaded the many days of red tape and bureaucracy that I knew lay ahead. I felt like a refugee from some war-torn country, without papers, without proof of identity, unable to travel. Despite my wool coat with its fur collar, I was cold and numb. I was astonished that not one of the cars that drove by stopped to offer help, but prostitution is rampant in and around Tehran. They probably think I am one of them, I thought ruefully, standing on a highway in the middle of the night.

I was startled when two men emerged from behind the bushes along the island dividing the highway. They, too, seemed to be wearing olive drab outfits. They spoke quietly to Modarress. Then, as suddenly as they had appeared, they left. I asked Modarress who they were. "They are members of the highway patrol," he said. I thought it strange that their outfits were seemingly identical to those of the men who had just robbed us. Besides, I had never heard of a highway patrol appearing on foot. I said as much to Modarress. He did not reply.

It took an hour for a police car to show up. Two officers, neat and businesslike in their uniforms, motioned for us to get into the back of the police car. I had been standing on the highway with Modarress as we waited for the police, not wishing to sit in our car after the robbery. I was now grateful to be out of the cold, but Modarress, mindful of Iranian protocol, preferred to stand outside and answer the officers' questions through the window. As we gave a detailed account of the robbery, the policemen shook their heads, as if in disbelief. They exchanged glances when Modarress described the make and color of the car and the clothes our assailants were wearing, but they continued to take notes and said nothing. They asked for and wrote down the usual particulars: my name, address, date of birth, place of birth, ID number, contents of suitcase, carry-on bag, and purse. They had me sign the completed report, gave me a copy, and told me to take it to the police station at Shahrak-e Gharb, a seven-minute car ride from Mutti's apartment. I didn't know how we were going to get to the police station or home, since Modarress had surrendered his car keys during the robbery. But Modarress said he kept a spare key in the car, and we drove off.

At two-thirty in the morning, the police station had an abandoned look to it. A sleepy guard registered our names and took away Modarress's cell phone. The sole officer on duty seemed uninterested in our story. "There is no one here," he said, sweeping his arm across the empty room, as if we needed convincing. "Go home and report back first thing in the morning."

All the lights were on in my mother's apartment in the otherwise dark building. The caretaker let me in. I sent Modarress home and told him to come back at seven a.m. He said he would go back to the scene of the robbery to look for my Iranian passport and papers, since it was quite common for thieves to take the money and valuables from a purse and throw everything else on the side of the road. He thought they would keep the American passport.

In the apartment, my mother was fully dressed, waiting for me. We embraced and repeated, more than once, that the important thing was that I was safe. I called Shaul and Hayedeh. I still thought this was a simple robbery, and Shaul agreed with me.

It was nearly dawn. Mother took two pills and went to bed. I collapsed on a sofa and dozed off in a fitful sleep.

❧ Getting a New Passport

Over the next three days, I went about the tedious business of getting my life back in order and replacing my stolen passport. Since I was familiar with Iranian bureaucracy, I began contacting friends, trying to find people who could intercede on my behalf to cut through the delays and red tape. My first call the morning after the robbery was to my cousin Farhad. "How's Vienna?" he asked. I told him I was still in Tehran. "Has something happened to Mutti?" he replied. I told him about the robbery. He was suddenly quiet. "I'll come over right away."

Farhad is several years younger than me. We grew up in adjacent houses. He had lost his father at a young age, and my father had watched over and mentored him. He was now the man of the family, shouldering responsibility for its elderly women: his own mother, Mutti, and another widowed aunt. Farhad was soft-spoken and gentle, courteous to a fault. But there was also a firm, steely quality to him, and he knew his way around Iranian bureaucracy. I dreaded making the rounds of government offices alone. Farhad ran his own small engineering firm, and I disliked taking him away from his work, but my mother insisted. "You need a man by your side," she said. "I know this country better than you do." I swallowed my feminist pride and asked him to accompany me.

Farhad arrived with his son, Kami. Only twenty-five, Kami was as gentle and soft-spoken as his father, but he was tall and well built, towering over everyone else. His height alone will intimidate everyone, I thought optimistically.

Our first stop, once Modarress joined us, was the neighborhood police station. At eight in the morning, the station was crowded and noisy. Men and women were there reporting burglaries, family disputes, and thefts of cell phones. Police officers walked in with men who had been arrested in a drug bust. A mother was desperately looking for her son, who had disappeared two days earlier. We made our rounds, from desk to desk, clerk to clerk. I had to repeat over and over the details of the robbery, fill out forms, secure signatures and official stamps. Farhad, having heard my story half a dozen times, was anxious to move along. Modarress, who usually took the lead when I needed to get things done in Tehran, uncharacteristically stayed in the background, restlessly shifting from foot to foot. We needed the signature of the police chief, but he was on a hajj, or pilgrimage, to Mecca, and his deputy had not yet come in. More waiting. The deputy finally arrived, read the report, remarked nonchalantly that "such things happen," signed the papers, and sent us to the revolutionary magistrate's court on my mother's street to have the police report certified.

On the way to the court, Modarress, who was following us in his own car, rang Farhad on his cell phone to say he was having a problem with his brakes and couldn't stay with us. That proved to be the last I saw or heard from our "loyal" driver except for a brief visit to my mother's apartment to collect his fee for our ill-fated journey to the airport. After that, he disappeared.

The two entrances to the revolutionary magistrate's court were separated by a curtain, denoting one side for men and the other for women. Farhad and I located the presiding judge. He wore pants and an open-necked shirt and jacket. Not a cleric, I noted to myself—no robe. A neatly trimmed beard—no stubble. He was polite and well-spoken—not rude. He offered me a seat, signed the papers, advised my cousin to make copies of everything, and sent us on our way. He, too, seemed to think he was dealing with a simple robbery.

The Ministry of Foreign Affairs, where I needed to go for a letter of authorization before my new passport could be issued, was housed in the former headquarters of the Anglo-Iranian Oil Company. The era when the British had exercised considerable power and influence in Iran was long gone. The street names around the building were also long gone. In a frenzy of post-revolutionary fervor, the names of Tehran's main avenues, great squares and parks, even nondescript side streets had been renamed to celebrate the revolution and its heroes. Shah Reza Avenue, named after the founder of the former ruling dynasty, was now Enqelab, or the Avenue of the Revolution. Kakh, or Palace Avenue, had become Palestine Avenue. And Roosevelt Avenue, named for the American president, had been changed to Mofattah, memorializing a clerical leader and martyr of the revolution.

We headed downtown to the ministry through the chaotic traffic. Hundreds of cars—some of them the expensive BMWs, Mercedes-Benzes, and Audis of Tehran's newly rich class, but mostly older cars, belching smoke from their tailpipes—competed with buses, motorcycles, cyclists, and pedestrians for the same space. Traffic lights changed color dutifully but went largely unheeded. Cars crept into blocked intersections, bringing traffic to a standstill. People shouted at one another, and occasional fistfights broke out between exasperated drivers. Policemen stood by, refusing to get involved, not even pretending to direct the traffic.

The passport bureau at the ministry was in a large, airy room. Five male clerks, in sweaters over open-necked shirts, with stubble on their cheeks, sat behind five desks. They shuffled about in slipper-like sandals, open at the back. Stubble and slippers, I came to learn over the coming weeks and months, were the hallmarks of the Islamic Republic. The outward scruffiness mirrored an inner reality: unhurried, sloppy in dress and in the performance of their duties, these men demanded as little of themselves as the bureaucracy demanded of them.

One of the clerks was expecting us. My countless phone calls to Shaul had borne fruit. Shaul had called a friend, Hadi, a professor of politics at the University of Tehran, who was currently a visiting scholar at the Wilson Center. Hadi had good contacts at the Iranian Interests Section in Washington, D.C., the office that handled Iranian consular affairs in the absence of full diplomatic relations between the two countries.

The clerk had in hand a fax from the interests section certifying that my stolen Iranian passport had been issued in Washington and providing the relevant passport details. The Foreign Ministry could now provide the authorization letter I needed. The clerk ordered tea and got down to work. By the time we were done with the formalities and the passport bureau chief had affixed his signature to the documents, it was past one o'clock in the afternoon—too late to get to the main passport office, which was already closed. But at least we had the name of the director, and that would give us an entrée the next day. "You'll have your new passport in two or three days," the clerk told me. I was elated.

Back at my mother's place, I called my travel agent and reserved a flight for Wednesday, three days away. I telephoned Shaul and told him to expect me. Many people had called my mother when they learned of the robbery, one of whom had even heard that I had been robbed, beaten, and hospitalized. A couple of close friends came by that evening. Like me, they had no reason to suspect anything other than that I had simply been the unfortunate victim of a robbery. They shook their heads in sympathy, remarked on the growing insecurity in the city, commiserated on the loss of my passports and papers, and assured me that it would all be behind me in a few days. Only my childhood friend Ferry and his wife were skeptical. "This was no ordinary robbery," Ferry's wife said. "It seems political to us." "Nonsense," I responded. "It was a robbery, pure and simple."

❧ The Passport Office

The next day, a Sunday, we went to the passport office on Sattar Khan Avenue in west Tehran. Farhad and I entered separately through the men's and women's checkpoints, divided by the usual tatty curtain. The female guard on my side of the curtain conducted a superficial search of my purse and let me through. She was friendly and smiling. In the first decade after the revolution, smiles on the faces of mid-level civil servants were rare, deemed a sign of frivolousness, unseemly in an Islamic state. Thanks to President Khatami, who was elected on a reformist platform in 1997 and spent two four-year terms fighting the hard-liners, the scowls of government officials were no longer de rigueur. (Tehran's wits referred to Khatami as Seyyed-e Khandan, the smiling cleric, a play on words in Persian that denoted both his sunny visage and his relative ineffectiveness.) During Khatami's presidency, university students—men and women—mixed more freely; women fought for and secured more freedom in matters of dress; color returned to clothing on the streets; young girls moved about the city with hair showing beneath their headscarves, their nails polished, a touch of lipstick on their lips. I realized how miraculous it was, two years into Ahmadinejad's far more restrictive presidency, that in a government office I was still encountering a smiling face.

Farhad and I headed straight for the director's office, past the queues of people waiting to hand in or pick up forms. We ended up in a large room, where, we were told, the final approval for a new passport would be issued. On the wall, as in all government offices, were pictures of the founder of the Islamic Republic, Ayatollah Khomeini; the current supreme leader, Ayatollah Khamenei; and President Ahmadinejad. Three women, one in a black chador, two wearing the ample scarf known as a *maghna'eh*—which covers the forehead, hair, and ears; fits tightly under the chin; then drapes over the shoulders and upper back and chest—sat behind desks. The lone man in the room, obviously in charge, sat at his own desk, at some distance from the women. We carried our growing file from desk to desk. There was more signing, registering, paper shuffling, and waiting. Finally, the man in charge called my name and handed me two letters. I was to take one back to the Foreign Ministry and one to "the President's Bureau." Each of these two offices, in turn, had to give me letters approving my application for a new passport. "Once you get these letters, you should expect to wait at least two weeks before your passport can be issued," he said.

I was shattered. I had been told it would only take three days. But far more important, I knew that "the President's Bureau" was a euphemism for the Ministry of Intelligence and Security. I was familiar with the ministry's fearsome reputation. It was responsible for internal security, and was the regime's political watchdog, its secret police. It harassed intellectuals, journalists, and even the mildest of dissidents; it made arrests. It had been responsible for disappearances, even assassinations. Still, I convinced myself this merely meant more forms and interviews and, certainly, more delays.

I was directed to see a Mr. Torabi in the same building. Farhad and I went downstairs, found the office marked President's Bureau, entered rooms which turned out to be quite well furnished, and asked for Mr. Torabi. I do not know if this was his real name or a fictitious one, as was often the case with Intelligence Ministry officials I later encountered. Mr. Torabi was not there. When I went in the following day, he was not there, either. "You just missed him. He won't be back till Wednesday," I was told. I felt that I was being sent after black beans, as the Persian expression goes—being given the runaround.

At home, I canceled my airline reservation and once again telephoned Shaul. "There will be a two-week delay," I told him. "We have to find someone who can expedite things." In Iran, contacts—and money—are crucial in situations like mine. Shaul promised to make phone calls. Over the next four months, I would make, cancel, and remake these same airline reservations several times, each one a marker on the barometer of my rising, and then dashed, hopes.

A Bleak New Year's Eve

I had expected to spend New Year's Eve with my husband and our family in Washington; I was now spending it with Mutti in Tehran. My mother loves festive occasions: birthdays, Christmas, New Year's, the Iranian new year festival, Nowruz. As a child I learned to love these chances to bring people together, to enjoy the company of family and friends, to laugh and tell stories, and, like Mutti, I was punctilious about observing them. In our household, failure to telephone a relative on a birthday or to mark a celebration was a serious matter. Shaul often teased me about the importance I attached to such gestures. Although Mother and I decided to stay home, I wanted to make New Year's Eve as joyful for her as possible.

I walked to the fancy new grocery store a block from my mother's apartment and bought salmon and caviar. We set the table with a beautiful tablecloth and Mother's best Rosenthal china, which she kept in a special cupboard in her apartment. Dinner, however, turned out to be a somber affair. Unease hovered over the table. Both my mother and I sensed that the normal order of our lives had been interrupted. Just how very deeply it had been disrupted, neither of us even dimly understood.

The next day I went with Kami to take care of my cell phone, which was now in the hands of my assailants. In Iran, you can buy a cell phone at a variety of stores, but a number has to be purchased from the government phone company. The number is encoded on a chip that is installed in the phone. I had to cancel my old cell phone number and purchase a new one. At the telephone company office, I handed over a batch of documents to a clerk: my "deed" of ownership, the barely legible Xerox copy of my birth certificate as proof of identity, and the police report, duly notarized by the revolutionary magistrate's court, attesting that my cell phone had been stolen. But here, too, bureaucracy was alive and well. They could cancel my old telephone number, I was told, but they could issue me a new number only if I produced a picture ID—the original, not a Xerox copy. I repeated the obvious: my ID card had been stolen; it would be months before I could obtain a new one. The clerk shrugged. It was not his concern. I'll be home in two weeks, anyway, I told myself as I left empty-handed.

Finally, on Wednesday, I saw Torabi, the man in the Intelligence Ministry's "President's Bureau," having called the day before to make sure he would be there. He went over the robbery with me again and asked me a few more questions. "Why don't you step outside and wait for my colleague, Mr. Ja'fari. He wants to talk to you," he said. I waited in the reception room. After about half an hour, the door behind me opened and a man asked me to come in.

Ja'fari was sitting at a table behind a laptop. He was in his mid-thirties, of medium height, with a bit of stubble on his face. He wore an open-necked shirt beneath a modified safari jacket. A smirk never left his face. His manner alternated between solicitous official—"Tell me again about the robbery"—and faceless bureaucrat—"Date of birth? Identity card number?" He appeared to be reading the questions from his laptop. At first he asked questions and simply nodded at my answers. Then he handed me a sheaf of blank paper, repeated the same questions and posed many others in writing, and instructed me to write down my replies.

Yet, still, I was only slightly uneasy: the attention of the Intelligence Ministry was never welcome, but I had been assured by friends that clearance by the ministry for lost passport applications was routine. Asking for my responses in writing cast the interview in a more serious light, but most of the information was ordinary enough: name, family name, husband's name, children, employer, salary. A few of the questions seemed unnecessarily intrusive: occupation and employer of husband, daughter, son-in-law, sister, brother. Ja'fari seemed overly interested in the details of my Wilson Center salary: amount, deductions for federal and state taxes and for Social Security and retirement, the biweekly method of payment. Concerned lest my salary, when converted into Iranian, rials seem to him exorbitant, I made all this as convoluted as possible. (Later, on the day of my release, when I saw Ja'fari's shiny, silver-gray Peugeot, I concluded that I need not have worried. The Intelligence Ministry took very good care of its own.)

I found it odd that Ja'fari wanted the names and ages of my granddaughters, as well as a list of the people I saw regularly in Washington. I came to understand only much later that, in the style of the now-defunct East German secret police, the Stasi, the Iranian secret police collected masses of information, no matter how insignificant or useless, on everyone who happened to attract their attention. As with the Stasi, such information contributed nothing to national security, but fat dossiers were regarded as proof of "thoroughness" and helped inflate the self-regard of the intelligence officers. When Ja'fari asked me if I was married to a Jew, an alarm bell should have gone off, but it didn't. I failed to catch the implied menace in the question. He has never met a Muslim woman who married a Jew, I thought. Trying to strike a friendly tone, I even offered to show Ja'fari around if he ever came to Washington. Notwithstanding a very few friends' skeptical attitudes, I still believed I was the victim of an ordinary robbery and this was routine clearance before a new passport could be issued.

Ja'fari ended the interview around noon. I went home, never expecting to see him again. I assumed that my passport would be issued in a few days. But when I picked up the phone in my mother's apartment the next day, it was Ja'fari at the other end of the line. He instructed me to appear Saturday morning, this time at an Intelligence Ministry office. Mr. Ja'fari, which may or may not have been his real name, was to become my constant but unwelcome "companion" in the weeks and months ahead—an unshakable and controlling presence throughout a terrifying interrogation that would stretch out over the next eight months, nearly four of them spent in solitary confinement at Evin Prison.

2.

AN IRANIAN CHILDHOOD

I WAS BORN MARCH 3, 1940, in Tehran. My mother is Viennese and my father is from Kerman, in eastern Iran. Father came from an old established landed family, many of whose members also served in the government. My paternal great-grandfather, Vakil ol-Molk-e-Dovvom, was the governor of Kerman in the 1870s, and my grandfather Raf'at Dowleh was vice governor of the province before becoming a member of parliament. My paternal grandmother came from a clerical family; her brother was the highest-ranking cleric in Kerman. On the European side, my maternal grandfather, who died in World War I, owned a hotel in Marienbad, in Czechoslovakia, and my mother's older brother was a cloth merchant in Prague.

For the first six years of my life I lived in Karaj, twenty-five miles from Tehran, where my father was a professor of botany at the College of Agriculture.

My father couldn't have chosen a better place than Karaj to ease his Austrian bride into Iran, which in the 1930s remained traditional and offered few amenities. The college was a small, closed community, with a river and beautifully landscaped wooded areas. The faculty lived either in two-story houses or bungalows separated by hedges. In the summer, the gardeners sprinkled water over the college's unpaved streets to help settle the dust and cool the air.

By the time I was born, Mother had spent two years in Iran. She had thrown herself wholeheartedly into the culture and customs of her adopted country. But she ran a European household, and we spoke German at home and followed European customs. The stories she told were of Snow White and the Seven Dwarves, Cinderella, and Hansel and Gretel. I learned Persian stories from my nanny, who doubled as cook and housekeeper.

I loved the garden for its small streams, square ponds, flower beds, rose gardens and old trees, especially the catalpa, poplar, pine, and plane trees. With my nanny in tow, I would play hopscotch in the walkways of the garden and games of hide-and-seek with other children. This was paradise, I thought; but every time I said as much to my nanny, she would scold me, take me by the hand, and make me rinse my mouth to wash away my "blasphemous" words.

It didn't take long for my outgoing mother to make friends with a number of the professors and their families. The members of the faculty were mostly European-educated and could converse with her in German or in French. Mother had an affinity for those who spoke her native language.

The Schricker family, headed by Hans Shricker, an Austrian forestry specialist, lived next door to us and their eldest son, Adalbert, married my father's sister, Touran. Mother had lost both her parents at a relatively young age and was raised by her sisters in Vienna. The Schrickers became her surrogate parents. Mr. Schricker, a skilled carpenter, built a bassinet when my mother was pregnant with me, and once I was born, Mrs. Schricker showed Mother how to bathe a newborn, and how to diaper and dress me. Under Mrs. Schricker's tutelage, Mother sewed and knitted clothes for me, since ready-made children's clothing was a rarity in those days. Mrs. Schricker—warm, loving, practical, and down-to-earth—eased the pain of living away from home.

Unlike traditional Persian homes, our garden didn't have a wall around it, but pine trees served to shield it from the street. We had a large living room and a dining room, several bedrooms, and a bathroom with a bathtub and a Persian-style toilet, basically a basin sunk in the floor.

In the evenings Mother and Father would sit in the living room and listen to the radio, while I would play in a corner with my toys. My parents' friends, especially the Schrickers, would come over to listen to the European news broadcasts. Hitler had invaded Russia in June 1941, and one flank of the German's three-pronged attack was aimed at the oilfields of the Caucasus on Iran's border. In Karaj they all worried that the German army would overrun the Caucasus and advance into Iran.

The Allies were already concerned about German influence in Iran. Once Hitler invaded Russia, they desperately needed Iran's overland routes to supply the hard-pressed Russian army. Unable to persuade a proud and stubborn Reza Shah—the military officer who seized power in 1921, sent the Qajar dynasty packing, and founded a new dynasty in 1925—to abandon Iran's state of neutrality and join the Allied cause, Russia and Britain invaded Iran in August 1941, the Russians from the north, the British from the south. When Russian troops appeared at Karaj, Father remained at his teaching post in the College of Agriculture, but he sent Mother and me to Tehran, to my grandparents' house. I was happy to be reunited with my older stepbrother, Siamack, who was going to school in Tehran and already living with my grandmother.

My Grandparents

By the time I was born, my grandparents were living near the University of Tehran. They had moved to Tehran from Kerman when my grandfather was elected to parliament.

My grandmother's home was another world, utterly different

from our European household, where we spoke German, followed strict rules, sat around the table to have our meals, and ate Austrian food—schnitzel, boiled meat, soup, roast potatoes, and creamed spinach. Grandmother—Khanum Jan as we called her—ran a traditional Persian household. While my grandfather, who passed away just four years later, when I was five, was no longer the wealthy man he had been (his extensive land holdings had been seized under the previous reign), there was a great deal of coming and going, with visitors from their hometown constantly bringing the best dates and Kerman's distinctive sweets and pastries. At any given time, the cook would prepare meals for ten or more people. My favorite place was the kitchen, which was dark and smoky from the woodstove, and where the cook would often slip me a spoonful of white rice from the cooking pot. I loved the rice, the *aash*, a thick soup made of greens; the white cheese and walnuts, yogurt, and the fresh *sangak* flat bread from the corner bakery that came with every meal.

At home, Mother had been so worried we would get typhoid she insisted on cooking all the fruits and vegetables. At my grandparents', I was free from all the don'ts I heard at home. We ate sitting crossed-legged around a rectangular tablecloth spread on the floor. Mother sat on a chair at a small table set up just for her.

The house had a large garden with a pond where the household, including my grandmother, made their ablutions before each of the five daily prayers. The garden was divided into four large triangular flower beds. In each, a persimmon tree or a pomegranate tree stood among the flowers, rosebushes, and forsythias. The walls of the garden were thick with grapevines. In the fall, Grandmother would have a servant climb up a ladder and put a small sack around each cluster of grapes so that they would keep, even as the cold weather set in. Before the first frost she would have the sacks removed and the grapes picked. That way, she always had grapes to serve out of season.

The servants' rooms and the outhouse were at the far end of the garden. There were two toilets in the house, but Grandmother was too old fashioned to let anyone use them. Peddlers came to my grandmother's door every morning with donkey loads of melons, string beans, cucumbers, and fruit. Then there was the itinerant purveyor of *shahr-e farang*, or "the wonders of Europe," which consisted of a copper viewing box on four legs topped with minarets and bells. For a few rials, we could look into the darkened box and view moving images of exotic places and people. The *shahr-e farang* man offered a running commentary as the pictures galloped across the tiny screen. "Oh, see the queen of England majestically sitting on her throne, her crown on her head," he would say in a singsong voice and in rhyming couplets. "Now see the fierce tiger of Africa and the lion, king of the jungle."

In the winter, Grandmother would set up a traditional Persian *korsi* in her sitting room, which consisted of a low wooden table, measuring about four feet by four feet, placed over a charcoal brazier and covered with a large square quilt. Narrow mattresses were arranged around the quilt, and cushions were placed along the walls to lean against. On winter evenings, the family practically lived around the *korsi*, snuggling under the quilt to keep warm, eat, read, chat, play word games, recite poetry, and occasionally sleep. Grandmother always retired to her bed, but sometimes allowed the grandchildren to sleep under the *korsi* as a special treat. The servants had their own *korsi*, but it was off limits to the children.

Every Monday a mullah would come to the house and conduct a *rowzeh-khani*, a recital of religious martyrs' tales. This was the only time we children were not allowed into the sitting room, when adult family members joined the mullah and the servants sat cross-legged by the entrance as he somberly recited the heart-rending tale of the martyrdom of brave Hossein, the Prophet's grandson and the third Shi'ite imam, on the plains of Karbala in the seventh century.

My time with Khanum Jan helped shape my Iranian-Islamic identity. She read the Quran and explained religion to me as best she could. However, like many in my own and even in my father's generation, I remained a secular Muslim. Father came of age during the reign of Reza Shah. The king regarded religion and the clergy as obstacles to his furious modernizing. He saw to it that the school curriculum glorified Iran's pre-Islamic past, not its Islamic heritage. For my father and other Iranians like him, education abroad took care of the rest.

Khanum Jan, whom I loved dearly and who was the most important woman in my early life next to Mutti, was extremely tolerant, despite her religious upbringing. Generally speaking, she was broad-minded and receptive to modern changes—with one striking exception. When the veil was banned by government order in 1936, she stayed home for five years rather than go out into the street unveiled, a reaction not uncommon among women of her generation. The ban was another of Reza Shah's Westernizing measures. He wanted to bring women into the public space, schools, and the workplace. But the abolition of the veil was a highly radical measure, shocking to traditional society and bitterly opposed by the clergy. One of the first steps taken by the Islamic Republic after the overthrow of the monarchy in 1979 was to reimpose *hijab*, or Islamic dress, on women. But by then, the situation was reversed. Middle-class women now fought the imposition of the veil rather than its removal.

Despite my grandmother's own protest, her progressive mind-set was evident in the fact that she let her daughters, my aunts, go to school and did not object that they went unveiled. And when I married Shaul in 1965, when marriages between Muslims and Jews were highly unusual, she gave me her blessing, along with a beautiful pair of pearl earrings.

I don't recall ever seeing Khanum Jan in a black chador. Her personality was mirrored in the light colors she loved, and she often donned white, flowery chadors, allowing a bit of her hair to show beneath her headscarf. She was kind and welcoming to both her foreign-born daughter-in-law and son-in-law, and with her death in 1973, a piece of the cherished Iran of my childhood vanished along with her.

Europe

In December 1945, when I was almost six years old, Mother took me to Europe. She had not returned to Vienna since coming to Iran—Europe had been at war—and she had been longing to go back. Her youngest brother had died in the war and her two older sisters had moved to the United States. Her older brother, my uncle Max, was a successful merchant in Prague and she was eager to see him and her beloved Vienna again.

Father arranged for us to fly to Moscow on a plane that was taking Iran's new ambassador to the USSR. From Moscow we were to take the train to Prague. For a child who had seen only Karaj and Tehran, taking an airplane, staying in a hotel, and traveling by train was a sensational experience. Yet all I remember of Moscow are the dreary, dark afternoons and the large, cavernous hotel. In the evening, Mother would take me downstairs to the near-deserted restaurant for dinner. There were always one or two couples on the dance floor, but they looked forlorn in the empty dining room. We would rush through dinner and hurry back to our room.

On the day of our departure for Prague, the Iranian ambassador arranged for his car to drive us from the hotel to the train station. A woman from the Russian Intourist Agency, who had made our arrangements, put us in a first-class compartment and gave us food for the long journey. There was none to be bought on the train. The conductor who checked our tickets told Mutti to keep the door of our compartment locked at all times. We were also given a small cooking lamp, which Mutti could use to warm our meals. I can't remember how long the trip to Prague took, but I was glued to the window. Images from the journey remain etched in my memory: a desolate, gray landscape; burnt and demolished towns and villages; people lying huddled in the snow along the railway tracks; signs of hunger and illness evident even to a young child. At each stop, a mass of people rushed onto the train and banged on doors. I huddled against Mutti, crying in fear. At the Czech border, the conductor carried our suitcases to the crossing as we walked beside him in the snow. We were among the first passengers crossing here since 1940.

Prague, to my eyes, was a miracle of a city. My uncle Max picked us up at the train station. He was a tall, handsome, and very elegant man. He wore his hat tilted to one side, unlike my father, who wore his hat flat on his head. Uncle Max's wife, Inka, was a beauty. They lived in an apartment of large rooms and high ceilings: there were Persian rugs on the floors, antique furniture, walls covered with paintings, closets full of very fine china. A plump maid in a neat black dress and white apron came every day. Mother, who did not believe in idleness, immediately enrolled me in the neighborhood school, where I learned to speak Czech. (I promptly forgot it once we returned to Tehran.)

Uncle Max took Mutti and me to the biggest toy store in Prague and bought me a fair, blue-eyed doll. I was bedazzled. I had never seen so many toys. After two hours Mutti and Uncle Max had to drag me out kicking and screaming.

The food in Prague was also a revelation. There was ham and salami and sausages for breakfast and fat-laced meat and different sauces for lunch and dinner. I loved the dumplings and the black bread covered with lard. Uncle Max even took us to Spiendelmuehl, a very posh winter resort in the mountains. I had never seen so much snow! A carriage drawn by two horses would take us from the hotel to the ski slopes. I learned how to sled, and Mother, elated to be back in Europe, skied the whole day.

Mutti was impatient to get to Vienna. Uncle Max tried to dissuade her or, at least, to prepare her for the devastation the city had endured from bombing during the war. But she was adamant. She wanted to visit her mother's grave and look up some of her old friends. Finally, he bought us first-class train tickets and packed two suitcases full of food to take with us. Food was scarce in Vienna, and people could not be expected to share their meager rations with visitors or strangers.

The train departed in the evening. At first, Mutti and I were the sole occupants of the first-class compartment. Uncle Max warned

Mutti not to accept any packages from strangers and not to engage in conversation with other passengers. A lot of counterfeit money, false documents, and contraband were being smuggled from Czechoslovakia into Austria.

We had been on the train for more than an hour when the door opened and a tall, well-dressed woman entered the cabin. She was wearing a mink coat and hat and leather boots; she carried a large leather bag. She sat across from us without exchanging a word. Mother continued to tell me stories in a very low voice. As we neared the Austrian border, the woman closed the curtain and turned off the lights. She needed to sleep, she told my mother. Suddenly the door of the compartment opened and three or four Austrian and Czech officers flipped on the light and asked to see our passports and our bags. They didn't bother much with us, but they went through the woman's suitcase and handbag, item by item. I started crying and clung to Mother, wishing again we had stayed in Uncle Max's beautiful apartment; the woman scolded the officers for frightening a child.

The officers left with our passports, and one of them soon returned and handed Mutti our documents but told the woman to follow him. I remember her saying in German, "*So eine Freschheit*"—Such rudeness. As she bent down to put on her boots, she threw a small package at Mother's feet and walked out. With a quick motion with her foot, Mother pushed the package under the woman's seat. All this took place in the dark and in a split second. An hour later, the woman reappeared and without turning on the light asked Mother where her package was. Silently, Mutti pointed under the seat. She retrieved her bundle, took her suitcase and hat, and walked out of the cabin without a word. Uncle Max was livid when he heard the story. Had they searched the cabin, he said, the woman would have denied the package, most probably counterfeit money, was hers, and we would have been in serious trouble.

My father had arranged for us to stay with an Iranian friend of his, Ali Asghar Azizi, who had married into a well-to-do Austrian family. When Mother presented the Azizis with our two suitcases of food,

Mrs. Azizi put the ring-shaped salami around her neck and danced across the kitchen with joy.

Yet Vienna turned out to be a journey into almost unbearable loss for Mother. I had never seen her this way, as if in mourning, the hurt written all over her face. Every day of our three-week visit, we would leave the house and take the tram into town. Holding me tightly by the hand, Mother would wander from street to street, from neighborhood to neighborhood, tears rolling down her cheeks. At every turn another piece of her heart would break. She would point at the ruin of a house or building: this was where she had lived as a child; this was where she had gone to school; this was the park where she played; the theater she attended. She kept on whispering, "*Mein armes Oesterreich*"—My poor Austria. We went in search of the building where Father had lived as a student and to the Faculty of Agriculture at Tuerkishenspark where he had gone to university.

We walked along the Stadtpark, where she and Father had danced the waltz, past the opera house and the very exclusive Sacher Hotel and Café Mozart. Vienna was an occupied city, divided into American, British, French, and Russian zones. One evening when we were going home, a group of Russian soldiers boarded the tram. An old man was sitting in the front, holding an empty tin in his hand. One soldier grabbed the tin, put it on his head, and ridiculed the old man. Even as a child I felt his shame and humiliation. Frightened, we got off at the next stop, ran to another street, and waited for an hour in a café before making our way back to the house.

Vienna was a wrenching three-week hiatus during what turned out to be an enchanted eight-month stay in Prague with Uncle Max. I saw beautiful shops, beautiful homes, and elegant hotels and restaurants. I saw my first puppet show and my first children's play. Mother took me to the opera to see *La Bohème* and *Madame Butterfly*. I was given dazzling picture books and toys. I loved the food and the sweets. In the spring, when we boarded a train for Ankara, where a cousin of my father served as the Iranian ambassador, then another train to Baghdad, and finally a bus to Iran, we left my fairy-tale city behind.

Tehran

By the time we returned from Europe, Father had decided to leave the academic world of Karaj and to join the Ministry of Agriculture. I was almost seven years old. Between the time I was seven and eleven years of age, we moved three times, each time to a slightly larger apartment, but for me life was becoming increasingly restricted. I had no garden in which to play and run around, except when I went to Grandmother's house or visited friends in Karaj. I was enrolled in Jeanne d'Arc, a Catholic school run by nuns. We followed a double curriculum—French in the morning and Persian in the afternoon. In the morning, I learned about the Alps and the Pyrenees, the river Seine and the river Loire. In the afternoon, I learned about the Zagros and Alborz mountains, the Zayandeh Rud River in Isfahan and the Karkheh River in Khuzistan.

My last year at Jeanne d'Arc coincided with the struggle led by Prime Minister Mohammad Mossadegh to nationalize Iran's oil industry, then controlled by a British enterprise, the Anglo-Iranian Oil Company (AIOC). The nationalization campaign pitted Iran against both the powerful company and the even more powerful British government, which was the majority shareholder in AIOC. The entire country was caught up in the David-and-Goliath struggle. Political parties—Mossadegh's own National Front; the Communist Tudeh Party; the ultranationalist Sumka Party, whose members, fascist-style, sported black shirts; the Toilers Party, headed by a politician from my family's ancestral home, Kerman—vied for popularity and power, while their adherents in secondary schools and Tehran University clashed with one another on the streets. New, highly partisan newspapers appeared and were shut down. Mossadegh, hugely popular, made fiery speeches before massive crowds on the great square outside the houses of parliament.

Even as an eleven-year-old I was caught up in these currents, as were the rest of the students at the normally staid Jeanne d'Arc. We had all become politicized and wanted the British out, and the oil industry in Iranian hands. Mossadegh was our hero, and we, like other students, took up the shout, "*Ya marg, ya Mossadegh*"—"Death or Mossadegh." Politicians considered insufficiently ardent on the oil nationalization issue, including Mossadegh's predecessor as prime minister, Ali Razmara, were assassinated. Razmara had signed an oil agreement with the despised British that ardent nationalists considered a sellout of Iranian interests; parliament rejected the agreement. His murder brought the mindless violence close to home. Razmara's daughter was a student at Jeanne d'Arc, and on the day her father was found dead, the whole school poured out into the schoolyard in sympathy with our classmate. Even the strict nuns could not keep us in the classroom.

The AIOC was finally nationalized by an act of parliament in March 1951, ending in one stroke decades of British control of Iran's most important industry. The country was jubilant. The Iranian government sent a team of officials to take over the oil company operations. It invited the majority of the British employees to stay on; but the British, in a huff and hoping to cripple the Iranian oil industry, pulled out their technicians and staff. The Iranian team was led by Mehdi Bazargan, a political colleague of Mossadegh, who nearly thirty years later was to become the first prime minister of the Islamic Republic. My father joined the team, seconded from the Ministry of Agriculture to head the oil company's agricultural department. Mutti, Siamack, and I moved with Father to the city of Abadan, where two years later, my sister, Hayedeh, was born.

❧ ABADAN

Abadan was the heart of Iran's oil industry. At the time, the Abadan oil refinery was the largest in the world. The very air smelled of gas and oil; at night, from almost any vantage point, one could see the flames from the flared gas of the oil wells licking at the tall chimney that towered over the refinery. The oil industry was by far the city's largest employer, and employees lived in oil company housing and socialized in oil company clubs. Abadan had also been, in many ways, a very British city. Thousands of Englishmen had worked for the AIOC and lived with their families in Abadan. There was Iranian staff, too, but with few exceptions the senior management and technical positions were held by Englishmen. The English and the Iranians worked together but led separate lives. The English lived in Braim; most of the Iranians lived in Bavardeh, a totally separate housing development. The English frequented the Gymkhana Club, the Iranians the Iran, Bavardeh, and Golestan clubs. The laborers, poorly paid Iranians despite AIOC's high profits, lived mostly in shantytowns. Abadan had its own *halabi-abad* and *hassir-abad*, "tin town" and "straw-mat town," named after the shacks made out of flattened oilcans or straw mats that were laid across scaffolding of sticks and wood.

When the oil industry was taken over and the British driven out, all these facilities were seized by the Iranian government. When we arrived in Abadan, we were assigned a house in the upscale Braim district.

Abadan had a different feel to it than Tehran or Karaj. I associated Tehran with the mountains and the plains that ran south and east to the Kavir Desert. The air was hot and dry in the summer, crisp and cold in winter. There was no hint of the sea, no touch of dampness in the air. Abadan, by contrast, was built on the Shatt al-Arab, the border river between Iran and Iraq, and abutted the Persian Gulf. It was a port city. There were palm and banana trees as well as lush bougainvilleas. The local people were dark-complexioned, seafaring. Most spoke Arabic and Persian with a pronounced Arabic accent.

But for a curious child, Abadan meant a recovery of freedom. Our house had a large garden surrounded by hedges. My parents joined the Boat Club, with its clubhouse on the riverbank built to resemble a boat, and the Golestan Club, within walking distance of the house. I could check out all the books I wanted from the club library. Mother didn't read Persian, and Father was too busy to notice. At the age of thirteen I read Victor Hugo, Anatole France, Albert Camus, John

Steinbeck, and Ernest Hemingway in translation, as well as a great many Persian novels. It was in Abadan that I developed my love for literature.

Despite the long British presence, there were no bilingual schools in Abadan, and I attended the local Persian elementary school. I walked into the schoolyard on my first day and saw students crowded around a little boy, perhaps eight years old, lying on his back with his legs in the air. The assistant principal was caning the soles of his bare feet. I was horrified. Jeanne d'Arc had been strict, but punishment had meant sitting alone in a corner or being banished from the classroom.

Yet the oil company itself retained a strong British feel to it. Senior Iranian staff who had worked for the AIOC and studied in England often spoke English to one another. They sent their children to English boarding schools. At the card table, my parents' new bridge partners referred to clubs, hearts, diamonds, and spades, rather than *trèfle*, *coeur*, *carré*, and *pique*, the French terms common among their friends in Tehran. Mutti arranged for me to take English lessons with a private tutor.

Since the summers in Abadan were very hot and humid, we would come to Tehran for a month, staying two weeks with my grandmother and two weeks with our extended family in villages in Arak, some two hundred miles northwest of Tehran. We rode donkeys and picked and ate fruits straight from the trees, and cucumbers from the long, straight rows of the cucumber beds. We wandered for hours in the fields and watched the villagers swinging their scythes and harvesting the wheat.

But politics intruded on our idyllic life in Arak and roiled the lives and opinions of our usually apolitical family. The British were determined to undo the oil industry's nationalization, which had meant the loss of a valuable asset as well as a challenge to their imperial authority. They feared a precedent that would threaten their other holdings (indeed, President Nasser of Egypt would nationalize the Suez Canal five years later). In retaliation for the nationalization of the AIOC, the British had frozen Iran's sterling assets, had successfully imposed a boycott on the sale of Iranian oil, and although we didn't know it then, were secretly plotting to overthrow Mossadegh and persuade the United States to join them in the scheme. As a result of the oil boycott and assets freeze, the economy was suffering, business was slow, and imports had dwindled. Mossadegh was also locked in a struggle with the shah over power and constitutional authority; things seemed unstable as demonstrators took over the streets.

In the evenings, my relatives heatedly debated the situation. The family was divided, some loyal to Mossadegh and others to the shah; some enthusiastic about oil nationalization, others worried about the direction in which Mossadegh was taking the country: "He is allowing the left and the Communists too much power." "No, he is the only politician who dared stand up to the British and defend Iran's honor." "Yes, but he is leading the country into anarchy." So went the arguments, back and forth. I remember a younger cousin, an ardent supporter of Mossadegh, accusing his aunts and uncles of caring more about their villages than about Iran. For the two branches of the family, the Bayats and the Esfandiaris, the issues were especially fraught. Mossadegh, the aristocrat who had emerged as a defender of the masses, was a close relative. His mother, Najm al-Saltaneh, a lion of a woman, was the second wife of my great-grandfather Vakil ol-Molk-e Dovvom and the grandmother of many Bayats. Mossadegh's son, Gholam Hossein, and his wife, Malekeh, were close friends of my mother and father.

The family was proud that once again one of their own was now prime minister; and they both admired and were awed by Mossadegh's crafty political maneuvering and the oratorical skills that turned him into a popular hero. But Mossadegh, irascible and headstrong, had also released radical forces. Workers were organizing and demanding higher wages. Talk of land reform was threatening to large landowners, including the Bayats and the Esfandiaris. The Tudeh, or Communist, Party was rising in popularity and influence. The endless political turmoil, strikes, and street demonstrations made members of the family nervous. Vigilante violence hit close to home. Brigadier General Mohammad Afshartous, Mossadegh's police chief, who was kidnapped and murdered, had married into the Bayat family. Worried by the rising radicalism and violence, the Bayats sent a family delegation to visit Mossadegh and to beg him to curb the disorder. He heard them out but did nothing to assuage their anxieties.

Mossadegh was also challenging the shah's authority, asserting the primacy of parliament and his prerogatives as prime minister. In July 1952, Mossadegh resigned when both he and the shah claimed the right to name the minister of war. After two days of pro-Mossadegh rioting, the shah stood down, and Mossadegh returned to office in triumph, more powerful than before. Members of the family were torn: they felt instinctive loyalty to their famous relative; some found attractive the idea championed by Mossadegh that authority should rest with the parliament and that the shah should reign and not rule. But they also feared for the stability of the throne and the long-term stability of the country; and Mossadegh's seeming radicalism made them uneasy.

Affairs between Mossadegh and the shah, and Mossadegh and the British, came to a head in August 1953. Early that year, the British government succeeded in persuading the incoming Eisenhower administration to join their plan to overthrow Mossadegh. The CIA and Britain's Secret Intelligence Service (SIS) went to work. A reluctant shah was brought on board. Royalist officers in the army were won over; newspaper editors, members of parliament, and politicians were paid off; the cooperation of political operators who could mobilize the street crowds was secured.

The plot was set in motion in August, and after two days of seesaw battles on the streets, the royalist forces finally prevailed. The shah, who had left the country for Rome when the plot initially appeared to have failed, returned to Iran to reclaim his throne. During that turbulent week, I happened to have gone with my parents to the Caspian city of Rasht. We arrived at the very height of the crisis and saw the statue of the shah, which had dominated the main city square, lying on the ground, smashed to pieces. It had been pulled down from its pedestal by anti-royalist crowds. A few days later, after royalist forces had prevailed, someone had put the broken-off head of the shah's statue back on its pedestal. There was the shah, albeit somewhat reduced in stature, gazing across the square again.

These momentous national events left the family with mixed feelings. They were devastated to see Mossadegh's home ransacked, and the prime minister put on trial and jailed. But they were relieved that the threat of upheaval had been averted, and that Mossadegh's immediate family had not been harassed. When we gathered in Arak during the summer of the following year, all talk of politics had come to an end and, at least to a child, life had returned to its normal, lazy rhythm.

3.

A CAREER INTERRUPTED

I WOULD NOT COME INTO contact with such fierce political loyalties again until I attended university—in Vienna, at my mother's insistence—five years later. Many of my fellow Iranian students were active in the opposition movement against the shah. The principal student organization, the Confederation of Iranian Students, was left of center rather than revolutionary, dedicated to the memory of Mossadegh and loyal to his political party, the National Front. But more radical currents, some Marxist, some Islamic, were already stirring among the students, and two decades of authoritarian rule in Iran would turn a future generation of students into outright revolutionaries.

While I stayed clear of the student movement (my father having instilled in me both patriotism and caution about getting mixed up in politics), my time in Vienna had a huge hand in shaping my intellectual development and my love for Western culture. I studied journalism, philosophy, and art history, but I also attended poetry readings and literary debates. I heard Sviatoslav Richter play the piano and Yehudi Menuhin play the violin; I even heard a young and yet unknown Zubin Mehta conducting a student orchestra. I spent a summer in London improving my English, and traveled to East Berlin, Munich, Rome, Venice, Paris, and Geneva. Even if I wasn't fully conscious of it at the time, it was during these years that I came to appreciate the value of freedom of thought and expression, the right to travel and explore, and freedom from authoritarianism.

Home, Again

I returned to Tehran in the summer of 1964 and was hired by the publisher of *Kayhan*, the largest daily newspaper in the country. Since I knew French, English, and German as well as Persian, I was assigned to the foreign news desk. When the publisher, Dr. Mostafa Mesbahzadeh, known to everyone as "Doktor," introduced me to my colleagues on the foreign news desk, I was met with skeptical stares. The foreign news veterans were all men in their early fifties, educated, but from modest backgrounds. Most of them, I later learned, were former Communists or had dabbled in left-wing ideologies popular among students and the new educated middle class in the postwar period. They had spent time in prison after the overthrow of Mossadegh, and some of them had been tortured. Times had changed, but they remained attached to their radical political beliefs.

I was twenty-four, the only woman on the foreign news desk, one of the very few in the entire newsroom. I was also from the wrong social class in their eyes, with a well-known family name and family members in senior positions in the civil service. These "enlightened radicals" clearly did not think a woman capable of doing their weighty work, and they were not comfortable having a woman in their midst. "Does this *zaifeh*—this weak one—understand anything?" an older reporter once sneered, using a traditional and derogatory term for women. With me around, the men had to watch their language and stop exchanging crude jokes and accounts of their escapades. The toilet in the building was for men only, meaning I simply could not go to the bathroom all day. At five-thirty in the morning, my colleagues would breakfast on a dish of sheep's brains and sheep's feet—a delicacy in Iran, but one whose sight and smell nauseated me. One or two of the men even topped off their breakfast with a glass of vodka. But my foreign language and translating skills were good, I was speedy, and gradually the men came to accept me. For a brief period, I even became the foreign news editor, and by the end of my decade at the paper, the environment had changed so dramatically that women were even given their own bathroom.

Kayhan was an afternoon paper, and except for major stories, the foreign news pages were put to bed relatively early. I arrived at work at five-thirty in the morning and worked until two-thirty in the afternoon. Depending on the volume of news, I sometimes stayed through the afternoons and evenings, as well.

The newspaper had no foreign correspondents of its own and relied on the wire agencies Reuters, the Associated Press, United Press International, and Agence France-Presse. We were still in the age of teleprinters, and dispatches came rattling through on long perforated sheets of paper. Every half hour someone would walk in with rolls of dispatches and give them to the translators. At noon, the mail boy would bring in newspapers flown in from Europe—the *Herald Tribune*, the London *Times*, the *Financial Times*, *Le Monde*, *Figaro*. In August 1968, when Russian tanks invaded Czechoslovakia, I remember huddling around the teleprinters as the dispatches rolled off the machines. Earlier that year, the new Czech leader, Alexander Dubček, had sought to loosen the hold of Soviet-style communism over the country. He had freed up the press, allowed non-Communist political parties to operate, and decentralized the economy. The "Prague Spring" seemed, for a moment, to herald a wave of change across the Soviet bloc. But what the Czechs welcomed the Russians feared, and that morning the news coming across the teleprinters was grim. More than 200,000 Soviet and Warsaw Pact troops had fanned across the country. Dubček and his colleagues as well as Czech activists and intellectuals had been arrested. The Prague Spring was being snuffed out. Even my leftist colleagues were hard put to justify the invasion.

The staff of the foreign news desk served principally as translators. The editor selected the stories he wanted to run, and we translated them in longhand. They were then typed and edited, headlines were written, and the type was set.

Just before the presses rolled at noon, the censor from the government's information office would show up with a list of stories that we were not allowed to run. The censor, Mahram Ali Khan, had held the job since the 1930s, and each day he went from newspaper office to newspaper office with the censor's list. He checked all the pages and read all the major stories. Sometimes he ordered the removal of a name or a paragraph, sometimes a whole story. We were not allowed, for example, to report student demonstrations in other countries, lest our own university students get ideas. We were not allowed to repeat criticism of the shah from abroad. Fortunately, Mahram Ali Khan had a sense of humor. One day, before I joined *Kayhan*, the journalists took advantage of Mahram Ali Khan's visit to the men's room, locked him in, and pretended they could not open the door. They quietly reinserted the stories he had removed and went to press before they let him out.

Within six months, the publisher, Dr. Mesbahzadeh, decided I would be more useful as a reporter than as a translator. I began to cover visits to Iran by ministers, officials, and foreign heads of state. I also reported on trips abroad by the shah and other high officials. Shaul, who would become my husband a year later, worked for the English-language newspaper of the Kayhan publishing house.

We ran across each other in the newsroom but really "met" when both of us were covering the visit to Iran of Ethiopia's emperor, Haile Selassie, who granted us an exclusive interview. At the end of the interview, after thanks and good-byes, I simply turned around and walked out, realizing only too late from the startled looks of Haile Selassie's courtiers that I had committed a faux pas. You were not supposed to turn your back on the emperor. I met Haile Selassie once more in the late 1960s, when I covered the shah's trip to Addis Ababa.

The emperor recognized me. "I am indebted to you," I said. "I met my future husband when interviewing you."

"Well, and are you happy with your husband?" he asked with a twinkle in his eye.

I had taken to Shaul immediately. He was already a prominent journalist, covering all the major stories for his newspaper and writing for the *Financial Times* and the *Economist*. He had a sharp intellect, fierce integrity as a journalist, and was infectiously enthusiastic about newspaper work. Covering stories with him was always an adventure. We were both interested in Iranian politics; we both loved literature. When we first met, he was deeply into the German playwright Bertolt Brecht, and he soon presented me with several of Brecht's plays in the original German, which would not have been easy to locate in Tehran's bookstores. He had studied in America and opened up to me a whole new world of American history, literature, and politics.

The decision to marry was not an easy one. We came from two different communities, and marriages between Jews and Muslims were extremely rare, virtually unheard of, in our two societies. Both Shaul's family and mine were deeply unhappy. We were breaking all sorts of taboos, and, looking back, I am amazed at our audacity. But we were young and determined, and once we were married, I was warmly accepted into Shaul's family and Shaul into mine. Shaul and Mutti grew especially close to each other.

Two years into our marriage, in 1966, Shaul decided he would like to return to Harvard, where he had gone to college, to study for an MA in Middle Eastern studies. He was covering the Middle East and wanted to study the region more seriously. Besides, he was unhappy with the creeping censorship of the press. We spent two years in Cambridge, basically exchanging our comfortable life as professional journalists for the more cramped circumstances of graduate students. Shaul's scholarship hardly covered our expenses, especially once our daughter, Haleh, arrived.

Shaul received his MA in 1968, but student life continued for the next three years as Shaul pursued his PhD, in Iranian history, at

Oxford University in England. I taught Persian while he completed his doctorate.

We returned to Iran and to our newspaper jobs in 1972. The Kayhan organization was enjoying a period of considerable success and expansion. *Kayhan* continued to be more "liberal" than Tehran's other large-circulation daily, *Ettela'at*, but it was no longer the bold and risk-taking newspaper I had joined nearly a decade earlier. The weight of censorship had grown heavier, and the freedom to write and publish more restricted. Mesbahzadeh's own liberal preferences remained in place, and as the publisher, he was always admirably protective of his editors and reporters. Pressured to fire journalists who had stepped on the censors' toes, he continued to pay their salaries and brought them back to the newsroom at the first opportunity. He kept jobs open for colleagues who went to jail, took care of their families, and reemployed them once they were released. He allowed reporters who were banned by the shah's secret police, SAVAK (the Persian acronym for Organization for State Security and Intelligence), to write for *Kayhan* under assumed names.

But the organization's very success was a kind of vulnerability, since the financial stakes were now huge. The staff and employees numbered in the hundreds. "If we are closed down, who is going to pay all these people?" Mesbahzadeh once asked Shaul, who was insisting he stand up more aggressively to the censors. The government was a source of advertising revenue, and it set policies that could affect everything from *Kayhan*'s ability to purchase newsprint abroad to Mesbahzadeh's considerable land holdings. Increasingly the shah and the government showed less tolerance for even the mildest criticism, and the grip on the media of the emboldened Information Ministry grew tighter. Dr. Mesbahzadeh continued to allow his editors considerable autonomy, but the editors were being hounded daily by the censors.

In 1973, rumors circulated at *Kayhan* that Mesbahzadeh was under pressure from Prime Minister Amir Abbas Hoveyda to name his protégé, Amir Taheri, a *Kayhan* reporter, as editor of the newspaper.

Taheri, who seemed all too willing in his reporting to do the prime minister's bidding, was to replace the highly respected, independent-minded Mehdi Semsar. The rumor proved true. One morning Taheri's appointment was announced to the staff. When he walked into the newsroom a few minutes later and took his seat behind the editor's desk, one colleague and I gathered up our belongings and walked out of the newsroom and the building. We quit. I subsequently had a long meeting with Mesbahzadeh, who tried to convince me not to leave. Editors come and go, he said, but *Kayhan* will endure. I was not persuaded; and I have never regretted my decision. Leaving *Kayhan* was difficult for me. It was the country's leading newspaper; I took pleasure in the work and in being part of the *Kayhan* family. Shaul and I needed both our salaries to make ends meet. But I am proud of having refused to work under a government-imposed editor who represented everything I disdained in a profession I loved.

An Unrepentant Feminist

I had grown interested in women's issues during my last years at *Kayhan*. When my friend Mahnaz Afkhami, the secretary general of the Women's Organization of Iran (WOI), invited me to join her team, I welcomed the opportunity to work with her.

The WOI, established in 1966, was the umbrella organization for almost all women's groups and women's activity in Iran. Mahnaz, a dynamic American-educated feminist, had taken over a dormant organization in 1970 and turned it into an effective instrument to promote women's causes.

The struggle for women's rights in Iran began in the late nineteenth century. Women took an active part in the Constitutional Revolution of 1906, but the constitution that was wrested from Mozaffar al-Din Shah of the former Qajar dynasty did not give women the right to vote. A handful of women campaigned for women's education, and established the first schools for girls in the early years of the twentieth century. Under Reza Shah, the government established a system of public elementary and secondary schools for girls as well as boys. When Tehran University, the country's first modern university, was established in 1936, it admitted both men and women. Reza Shah had already ordered the abolition of the veil. He saw it as a symbol of Iran's backwardness and a barrier to the education of women and their introduction into the workforce and society. The marriage age for girls was raised from nine to thirteen—a radical step at the time. Women entered the workforce, initially in the civil service.

This process continued under his son, Mohammad Reza Shah, much to the discomfort and sometimes the fierce opposition of traditional members of the clergy, who, for example, forced the government in 1962 to withdraw a modest proposal to allow women to vote in local council elections. In his commitment to the principle that traditional restrictions on women should be removed, the shah was encouraged by his wife, Queen Farah, and by his twin sister, Princess Ashraf. Women in Iran's burgeoning and better-educated middle class pushed for change as well. Similar movements were under way in other countries of the region, including Egypt and Tunisia, but Iran was breaking new ground.

Despite clerical opposition, women received the right to vote in 1963. The 1967 Family Protection Law, amended and expanded in 1975, restricted the ability of men to take more than one wife and to secure divorce on demand. It gave women the right to seek divorce, and strengthened women's rights in child-custody cases. The marriage age for girls was raised from thirteen to fifteen, and then to eighteen. Women's employment grew fairly rapidly in the 1960s and 1970s, and the number of girls in schools and higher education expanded dramatically. Whereas women had made slow, steady progress in previous decades, the WOI accelerated this process, giving it direction and taking it into new fields.

During the period when I was involved with the organization, the WOI made working-class women its focus. It established branches and family welfare centers all over the country. These provided working-class women with literacy classes and vocational training, helping them earn a living independent of their husbands. It ran family-planning clinics; it provided women with legal advice; and guided them on their rights in child custody, divorce, and spousal-abuse cases. It made inroads at establishing day-care centers for working-class women. It lobbied with the government and the private sector to open up more executive and managerial positions to women.

None of this was easy. Resistance to change and skepticism that it was necessary or practicable were widespread. Both phases of the family-protection law required patient negotiation with cabinet ministers and members of parliament. The endorsement or acquiescence of leading members of the clergy was crucial for new legislation affecting women. In 1967, the minister of justice journeyed to the shrine city of Najaf in Iraq, the center of Shi'ism's most prestigious religious seminaries, to persuade Ayatollah Kho'i, then the highest-ranking and most eminent clerical leader in the Shi'ite world, to lend his support to the new family-protection law.

My responsibilities as deputy director for international affairs included disseminating information about the WOI's activities and sponsoring programs to educate both men and women on women's issues. I traveled fairly widely inside the country. I found the women eager, but the men resistant. On one trip, for example, the driver of the car that was taking me to Qom was loud in his praise of the cleric, Ayatollah Khomeini, then living in exile in Iraq, for his opposition to the 1962 attempt to extend limited suffrage to women. I was also responsible for the WOI's relations with international organizations and women's groups abroad, which enabled me to travel to China, Thailand, and the United States for meetings and international conferences, and I established links between Iran and the international women's movement.

Just before I left the WOI in 1976 to accept a new position, I took part in drafting the National Plan of Action on the Improvement of the Status of Women in Iran. Approved by the cabinet, the plan called for the full integration of women into all aspects of social and economic life. It was, of course, a statement of goals that were yet to be accomplished, but it committed the government itself to work toward women's equality in several areas.

The WOI was subsequently criticized for a strategy of change from above, for relying too much on official support, rather than organizing middle- and working-class women. But the criticism was misplaced. We were not in the business of organizing mass political movements, which would have been impossible in Iran at the time. As an activist organization, the WOI was in its infancy. Opposition, especially from the clergy, was considerable; and the support of the shah, his wife, and his sister was crucial if the government was to be persuaded to risk taking measures that challenged tradition. Much of the WOI's work in the last decade before the revolution benefited working-class women far more than members of the elite. Elite women had education, were aware of their rights, knew how to get divorces, understood birth control, and could obtain employment. It was working-class women whose lives were changed the most by the WOI's victories.

After the revolution, the clerics sought to undo as many of our accomplishments as they could. But even Ayatollah Khomeini and the clerics who had fiercely opposed the extension of suffrage to women in 1962 and 1963 realized they could not turn back this particular clock. They continued to allow women to vote. The new government, however, suspended the Family Protection Law, encouraged women in the civil service to take early retirement, and discouraged women in general from working. It barred women from judgeships and certain fields of higher education and specialization; lowered the marriage age for girls to nine (the age of puberty in Islam); tried to dictate what women wore; and segregated men and women in university classrooms, beaches, ski slopes, and public transportion. It even inserted clauses into the constitution defining the principal role of women as mothers and housewives.

Iranian women, young and old, from all classes, courageously resisted these measures. Young women fought the Islamic dress code, wearing loose headscarves rather than the chador or the *maghan'eh*, showing a bit of hair under their scarves, the bottoms of bluejeans underneath their robes, and a hint of lipstick on their lips. In this, they risked arrest, even lashings, but gradually won for themselves more freedom in matters of dress. Women voted in large numbers. Working-class and traditional women continued to be at the forefront of the struggle to reinstate the Family Protection Law. It was principally women from working- and lower-middle-class families who embraced opportunities for education, pushed for places in the universities, and demanded and seized opportunities for employment. That women fought back was partly the result of the revolutionary upheaval itself, which politicized society and, contrary to the intention of the clerics, thrust women into the public sphere. But I believe the WOI played a role in making a new generation of women conscious of their rights, and these women were determined not to be relegated to second-class status again. For these reasons, my three years at the WOI remain among the most rewarding of my working life. I became, and remain, an unrepentant feminist.

In 1975, I was thrust into the world of art and public culture when I accepted an offer to join the Shahbanou Farah Foundation, established under the sponsorship of the queen, which oversaw a number of major museums and cultural centers. The museums in my charge included the Carpet Museum of Tehran, the Tehran Museum of Ancient Iranian Ceramics and Glassware, the Tehran Museum of Contemporary Arts, and the Khorramabad Museum of Ancient Lurestan Bronzes. We were also running cultural centers in the capital, where we organized art exhibitions, art workshops, lectures, and seminars. I was only in my second year at the foundation when the clouds of revolution began to loom over the country.

REVOLUTION

In the 1960s and 1970s, Iran seemed to be prospering. The country was stable. The economy was booming, and while wealth distribution was uneven, Iranians in general were better fed and clothed. Increasing numbers of people had access to education as well as cars, refrigerators, TV sets, and other modern conveniences. The shah had managed his foreign relations well and, in a much-divided world, enjoyed good relations with both the United States and the Soviet Union, as well as with China, India, and Pakistan, and Israel and the Arab states.

Yet political stability had been purchased at a price—repression. A growing educated middle class chafed at the lack of freedoms and input regarding how the country was run. The explosion in oil prices in 1973–74 dramatically boosted government revenues, but the rapid injection of that money into the economy led to inflation, rising food prices, and a real estate boom that pushed affordable housing out of reach for most ordinary families. Rural migrants crowded into the capital and other major cities in search of jobs and found themselves living in crowded shantytowns lacking electricity and piped water. For newcomers, life in Tehran, a messy, sprawling metropolis, meant a bewildering sense of cultural dislocation and a shock to traditional and religious sensibilities.

Since other avenues for the expression of discontent—political parties, trade unions, an independent press, professional associations—were suppressed or strictly controlled, people flocked to mosques, where clerics used a religious vocabulary to preach barely disguised condemnations of the state and its policies. When the shah responded to these murmurs of discontent by easing up on controls over speech and political activity, opposition elements quickly seized on the opening.

By 1977, for example, Tehran's "poetry nights" at the German-sponsored Goethe Institute had taken on a decidedly political color. Large gatherings listened while poets read from works praising liberty and criticizing oppression. Lawyers and intellectuals addressed open letters to the prime minister and the shah calling for the reinstitution of basic freedoms and the release of political prisoners. These letters circulated widely in Xerox form, even if they could not be published in the daily press. In January 1978, under government pressure, one of the two leading newspapers in the country published an article scurrilously attacking Ayatollah Khomeini, the shah's principal opponent abroad. The article led to protests by seminary students and clashes with the authorities in the shrine city of Qom. Khomeini had risen to prominence in the early 1960s for his uncompromising denunciations of the shah's policies. He rapidly achieved a name for himself.

His arrest in 1963 had led to widespread riots, shaking the government to its foundations. The following year, free again, Khomeini used a sermon to denounce the status-of-forces agreement (SOFA) Iran had signed with the United States. It gave American military personnel and their families in Iran immunity from prosecution in Iranian courts, and was hugely resented by politically inclined Iranians. He was sent into exile and eventually made his way to Najaf, in Iraq, where he took up teaching, attracting a wide circle of seminary students with his learning and his ability to give potent political meaning to traditional Islamic teachings. He continued his attacks on the shah's regime, eventually describing monarchy as hateful to Islam and calling for the establishment of an Islamic republic under clerical leadership. In Iran, he gained a wide if not always public following and a clandestine network of clerical devotees who spread his message.

When demonstrations against the government broke out in January 1978, triggering further protests, Khomeini was well poised to seize control of the nascent opposition movement. In February, demonstrators in Tabriz went on a rampage, trashing government offices and the headquarters of the ruling party. They also attacked the symbols of "modernity": nightclubs, cinema houses, liquor stores, and banks. The protests accelerated with astonishing speed. Six weeks later, similar riots erupted in half a dozen major cities. In September, over a hundred thousand joined in a protest march and communal prayers in Tehran. On Friday, September 8, after martial law had been declared in the capital, dozens were killed in clashes between protesters and troops. "Black Friday," as it was instantly dubbed by the shah's opponents, proved a watershed in the trajectory of the growing protest movement, which brought together varied political organizations and social classes: traditional and radical clerics, centrists from Mossadegh's old National Front, Communists of the Tudeh Party, as well as men and women associated with underground guerrilla movements, civil servants hurt by inflation and stagnant salaries, intellectuals eager for more freedom, and shopkeepers and bazaar merchants chafing at government attempts to control prices.

Khomeini's clerical lieutenants came to dominate the movement, and Khomeini emerged as its undisputed leader. Charismatic, adept at a rhetoric that resonated powerfully with the public, rejecting every compromise, and unrelenting in his determination to unseat the shah, he transformed what began as a call for the restoration of constitutional guarantees into a call for revolution. He united this disparate collection of opposition groups behind one goal: the overthrow of the monarchy.

In the fall and early winter of 1978, the shah's regime seemed to be unraveling before our eyes. Heavily armed troops appeared helpless to stop the mounting demonstrations and the imaginative forms of civil disobedience adopted by a thoroughly roused public. Civil servants went to work every day, but sat in their offices and did nothing, gradually bringing much of the government to a standstill. The mail could not be delivered, nor could imported goods be processed through customs. Oil-industry workers went on strike, reducing production to a trickle, which caused massive shortages of fuel and grounded truck transport. Factories shut down. Workers at Tehran's major electric power plant turned off the city's electric supply at will, plunging the capital into darkness. Schoolboys in Tehran stalled cars in the middle of major crossroads, snarling traffic and causing massive traffic jams. Tehranis took to their rooftops at night to cry out *Allah-*

o-Akbar, God is Great, into the December night, as if calling on God to rid the country of the shah.

Many of our friends were caught up in the revolutionary fervor, somehow imagining that the regime could be overthrown, the shah replaced by Khomeini, and that their own lives—comfortable, privileged—would remain unchanged. "Let him go," one of our friends said. "Anything will be better than the shah." Shaul and I, and a small circle of our closest friends, however, witnessed these momentous events with mounting trepidation. A political earthquake was taking place. The future seemed full of uncertainties. Deep down, Shaul and I sensed that that our lives would never be the same again. Shaul returned from a trip to London in early November. I could not pick him up at the airport because martial law had been declared and a curfew was in force. He took a cab home. No one at the airport seemed to be in charge at passport control or customs, he said. Troops patrolled the nearly deserted night streets, but they were lackadaisical in enforcing the rules of martial law. Back home, Shaul silently took in the familiar objects of our living room and library—the books, the frames of Persian calligraphy on the walls, the glow of lamps on the sofas. He seemed moved by the sense of calm and order inside the house, compared with the rising chaos on the streets. I could read his thoughts from the look on his face. "Are we going to have to give all this up?" he finally asked.

Clerical and other opposition leaders called for massive protest rallies on December 10 and 11, to coincide with the days of religious mourning. The government banned the marches, and fear of violence and bloodshed was widespread. Shaul and I decided that, as a precaution, I should take our daughter Haleh to London for two weeks and wait things out. I left Tehran for London in early December. The exodus of the middle class had already begun, and the airport was jammed with Iranians and foreigners leaving the country. Panic was in the air. Still, I did not feel I was leaving Iran for good.

In London I waited anxiously for news. The regime, hammered by strikes, shutdowns, demonstrations, and violence on the streets, was in a hopeless situation. Shaul and I spoke on the phone; repeatedly we postponed my return, our mood wildly gyrating between unrealistic hopes that things would calm down and mounting evidence that the regime was near collapse. My two-week stay stretched into three, then four and five weeks. The shah left Iran on January 16, never to come back; Khomeini returned to Iran on February 1, 1979, greeted by a crowd of more than a million. Ten days later, with the army having declared its "neutrality," people in Tehran rose up and overran government ministries, military barracks, police stations, and the radio and TV broadcasting centers. The monarchy had collapsed; an Islamic republic had taken its place.

Revolutions such as Iran's are huge upheavals in the life of nations, overturning not only governments and institutions but the lives of every individual and family caught in the vortex. Both Shaul and I were deeply rooted in Iran. Everything we had built over a lifetime was there. On the other hand, the country was in turmoil. Armed revolutionary committees roamed the streets. Every day, grisly pictures appeared in the Tehran papers of executed members of the old regime—many I had known personally or had covered as a journalist. Farrokhrou Parsa, the first woman cabinet minister in Iran and a former minister of education, was charged with "prostituting young girls," placed in a sack, and executed by firing squad. Prime Minister Hoveyda, a friend of my parents whom I had known as a child, was given a summary trial and shot—in the middle of the night, on the rooftop or backstairs of a prison, it was reported. The Kayhan Organization, where Shaul worked, had been seized by the revolutionary government. Shaul had been offered a one-year visiting professorship at Princeton; reluctantly we decided that he would accept. Without admitting it to ourselves, we had decided to leave Iran.

Shaul joined us in London in January 1980. He had managed to salvage a few of our belongings; but everything else—our home, property, careers, friends, family, the feel of the familiar—we left behind.

America

Shaul left London for Princeton in late January, and I followed in July, after Haleh finished school. Princeton was a quiet university town, very different from Cambridge, Massachusetts. The Princeton campus was self-contained, and university life did not spill out into the small town very much. There were few coffee shops and fewer bookstores.

We lived for a year in a tiny two-story town house owned by the university, amid rented furniture and an assorted collection of dishes, cutlery, and kitchen appliances loaned by friends. Shaul had a one-year contract, but we had no certainty of employment beyond that. The news out of Iran was uniformly grim. Disorder continued on the streets, on university campuses, and in government offices. I worried about my parents in Tehran, yet I felt helpless to do anything for them.

During my first week at Princeton I met Janina Issawi, whose husband, Charles, was a professor. Janina knew what it meant to be an exile. Polish by birth, she and her family had been rounded up by the Soviet army in World War II and sent to labor camps in Russia. Somehow, the family made it overland to Iran, then to Lebanon, where she studied at the American University of Beirut and met her future husband.

"Get yourself a house; put down some roots," she told me, an easier proposition for Shaul than for myself, since he had attended boarding school outside of New York City as a teenager, as well as doing both his undergraduate and graduate work at Harvard. Except for the eighteen months I spent in Cambridge in the mid-1960s, when I was preoccupied with a new baby, I did not know America. I had to get used to its sky, soil, and rhythms, to hearing English rather than Persian spoken around me. I had to start a new career. Yet I vowed to follow Janina's sensible advice. We registered Haleh in school. We made a down payment on a house outside Princeton, got ourselves a secondhand car, planted our garden, and asked friends over. We began to put down roots, even though a bit of replanting from time to time proved inevitable.

Shaul taught at Princeton for two years and held fellowships at various research institutes for three, spending a year in North Carolina and another in Washington, D.C. This meant separation and long commutes. I started teaching Persian at the university, initially for only a couple of hours a week. Soon I was carrying a full teaching load. It was very satisfying work. I was eager to share my love of Persian language and literature with the students, and I formed strong bonds with many of them.

In 1985, Shaul was offered a professorship at George Mason University in Fairfax, Virginia, not far from Washington. We moved again and purchased a house in Potomac, Maryland; but for the next few years I continued to teach at Princeton, and Shaul and I took turns commuting between Princeton and the Washington area.

In 1992, my teaching came to an end. I used two back-to-back fellowships from the John D. and Catherine T. MacArthur Foundation and the Woodrow Wilson Center to write my book *Reconstructed Lives: Women and Iran's Islamic Revolution*. Based on interviews, the book profiled a number of Iranian women and the strategies by which they coped with the revolutionary upheaval in Iran. At the end of my Wilson Center fellowship, Robert Litwak, who directed the Division for International Studies, asked me to join his team on a part-time basis to start a small project on the Middle East. I plunged into my new task with energy. We began very modestly, but within a few years, the Middle East Program was one of the most active in the Washington area. We organized seminars, lectures, and conferences and invited speakers and participants from the Middle East, including Iran. I was pleased to be fostering dialogue between Iranians and Americans. I never imagined, in my wildest dreams, that such work could be construed as subversive by the country of my birth.

But as Ja'fari's summons on that January morning reminded me, this was precisely the prospect I faced as I prepared for another round of interrogations at the Intelligence Ministry.

4.

THE INTERROGATION

Mr. Ja'fari had given me an address in affluent north Tehran, off Africa Avenue. I realized when I stepped out of my taxi that this was a building I knew, even though I had never been inside. Before the revolution, it had been the home of a member of one of Iran's leading industrial families. The house had been modeled after the Petit Trianon, the eighteenth-century palace Louis XV had built for his mistress Madame de Pompadour at Versailles, outside Paris. Expropriated by the new regime after the Islamic Revolution, it had been used for a time as a rehabilitation center for prostitutes. Rooms where the family had lived, raised children, and entertained their well-heeled guests were now a Ministry of Intelligence interrogation center. The walls around the garden were topped by barbed wire, naked and jagged against the blue Tehran sky.

The Intelligence Ministry has houses like these—anonymous, tucked away in residential areas—scattered about Tehran. The ministry, friends told me, even has rooms and suites in hotels, to keep an eye on foreign visitors and fellow Iranians. It was not uncommon, they said, to be summoned to a hotel for questioning.

I went not to the main gate of the "Petit Trianon" but, as instructed, to a side door, which had perhaps served as the servants' entrance in the old days. A small sign by the door said only Passport Office—the kind of circumlocution beloved by the Intelligence Ministry, as if they wished to hide from Iranians and even from themselves the nature of their reprehensible business. Ministry of Intelligence offices in various government buildings were called "the President's Bureaus." My interrogator, Ja'fari, referred to himself and was known to others as the *karshenas*, "the specialist." His superior didn't have a name at all and was known simply as Hajj Agha, an honorific for a man who had performed the pilgrimage to Mecca.

I rang the bell. The door was opened by remote control. A young soldier in a glass cubicle set aside the book he was reading, took down my name and other particulars, carefully noted the time of my arrival, and pressed another buzzer to open a door to my right. I hardly knew what to anticipate.

I walked into a large, windowless waiting room. It was furnished with easy chairs and a sofa. In one corner a TV was broadcasting a program on some Iranian province; unread newspapers sat on a coffee table by the sofa. A man I took to be the receptionist sat behind a desk, on a slightly raised platform facing the door. To his right, a closed door led to what turned out to be a series of interrogation rooms. I went up to the receptionist (I realized only later he, too, was a senior intelligence officer) and gave Ja'fari's name. He was untypically polite, even standing as I walked in the room. "Why does Mr. Ja'fari want to see you?" he asked. I explained what had happened to me on the night of December 30. He listened very carefully. "Everything will be okay," he said. "But please answer the questions they will ask you truthfully." I nodded.

He invited me to have a seat. I chose the brown sofa closest to the exit, despite knowing that the door was locked, and that I would leave only when they decided to let me go. I recalled the Persian saying: "Your coming is in your hands, but your leaving is in the hands of God." In my case, leaving was in the hands of the Intelligence Ministry's agents.

The room was warm. I removed my raincoat and sat in the black robe I was wearing over my pants and T-shirt. As usual, I was early, nervous that Tehran's chaotic traffic would make me miss my appointment. I spent a desultory half hour waiting for Ja'fari, unable to concentrate enough to read the day's headlines. The door opened, and a woman wrapped in a chador walked in. She went straight to the receptionist and in a loud voice said, "When will you let go of my brother? You have held him long enough. I have not seen him since you took him in. What are you doing to him?" My heart sank. The building, I thought, must have its own detention facility. I had heard reports that the Intelligence Ministry, the Revolutionary Guards, the Basij paramilitary forces, and shadowy vigilante groups maintained their own detention centers all over the city.

The door opened again to let in a young man who seemed familiar with the place, as if he had been here on numerous occasions. He was soon summoned inside by a middle-aged man in a dark suit, sandals, and no tie. Through the now-open door behind the receptionist's desk, I caught a glimpse of Ja'fari, carrying his laptop case on his shoulder, moving toward an interrogation room. My turn had come. The man behind the desk called my name, "Khanum Esfandiari"—Ms. Esfandiari—and directed me to the room Ja'fari now occupied.

Mr. Ja'fari

I walked in through the open door and heard Ja'fari's unmistakable voice: "*Salaam*"—Good morning. His *salaam* was curt, elided to one syllable. He was sitting behind a long desk; his laptop was already open before him and he was removing papers from an attaché case, which sat on the floor next to his chair. He asked me to tell him again what had happened on the night of the robbery. He had heard my account before and was probably trying to catch me in inconsistencies. Instead, I saw an opening. "I am very disturbed," I said. "I need my passport. I want to rejoin my family." Since I was a resident abroad,

I insisted, they should be able to issue me a new passport in a few days. I also asked his help in retrieving my belongings. "The men who robbed me were rude; they threatened me. How can such a thing happen on the road to the airport?" I had by now reluctantly concluded that agents of the Intelligence Ministry had staged the "robbery." Ja'fari's summons had hardened my gnawing suspicion into certainty. I wanted Ja'fari to know that I suspected the truth.

Ja'fari was unmoved. "Where you live is of no importance. We don't have first- and second-class citizens in the Islamic Republic." The law, he noted, says an Iranian has to wait six months to replace a lost or stolen passport. "That is how long it will take." As to my belongings, he referred me, as he had done before, to the *agahi*, the detective branch of the national police. I felt certain that Ja'fari and his colleagues had already combed through my belongings, dividing my clothes and knickknacks among their wives.

With the formalities over, Ja'fari began to question me in detail about my career in Iran before the revolution, including my years with *Kayhan* (this once relatively liberal newspaper had become the organ of the most hard-line elements in the Islamic Republic and a mouthpiece for the security services), with the Women's Organization of Iran, and with the Shahbanou Farah Foundation.

Ja'fari questioned me about each of these activities, but I sensed he was going through the motions. "Skip that," he would bark about any parts of my career that he couldn't use against me. Naturally he focused on the fact that the honorary head of the WOI had been Princess Ashraf, the shah's twin sister, and that the queen herself had been the moving force behind the foundation for which I later worked. "Oh, so you worked for the royal court," Ja'fari remarked with his usual smirk. He tried to link my work for women's rights before the revolution thirty-five years earlier with the current women's movement in Iran—a movement to which the intelligence services were hostile. The previous summer a number of prominent female activists had been arrested during a demonstration demanding broader rights for women. They had been charged and were awaiting trial.

It was four in the afternoon by the time Ja'fari was finished with my employment history. I returned to my mother's and called Shaul. The line was very bad; I suspected they were already tapping the phone. Access to e-mail and the Internet was also erratic, probably for the same reason. I spent an uneasy night and reported again the next morning, as instructed, to the "Petit Trianon."

"Conspiracies"

Except for the receptionist, the waiting room was empty. Ja'fari showed up late, as he had done the previous day—an act of deliberate discourtesy designed to upset me and to underline that he was in control. After we settled down, Ja'fari leaned back in his chair and said, "Let's talk about *Markaz-e Wilson*—the Wilson Center."

I reminded him I had taught Persian language and literature at Princeton before I came to the Wilson Center. "We know about that," he said with a dismissive wave of his hand. He cared little for my ten years at Princeton. He wanted to know everything about the Wilson Center: the composition of its board of directors; the names, responsibilities and backgrounds of the director, the deputy directors, and the heads of the programs; the budget and the organizational structure. He even made me draw an organizational chart. "Who are these people?" he demanded. "Write everything you know about them."

I knew little about the earlier careers of my colleagues at the Wilson Center other than what I picked up casually from conversation. As to the Wilson Center director, Lee Hamilton, he impressed me with his leadership style. Invariably courteous and considerate, he exercised authority quietly but firmly. Yet he had an easy relationship with his staff. He lunched with us in the Wilson Center dining room almost every day, making sure to move around the tables to chat with many different groups of people. His door was always open, but I had little need to see him often because he delegated well and gave his program directors considerable autonomy. While we could count on his unstinting support, I learned that he did not suffer fools or substandard work. I came to admire his excellent judgment and his willingness to speak his mind, even if this ran against conventional wisdom. These qualities were amply evident in *The 9/11 Commission Report* and in *The Iraq Study Group Report*, both of which he coauthored and which examined the U.S. handling of domestic security after the 9/11 terrorist attacks and of the Iraqi occupation after the overthrow of Saddam Hussein.

But as I told Ja'fari, as to Hamilton's earlier career, I knew only what I had read in the papers: He had been a congressman for many years and had chaired the House International Relations Committee. He had been appointed president and director of the Wilson Center after retiring from Congress. When I wrote down that bit of information, Ja'fari's eyes lit up. He leaned back in his chair as he always did when he imagined he had reached a turning point in the interrogation. "Well, first the Congress, and now the Wilson Center," he said, as if he had led me to concede a point of great significance. The "revolving door" between the U.S. government and Washington think tanks and research centers was one of Ja'fari's obsessions—proof that the administration shaped and directed the policies of these institutions. The appointment of Hamilton to head the Wilson Center after he left Congress confirmed his suspicion. "Appointed by whom?" he asked me belligerently.

Motioning to the amateurish organizational chart I had drawn, I wondered what possible interest it was to him that David Biette was head of the Canada Institute, or that Blair Ruble was the head of the Kennan Institute. But Ja'fari focused on the names. "Is he Jewish?" he asked. "Is she Jewish?" I said I did not know. "Can't you tell by the name?" he persisted, as if I were denying the obvious. My answer was still no.

Around noon, Ja'fari asked if I wanted lunch. I declined. I didn't much feel like eating. He shrugged, gathered up his papers, and walked out, closing the door behind him. He left a few notes on his desk, perhaps to test whether I would sneak a look. I didn't. I was sure they had a hidden camera in the room.

Ja'fari continued his questioning in the afternoon. "We know all about the obvious stuff," he said. "Now write down the hidden agenda. Tell us about the meetings you had behind closed doors in Hamilton's office." I told him I knew of no hidden agenda, and that I had never been at a single private meeting with Chairman Hamilton. He didn't believe a word I said. "You're talking about the surface things, the superficialities," he insisted "We want to know about the core, the kernel, the hidden layers. Tell us about the hidden layers." With alarm, I began to see the shape of Ja'fari's fantasies and the case he was trying to build against me. He imagined that the Wilson Center was an agency of the American government, that we were implicated in some nefarious plot against the Islamic Republic, and that we routinely held secret meetings to plan strategy to this end. His references to secret meetings and hidden agendas were absurd, but the implications for me were menacing.

At four in the afternoon, after repeatedly accusing me of being uncooperative, Ja'fari called it a day. He made me sign the bottom of each of his interrogation sheets and each of my answers. As I was getting ready to leave, he said ominously, "Your answers are not satisfactory. The interrogation will continue every day for the rest of the week." I collected my coat and the book I had brought with me and walked out. I was drained and exhausted from seven hours of interrogation, the tension, and the tedious back-and-forth. My hand ached from hours of writing; the cramped position in which I had to sit and write had taken its toll on my back. The receptionist allowed me to use his phone to call my mother. I wanted her to know I was leaving in case I met with another "accident" on my way home.

Outside, there was snow on the ground, and the sky was gray and bleak. The gathering twilight mirrored my inner gloom. I stopped at a friend's house. I needed to rest, to compose myself, lest my mother sense my anxiety, and to take stock of my predicament. The interrogation was taking a frightening turn. I was being entangled in a web of the Intelligence Ministry's making and I could not see my way out.

"Smooth and Horrible"

From my mother's apartment, I e-mailed Shaul about the interrogation. "It was smooth and horrible," I wrote, thinking of Ja'fari's style, which managed to be both slick and sinister at the same time. "If they don't put a stop to this now, I am stuck." Over the next several days I bombarded Shaul with similar messages. I insisted Shaul, or someone, conjure up a powerful official to order Ja'fari to stop and the Intelligence Ministry to let me go. I was being unrealistic; the Intelligence Ministry was not often answerable to others, but I was desperate enough to clutch at straws. "Another day has passed and I feel drained and lost," I e-mailed Shaul on January 9. "I see myself in that horrible place," I wrote, picturing Evin Prison. Two days later, again referring to Ja'fari, I wrote, "Either one stops him now or he plans to keep me for months—yes, for months."

Shaul had learned from a friend with good contacts in Iran that I had fallen into the hands of counterintelligence, one of the most hard-line units in the security apparatus. "No one," he was told, "can tell these people to lay off." It was urgent that we stop Ja'fari before they had fabricated a serious case against me, yet our friends and acquaintances in Tehran were academics: university professors, researchers, members of think tanks. We had met them at conferences in the United States. They had given talks at the Wilson Center and other Washington institutions, spent time at American universities, or taken part in Track II Diplomacy—meetings between nongovernment Iranians and Americans. They had little influence and no power, but they knew people in the government who we hoped might in turn know people in the security services. They could vouch for me and the Wilson Center, explain the nature of my work.

At the same time, Shaul and I decided that, at this stage, we would keep my plight out of the American and foreign press. Friends who supposedly knew how these things worked in Iran almost invariably advised us to try to resolve my problem with the Intelligence Ministry quietly. Not unreasonably, we feared that an outcry abroad would only make the Intelligence Ministry more stubborn and determined to "prove" I was being interrogated with good reason.

While Shaul placed calls in Washington, I telephoned Nasser, a good friend and a Tehran university professor, and described the worrisome direction the interrogation was taking. "These people don't understand the nature of my work," I told him. I hoped his contacts could explain to the Intelligence Ministry that the Wilson Center was a nonpartisan think tank, not an arm of the U.S. government. On the contrary, as hostility toward Iran was widespread in official circles in the United States, and proponents of overthrowing the Iranian regime became plentiful, the Wilson Center at least provided a forum where a variety of views on Iran could be heard, including the views of scholars, civil society activists, and journalists from the Islamic Republic. "Tell them that," I said. I called Mostafa, a researcher at an Iranian think tank who had once visited the Wilson Center, and urged him to see what he could do. We were also hoping that Javad Zarif, the Iranian ambassador to the United Nations in New York, who was acquainted with me and the Wilson Center, would weigh in with the authorities in Tehran.

Virtually everyone we spoke to, including Nasser, came back from their inquiries with the same message: they could do nothing to help. The interrogation had to take its course. "Tell them the truth," they advised me pointlessly, as if I had any intention of doing otherwise, certain that once the Intelligence Ministry had completed their inquiries, I would be released. They believed nothing untoward would happen to a visiting scholar with an American passport. But they were not with me in the room with Ja'fari. They could not see the menace in his eyes or sense his almost palpable intent to harm me.

In the two weeks following my initial encounter with Ja'fari, I returned nearly every day for interrogation at the "Petit Trianon." These sessions could last nine or ten hours; occasionally Ja'fari stopped after three or four. The daily routine was always the same. I would report at nine a.m. Ja'fari—usually late—would begin with a few oral questions and answers; he would then require me to respond to his extensive questions in writing. The process was tedious and tiring. Ja'fari would hand me a loose sheaf of papers. On top of each page, the words "Interrogation Sheet" and a file number appeared in Persian. I entered my name and the date on each page. Ja'fari would write down his question; I would write down my cryptic reply. Ja'fari would read each answer, write down another question, and hand the sheet of paper back to me. By the end of each day, we managed to fill pages and pages of questions and answers. Each day, I was required to sign every page. While I wrote, Ja'fari fiddled with his cell phone or with the tape recorder that he sometimes brought with him; he sipped at the tea which the tea boy brought him several times a day. Sometimes, he stepped outside briefly to take a call on his cell phone.

At noon, he would break for lunch. I refused to have anything. The tea boy—actually an old man—was distraught that day after day I did not eat. One day, he brought me two tangerines. "For the sake of your forebears, for the sake of your children, eat," he said. "You're wasting away." I took the two tangerines because I did not want to break his heart, but I was too tense to eat. While Ja'fari lunched, I remained alone in the interrogation room, mentally going over the ground we had covered, revisiting the questions and answers, anxious lest he pick on a stray fact or an innocent remark and use it to accuse me of some subversive activity. In preparation for Ja'fari's next barrage of questions, I tried to recall events, meetings, and discussions stretching back nearly ten years.

In this environment of menace, threat, and intimidation, Ja'fari continued to grill me on the Wilson Center and the activities of my Middle East Program. He had Googled the Wilson Center, and he had also Googled me and Shaul and a few other people who had spoken at the Wilson Center. He would often arrive in the morning with downloaded information, which he then expected me to explain to him. For example, on my third day at the "Petit Trianon," he plunked down several invitations to meetings we had e-mailed to our list of participants. He then demanded a description of each meeting, the reason for the choice of topic, the identity of the speakers, and the content of the talks. "We will go over every single meeting your program held," he told me, and I envisioned—accurately as it turned out—days and days of interrogation regarding meetings at the Wilson Center going back many years, whose details I could not possibly remember.

Except for the earliest years of the Middle East Program, all the information about our programs was readily available on the Web. But due to laziness, inability to navigate our Web site, or inadequate English, Ja'fari and his colleagues did not do their homework. It was left to me to provide him with lists of our meetings, initially on Iran and later on several other countries, with summaries of talks delivered at these meetings, and with a great deal of other material, all of it in the public domain and readily available on the Wilson Center Web site.

Shaul and I established a workable but ridiculously time-consuming routine. I would get home at night and call or e-mail Shaul, explaining Ja'fari's requests. He would contact my Wilson Center assistant, Azucena Rodriguez, who would compile the information and e-mail it either directly to me or to Shaul. Slow Internet connections and a bad telephone line meant agonizingly erratic transmissions. Since Ja'fari's English was inadequate, I would spend hours translating this material into Persian. In the morning, after only a few hours' sleep, I handed the material to Ja'fari, who would use it for a new barrage of questions. I was thus forced to facilitate my own agony.

There was virtually nothing that didn't feed Ja'fari's insatiably suspicious mind-set or that he couldn't fit into his conspiracy theory about the Wilson Center's involvement in a plot aimed at the Islamic Republic. To Ja'fari, a meeting at the Wilson Center to analyze the results of Iran's parliamentary elections or to discuss the aspirations of the younger generation in Iran—the everyday subject of numerous newspaper articles—was evidence of an attempt to understand the Islamic Republic with the motive to undermine it. From a long lecture on Iran's economy, he would zero in on a few sentences critical of Iran's economic policy, highlight them, and then instruct me to read these sentences, and only these sentences, into the interrogation record. Despite the mass of information I produced, Ja'fari continued to insist I was not revealing everything. When I suggested he check our Web site himself, he replied that there were closed meetings not reflected on the Web site.

❧ "You Can't Fool Me"

The fact that the Middle East Program was, at its inception, called the Middle East Project, and that I was first designated a "consultant," caused me endless problems. To Ja'fari "consultant" had sinister implications, and "project" implied an elaborate plan, entrusted to me and designed to subvert the Iranian government. He pronounced "project" as *perozheh*, Persianizing the French form of the word. He would lean back in his chair and narrow his eyes and say, "Now tell me, how were you going to *piyadeh*—implement—this *perozheh*?" The explanation was simple. The Middle East Program initially was very small, had no staff aside from myself, and did not qualify as a full program. It was designated a "project" because no one knew what else to call it, but to Ja'fari's conspiratorial mind, simple explanations did not wash.

Grinning as if to say, "You can't fool me," he proceeded to provide me with his version of the "facts." "Let me tell you," he said, "you were recruited, not hired. You were given the assignment because they wanted you to focus on Iran. If they didn't have a plan for Iran, why did they choose you, an Iranian woman, to run this *perozheh*?" I was insulted by his suggestion that I was hired not because I was qualified but out of ulterior motives, as if no Iranian, particularly a woman, merited such an appointment; but Ja'fari cut me short. "What did they instruct you to do when they hired you?" he asked. Despite myself, I burst out laughing, recalling that I was hired part-time, on a meager budget, and initially asked to organize just one meeting a month. My laughter upset him. "What did Hamilton instruct you to do when he hired you?" he persisted. He was disappointed to learn I was hired not by Hamilton but by his predecessor, Charles Blitzer. "Mr. Hamilton inherited me," I told a deflated Ja'fari.

He was also convinced that I had a close relationship with AIPAC, the strongly pro-Israel research and lobbying organization, and that I traveled frequently to Israel. I had no connection to AIPAC and had never been to Israel, but Ja'fari refused to believe me. "Check my American passport. You will see I have never traveled to Israel," I told him. Ja'fari had a ready reply for that inconvenient fact as well. The Israelis, he said, issue visas to "their agents" on separate pieces of paper. This was one of the few times I allowed myself to show the seething anger I felt toward Ja'fari. He was implying I was a spy. "Don't you ever accuse me of being an agent of Israel or any other foreign country," I snapped. Ja'fari was taken aback, but this did not prevent him from reverting to similar charges later in the interrogation. "You are married to a Zionist," he told me on one occasion, referring to my Jewish husband. "You work for the Zionists."

Ja'fari hammered away at a perceived connection between the Wilson Center and the CIA. "Who are these men in uniform who come to your meetings?" he asked, I assumed in reference to some photo he'd come across online. "Who are the CIA people? Who comes from the State Department and the Defense Department?" Except in a general sense, I really had no idea who came to our meetings. Our meetings are public; our e-mail list is extensive. As to Ja'fari's CIA preoccupation, I tried humor. "Even if CIA people attend our meetings, they don't give me their names and particulars. You haven't told me *your* real name; and I still don't know where *you* work." Ja'fari was not amused. In what he considered another "gotcha!" moment, he produced an invitation to a conference sponsored jointly by my program and the program Judith Yaphe ran at the National Defense

University (NDU). Judith, Ja'fari discovered through Google, had worked as a senior analyst on the Middle East and the Persian Gulf at the CIA; but she had quit over a decade ago to join the NDU. To Ja'fari, she was still CIA. Besides, National Defense University was a name calculated to feed Ja'fari's conspiracy theories.

Ja'fari was interested in the other institutions with which we had cooperated, including the Hoover Institution at Stanford and the Center for International Studies at M.I.T. But it was the National Endowment for Democracy and the Open Society Institute (OSI) that earned Ja'fari's most intense scrutiny. The OSI was part of the Soros Foundations, founded by the philanthropist George Soros, and dedicated to promoting open societies throughout the world. The foundation had been active in newly independent countries of the former Soviet Union, including Ukraine, Georgia, and Kazakhstan. In these countries, mass popular movements led by intellectuals and opposition parties had succeeded in bringing down Soviet-style governments. These movements became known as "velvet revolutions" or "rainbow revolutions" because of their peaceful, nonviolent nature and because protesters had adopted a particular identifying color—orange in the Ukraine, rose in Georgia, for example. In the twisted mind of Ja'fari and his colleagues, the Soros Foundations had caused these velvet revolutions, and since George Soros was a Jew, a shadowy, Jewish conspiracy hovered in the wings. Because the OSI had funded some of my programs on Iran, it followed that the Wilson Center was part of a conspiracy to bring about a velvet revolution—a "soft overthrow," as Ja'fari sometimes put it—in Iran as well.

Such was the web in which Ja'fari was trying to entrap me. Initially, I was bewildered by Ja'fari's references to "velvet revolutions" and "soft overthrows." The terms were not familiar to me in Persian, and I had not followed closely the upheavals in Ukraine, the Caucasus, and Central Asia, which preoccupied Ja'fari. But with a sense of mounting panic, I grasped the thrust of Ja'fari's thinking. He pressed me to confess falsely that I was part of the conspiracy. When I refused, Ja'fari tried to intimidate me. "Khanum Doktor Esfandiari," he said, his voice dripping with sarcasm as he addressed me with my full title in Persian. "For twenty years you have come and gone and plotted. This is now finished. We will keep you here. We will take you before a judge."

The prospects were terrifying. "They are planning a show trial, a 'confession,' and a jail sentence," I e-mailed Shaul on January 13. Over the telephone, Shaul tried to reassure me. "They won't dare put you on trial," he said, but I wasn't convinced. Ja'fari tried another, even more sinister tack. He offered to leave me alone if I implicated the Wilson Center. "They want me to say the center is part of a network for soft overthrow [but that] I didn't know and was fooled," I said in e-mails to Shaul two days later. "I won't say that. . . . I refuse to go down this line." Shaul was in full agreement with me. "You must never take that road," he said.

The next day, after a particularly unsatisfactory session for Ja'fari, his parting words were ominous: "We are not satisfied with your replies. Things will get worse for you."

The next morning, Wednesday, January 17, when I reported at the "Petit Trianon" as usual, there was no sign of Ja'fari. It was the "receptionist"—who I now concluded was actually in charge—who met and spoke to me. "We called your mother's apartment to tell you not to come in, but you had already left," he said. "The interrogation is over. Go back home. Go to the passport office and get your passport." I could barely suppress the sense of relief, the excitement, that was welling up inside me. Yet Ja'fari's parting words still echoed in my head. "But the interrogator didn't say anything to me about this," I said. He paused very briefly. Perhaps I only imagined the hint of surprise in his face. "That is not a problem," the man said. "Don't hurry. Don't contact them. Go have some fun, visit your friends, and wait for their call."

I didn't realize at the time that two branches of the Intelligence Ministry were feuding over me, one ready to let me go, the other determined to hold on to me. Only the good news registered with me that morning. I raced home to share it with my mother. I called Shaul and told him, "I think it is over."

The Raid

On the morning of January 19, I woke up feeling lighthearted. It was a brisk and brilliantly sunny Tehran morning. The usually noisy street was quiet on Friday, the Iranian sabbath. No vans were unloading goods; no impatient drivers pressed down on their car horns; schoolchildren were not clambering down the stairway on their way to school. Even the two noisy young boys in the apartment above ours were mercifully silent.

I walked to the corner of the street and took a cab to the home of my friend Shideh. We went for a walk in the large garden of her apartment complex. Shideh had made a *nazr*—a vow Iranians make to themselves to engage in a charitable or religious act if their prayer is answered. Shideh had vowed to give money to a charity when I was reunited with my family. Several friends had made a similar *nazr*. My mother had promised herself to make a donation to the school for the blind in Isfahan. Another friend had pledged that if I were let go, he would make a pilgrimage to Imamzadeh Saleh, a small shrine in Tajrish, in north Tehran.

Refreshed by the walk, I returned home, and took Mother to a family lunch arranged by a cousin. Naturally, the first question my relatives put to me was "When are you leaving?" I thought I would be gone in a week, but not wanting to jinx things, I noted that it ordinarily takes six months to issue a new passport. "That is what I am told," I said with a shrug.

After lunch, Mother, feeling upbeat like me, wanted to walk. The sidewalks were bustling. Shops were crowded. Small cafés were full of young people. Street food vendors were hawking sandwiches, pretzels, pistachios, soft drinks, and fruit juice. Mellat Park, just across the street, was crowded. The park was a favored meeting place for young people and college students during the week, families on weekends, and political demonstrations when they were permitted. It was here that women's rights demonstrators had been attacked, beaten, and hauled off in police vans earlier in the summer. On this Friday, the morals police, always on the lookout for young girls showing hair beneath their scarves or young men and women fraternizing, were out among the crowds, but they seemed inclined to leave people alone.

After our stroll, two of my cousins came to the house for coffee. They left around four. I told Mother I would like to take a nap, a rare thing for me to do. An hour later I was startled from my sleep to see three strange men, disheveled and brutish-looking, staring into my bedroom, one of them with a video camera in his hand. "She is sleeping; she is not even dressed," my petrified mother was saying. One of the men pushed her aside. "Get up," he said to me. "Put on your chador."

I sat up, stunned, clutching my blanket around me. "I don't have a chador," I said, "and I need to get dressed." He threw my raincoat at me. "Wear this." I told him to close the door. I slipped my raincoat over my nightdress, put on my slippers, and came out of the room. The three men were standing in the living room. My mother was as white as a sheet: "Who are you? What do you want? Why are you here?" she kept asking. Like me, she thought they had come to arrest me. "Cover your hair," one of them ordered. I was determined not to carry on a conversation with them in my nightdress and raincoat. "I need to get dressed," I repeated. They exchanged glances, and the man who appeared to lead the team nodded. "Okay." The commotion had attracted attention. A neighbor and friend of my mother's stood next to her. The building caretaker stood at the door, anxiously peering in. The three men had insisted the caretaker accompany them to the apartment; they needed him to lead them to the right door and to give them legal cover. When my mother answered the doorbell, one of the men had stuck his foot inside the door to prevent her from closing it.

I went to my room; picked up a blouse, a pair of trousers, my coverall robe, and a scarf; and got dressed. Back in the living room, the team leader showed me a search warrant. He would not even let me make a copy. "You can only read it," he said. He made both Mother and me sign it. This done, he dialed a number on his cell phone and mumbled something into it. Within minutes, a smirking Ja'fari was at the door. "I told you it would get worse," he said.

Ja'fari took off his shoes by the door and asked which was my room. He hurried in with two of his henchmen. One man opened my closet and took out every scrap of paper I had there, and went through my clothes, including my underwear, and even my shoes. Ja'fari went through the papers, discarding some and keeping others. Among the papers he took was an invitation my parents had received to a reception to mark the coronation of the shah in 1969—nearly forty years earlier. To Ja'fari the invitation was no doubt damning evidence of connections to the royal court. Ja'fari, I noticed, showed no interest in a framed letter from the minister of agriculture of the Islamic Republic honoring my father for his services to the field of Iranian botany. Ja'fari was adept at cherry-picking his evidence.

Ja'fari also started to put away some clear white wrapping paper I had brought with me from the United States. "Why are you taking that?" I asked. "There's invisible ink writing on it," he said. I laughed, despite the gravity of the situation. "It's wrapping paper," I said. "It comes in many colors." Embarrassed, he left the wrapping paper behind.

Of five or six books I had borrowed from a friend, he took a book on the Iranian revolution by the French scholar Yann Richard, a guide to the city of Tehran I had purchased at a local bookstore, a copy of the literary/political journal, *Goft-o-Gou* (*Dialogue*), and an issue of the official gazette that published full transcripts of parliamentary debates and to which I had a subscription. Ja'fari seemed to regard *Goft-o-Gou* as a subversive journal, even though it is sold at newsstands all over Tehran, and to think it suspicious that one should read the parliamentary debates, which are open to the public and broadcast on radio and television.

Ja'fari also took my laptop computer and eyed with considerable suspicion the Skype phone attached to it. The phone can be used to make telephone calls over the computer at almost no cost. "Are you sending messages to anyone?" he asked. I explained that it was a computer phone; I used it to call my husband. He took the Skype phone with him too, leaving only the computer mouse on the table. The three men then searched my mother's study, examined all her German books and the family pictures, and checked the bathroom. The whole operation was filmed by the man wielding the video camera, even while the group leader sat in the living room, incongruously trying to make small talk with my visibly trembling mother.

Watching these trespassers moving about my mother's apartment—opening our closets and drawers, pawing through my clothes and belongings, reading our family letters, casting a prowler's eye over our family pictures—I was swept by conflicting emotions. I was scared, of course; they might cart me off to jail. I feared my mother might at any moment suffer a heart attack. I viscerally felt the violation of my privacy, almost physically, as if I had been raped. I felt a hatred for the men who were doing this to us, with an intensity that astonished me.

Once they had completed their search, the men drew up a list of the items they were taking from us. They made my mother sign the list and walked out. "You will hear from us soon," Ja'fari said. During the entire ordeal, the smirk had never once left his face.

5.

"THINGS WILL GET WORSE"

Ja'fari called the very next day, a Saturday, and instructed me to report on Sunday not to the "Petit Trianon" but to the central headquarters of the Intelligence Ministry. The change of venue was deeply disturbing; it signaled a ratcheting up of my interrogation and my case. At the Petit Trianon, there was still the pretense that I was being questioned in the "passport office." At the Intelligence Ministry's headquarters, that pretense was abandoned. Friends who knew something about the workings of the intelligence community told me that at the senior levels of the Intelligence Ministry, two factions were engaged in a tug-of-war over policy—and over me. The more moderate group argued that holding and interrogating me was of no benefit to the Islamic Republic and would only damage Iran's image abroad. I should therefore be let go. A hard-line faction believed they had caught the "big fish," a mastermind in the plot to overthrow the Islamic Republic. The interrogation, therefore, should continue until I talked.

The moderate faction had prevailed on the previous Wednesday, when I had been told at the "passport office" that my interrogation was over and that I was free to go. But the hard-liners succeeded in overturning that decision. The Friday raid on my mother's apartment and the change in venue meant that I was now in the hands of the hard-liners and the target of a serious intelligence investigation. Friends and acquaintances who had generously and courageously interceded on my behalf understood perfectly well the meaning of this new phase. Their behavior changed. With one or two exceptions, they began to keep their distance; they could not risk being associated with me. One schoolboy friend of President Ahmadinejad's who had vouched for me through his contacts in the National Security Council and the Foreign Ministry even received a message from the president: "Tell him to stop beating the drum of the Americans," he was told. I understood why people stopped calling and wished to avoid me. But this sense of abandonment was especially hard for me to bear. I felt alone, forsaken and without support in my own country.

At the Intelligence Ministry

The Intelligence Ministry had located itself in the building that used to serve as the headquarters of SAVAK, the secret police under the monarchy. It was a nondescript hulk of a building, off Khajeh Abdollah Ansari Avenue, in a lower-middle-class district in the eastern part of the city. I got out from my taxi a few blocks from the building, a practice I followed each day over the next several weeks, whether I came by cab or a friend drove me. I didn't want the cab service I used to spread the word around my mother's neighborhood that I was going to the Intelligence Ministry every day. I didn't want friends who dropped me off to come to the attention of the ministry. Such precautions, I discovered, become second nature when you are entangled with the secret police.

I had done my best to look inconspicuous. I wore my long, navy raincoat over a black robe and black slacks. A black scarf covered my head. I wore no makeup, not even neutral nail polish. Yet I felt and no doubt looked out of place. I was the only woman in a robe and scarf; all the other women on the street were covered head to toe in chadors. I even walked differently, I realized.

I arrived early and used my spare thirty minutes to walk around the neighborhood. It was not an affluent part of the city. There was the usual storefront taxi service, a traditional greengrocer, a food store, a small shop selling stationery and household goods—brooms, dustpans, cleaning cloths. The window of the stationery store was dirty; the notebooks, pencils, and pens on display were covered with a thin film of dust. The grocery had not made the transition to the modern-style supermarkets that proliferated in affluent north Tehran. The vegetables and fruits—small tangerines and apples, carrots, potatoes and beans, piles of greens—were of modest quality. Here, there was none of the broccoli, brussels sprouts, and pineapples that pleased the palates of the capital's wealthier residents. The canned goods were local, not the American or European foods imported or smuggled across the border from Turkey or across the Persian Gulf from Dubai.

People were going about their morning business: buying bread, queuing up for milk, selecting vegetables, taking a child to school. I felt an uncharacteristic pang of envy at these people doing ordinary things on an ordinary day. Ordinary had disappeared from my life. My days were defined by the demands of interrogators. I could return to my mother's apartment every night, but I could not go home to Shaul. For a moment my mind drifted to my morning routine in Washington. I would get up at six, and by the time I came downstairs, the aroma of the cappuccino Shaul had prepared for me filled the kitchen. While having my coffee, toast, and feta cheese, I would speak to Mutti on the phone and glance at the headlines in the *Washington Post*. By seven, Shaul and I were out of the house, Shaul headed for George Mason University and I for the Grosvenor or Bethesda Metro station, from which I took the subway to work. By nine in the morning, I would have already been in the office over an hour reading and writing e-mail, going over my schedule, planning my day.

I often spent my lunch hour walking briskly on the Washington Mall, and I walked every evening and weekend in our Potomac neighborhood. But today I found myself maneuvering between potholes on the sidewalk in an ugly part of Tehran. All I could see in my dark mood were the shabby apartment buildings on both sides of the road and the *joub*, or open canal, with its muddy water, in the middle of the street.

I felt the country I had cherished all my life was no longer mine. I had loved Iran with a passion. I loved its brilliant blue sky and its brown earth. I loved the desert and the sea. Nothing to me was more beautiful than the clear night sky of my ancestral home in Kerman. The great ruins at Persepolis had made me proud; the poverty in Zahedan had made me weep. The beauty of Isfahan's mosques took my breath away. Yet these horrible people had made me feel alien in my own homeland.

I WENT UP THE steps of the ministry with considerable trepidation. Will I ever get out of this place? I thought. Will I ever again see Shaul, my daughter, Haleh, and my grandchildren again? I was utterly alone. Suddenly I heard Shaul, my pillar of strength in difficult times, and his familiar, "Pull yourself together, Plums." I swallowed the lump in my throat and rang the doorbell.

A voice over the speakerphone asked my name; an automatic buzzer opened the door. I stepped in to find a man behind a glass kiosk next to a metal detector with a conveyor belt. I showed the man the faded copy of my birth certificate I used as ID, placed my bag and book on the belt, and walked through the metal detector. The man muttered that the conveyor belt was not working, and after fiddling with it for a while, he gave up and handed me my bag and book uninspected. I followed him to a tiny, windowless room; there was a desk and chair for the interrogator and a combination chair and desk, the kind seen in schoolrooms, for the person under interrogation. I could have touched both walls from where I was standing. A friend later described being interrogated at length in this very room, sweating profusely in the heat and under the glare of lights in his face and eyes.

Ja'fari suddenly walked in, with his ubiquitous laptop, and motioned for me to follow him. He led me to a larger, airier room. The two windows were barred. There was a large desk, behind which Ja'fari sat, and a shabby sofa, which I used. On a low, round table in front of the sofa was a box of biscuits, a pitcher of water, and paper cups. "For you," Ja'fari said, pointing. The water looked stale and gray; I never drank it. He also pointed to the bathroom in the corridor, which I never used, fearing hidden cameras. I waited for him to begin. In my morbid state of mind, I thought of the Canadian-Iranian journalist, Zahra Kazemi, who had died under interrogation four years earlier in Evin Prison at the hands of these same people. Her case made world headlines. She was hurriedly buried by her killers; her family was denied a request for an autopsy. Will I suffer the same fate? I asked myself.

❧ Emptying Me of Information

The Intelligence Ministry, I learned, conceives of its interrogations as taking place in two stages. The first stage is *ta'yyin-e hoviyyat*—"establishing identity," or collecting every bit of information possible about the individual under investigation. The second stage is *takhliyyeh-ye ettela'at*, a term which in Persian has a much more sinister meaning than "debriefing," the term from which it presumably derived. It literally means, "emptying of information." This is what Ja'fari set out to do with me at the Intelligence Ministry's headquarters. He came armed with new material he had downloaded from the Internet: articles I had written, and talks that people had given at the Wilson Center on Iran's nuclear program, economy, parliamentary and presidential elections, foreign policy, relations with Syria and the United States, and support for groups like Hizbollah in Lebanon and

Hamas in the Palestinian territories. He dumped all this material in front of me. He said once again, "We will go over each of these items, one by one."

At the "Petit Trianon," Ja'fari had concentrated primarily on the Wilson Center's Iran program. Here, he wanted to cover the whole Middle East. Over a period of two or three weeks, he demanded material on all the meetings we had held over four or five years on Israel and the Palestinians, Syria and Lebanon, Iraq and Afghanistan. We had organized a few workshops for Iranian women in Tehran and two or three in provincial capitals. We had organized similar workshops in Amman and Beirut for women from the Arab states. Ja'fari wanted dates, duration, names of participants, names of trainers, sources of funds. We had cosponsored three meetings on Iran with the Hoover Institution at Stanford University; these too became a focus of Ja'fari's attention, as did a series of meetings we held on the Iran-Iraq war, part of a larger cold war project that was examining the Korean War, the Cuban missile crisis, and other conflicts, using archival material and bringing together some of the original key players.

Shaul, clear-minded and logical, warned me not to fall into the trap of explaining what organizations other than my own were doing. He also strongly urged me not to do translations for them. "Tell them to do their own homework," he wrote. But Shaul could not appreciate the relentless pressure I was under in the interrogation room. I was facing the possibility of formal charges, imprisonment, and trial. Ja'fari had a nasty, vengeful streak. I didn't want to open another door of dispute with him; I was focused on fighting him on more important fronts.

A Theater of the Absurd

Ja'fari's voracious appetite for information—almost all of it already in the public sphere—seemed insatiable. Like some manic agent of the Soviet secret police or the East German Stasi, he was intent on amassing detailed information, no matter how insignificant, on every Iranian I had ever known. Along with his colleagues, he imagined that if he piled up enough information and stitched it together in charts and timelines, he could finally figure out America's plan for overthrowing the Islamic Republic.

I took Ja'fari's questions one by one and wrote my replies bent down on the low table in front of me—an exercise that was playing havoc on my back. Ja'fari, in the meantime, swiveled left and right in his chair and fiddled with his cell phone, which seemed to be ringing all the time. In a rare light moment, I told him I felt I was in a doctor's office. On the phone, he spoke in unexpressive monosyllables. I gathered that in addition to being an interrogator, he was some kind of a teacher, maybe, I thought, in night school. "Yes, we will meet for class," he would say into the phone. "No, we won't meet today." (He later informed me he was a university professor.) Occasionally, he walked out of the room and took a call in the hallway, out of my hearing. At times, he received a text message in English and, bizarrely, asked me to translate it for him. One of his text messages was a quotation from Ralph Waldo Emerson; other messages were in a similar vein—a colleague sending him tidbits of American and worldly wisdom.

I became sharply attuned to his methods. He would ask me the same question again and again, sometimes days apart, hoping to catch me in an inconsistency or to wear me down. In order to disorient me, he would jump from topic to topic. One minute he would be detailing my husband's hostility to the Islamic Republic and his supposed Zionist and AIPAC connections; the next minute he wanted to discuss Lee Hamilton: his political party affiliations, his appointment to head the Wilson Center, and his selection as co-chair of the 9/11 Commission and of the Iraq Study Group.

He repeatedly tried intimidation. "We will keep you in Iran for years," he threatened. "We can make life difficult for you." He claimed the Intelligence Ministry was in possession of incriminating documents against me, so sensitive that "we will show them to you in another place," clearly implying Evin Prison, where "you won't be free to come and go as you do now." Repeatedly, he reminded me that no one could help me. "The key is in your hands," he told me on another occasion. "But on sensitive issues, you don't cooperate." Only if I "confess," he insisted, would I be let go, allowed to go home.

He asked questions that were wildly off the mark but sinister in their implications. "Tell us how the U.S. intends the overthrow the regime," he repeatedly asked. "How often does Hamilton go to Congress and the State Department to get his orders and pass them on to you?"

His other technique was to quote selectively and out of context and to twist the meaning of what I or others had said or written. One day he triumphantly produced a sentence from the blurb on the back cover of my book *Reconstructed Lives: Women and Iran's Islamic Revolution*. The sentence read, "She and her informants describe strategies by which women try and sometimes succeed in subverting the state's agenda." The words conjured up all kinds of nefarious plots in Ja'fari's head. "What *e-steratегy*?" he asked rhetorically, using the Persian pronunciation. "What subversive acts? What did these women want? Ha! To overthrow the regime. This was their agenda, and you encouraged them."

He produced a 2004 talk I had given at the Washington Institute. He had underlined the last sentence of my remarks, in which I said the invasion of Iraq had "a sobering effect" on many Iranians. I concluded that "most Iranians would prefer talks with the United States over confrontation, on the one hand, or a U.S.-led regime change on the other." He didn't understand the structure of the sentence, and it drove him into a paroxysm of accusatory fury. "You are saying people want regime change," he insisted. We went back and forth, arguing at length. I could not get him to understand the English.

When I was first summoned to the "passport office," friends assured me I had nothing to worry about; it was the routine hassle of replacing a lost passport. When I was forced to report to the Intelligence Ministry, I was told Ja'fari was finishing up, that while I was clearly being harassed, I would never be arrested. But I now realized Ja'fari was building a case against me, not winding down. I knew I was right to fear the worst, and I relayed my anxieties to Shaul. "They are planning a show trial, confession, and a jail sentence," I e-mailed him in January. Again in early February I wrote: "You are not aware how they are building a case against me. . . . My gut feeling is the next step is Evin [Prison], incarceration, and appearing in court."

Shaul and I still stuck to the strategy of avoiding press coverage, publicity, or any statement about me by the Wilson Center, which we were convinced would backfire, bringing even harsher treatment from the hard-liners, but it was proving difficult. "I had another call from a newspaper today," Shaul told me on the phone in mid-February. "We cannot keep the story out of the press much longer."

Coping

Facing a barrage of intimidating questions, day after day and week after week, I developed strategies and mechanisms to cope, to protect myself. This was not an idle exercise on my part. Ja'fari had threatened to put me on trial. As I e-mailed Shaul on February 12, Ja'fari was laying the groundwork for charges against me. Each morning I tried to anticipate the day's questions. I struggled to recall events going back five, sometimes ten and twenty years, in case Ja'fari asked. I asked my assistant at the Wilson Center for material in anticipation of the new and unreasonable demands Ja'fari was bound to make. Each evening I carefully went over in my mind the course of the day's interrogation, trying to discern where Ja'fari was headed and what traps he had laid for me, and making sure I had not inadvertently slipped up somewhere.

From the beginning, I decided to provide the information Ja'fari asked for, no matter how routine. I occasionally reminded him that everything he wanted to know was already on the Web. But I did not volunteer information he did not ask for. There was no point in adding grist for his interrogation mill.

I also made it a point never to allow false accusations or inaccurate characterizations of myself or Shaul to go unanswered. On the other hand, I refused to get involved in discussions about my husband's political views, his writings, or remarks he had made on Iran or Middle East issues. My husband's views were his own, I insisted. I could only speak for myself. I took a similar position regarding views others had expressed at the Wilson Center.

Ja'fari would underline sentences in the text of remarks I had made or talks others had given at the Wilson Center and ask me to read these, out of context, into the record. I always made sure to copy down the longer passage in which these sentences were embedded in order to provide context, to show there was balance in the presentations. He routinely referred to my replies to his questions as "confessions." I made it a point in my written responses to correct him and to substitute the word "answer" for "confession."

I also avoided getting involved with Ja'fari in broader discussions, say, on American policy or—a subject dear to his heart—currently fashionable political theory and analysis. For example, Ja'fari wanted to discuss American policy toward Iran, and invited me to describe the major issues between Iran and the United States. I kept my answers brief. I could not discern his intentions with this line of questioning and, frankly, discussions with him on almost any subject tried my patience.

Ja'fari fancied himself something of an intellectual. He was familiar with some of the theoretical literature on revolutions, the nature of democratic transitions, the durability and vulnerability of autocratic regimes, and the makings of civil society. In the West, this literature, once confined to the university, had gained currency outside academia after the collapse of the Soviet Union and the emergence of democratic regimes in the former Soviet empire. Ja'fari was also familiar with the names of some leading political theorists, such as Crane Brinton and Theda Skocpol on revolution, Francis Fukuyama on the so-called end of history and the emergence of democratic polities, and Michel Foucault on forms of Western hegemony and the hegemonic power of various forms of discourse.

Ja'fari, I assumed, had encountered this literature in university courses, or perhaps in classes at the Intelligence Ministry, or through exchanges with other intelligence services. The Russian intelligence services, with whom Iran's security agencies were in contact, had theories about the causes of the "velvet revolutions" that were taking place in their former empire. They regarded them as the work of outsiders, specifically of the United States. Iran's intelligence officers seemed to share these suppositions. Ja'fari often employed a faddish vocabulary that smacked of the university classroom. He may also have been reading Iran's more serious newspapers and journals, which introduced these thinkers and their ideas to a wider public. He wanted to discuss these ideas and thinkers with me, either to show that he too was a well-read intellectual, or in order to lead the discussion back to the subject of my interrogation: what the United States planned to do in Iran, how I envisioned Iran's future, how I thought political systems evolve, and where my political preferences and inclinations lay.

I studiously refused to go down this path. I am by nature a practical person. I do not have a theoretical bent. I had not studied the people Ja'fari mentioned. I had no interest in getting involved in a discussion of abstract issues with secret police interrogators; and I did not want Ja'fari and his colleagues to twist something I might say on politics in general into another charge against me. Whenever Ja'fari tried to discuss "ideas," my ready answer was "I have not read Foucault," or "I have not read Fukuyama." I often simply said, "I have no idea what you are talking about." This proved endlessly frustrating to Ja'fari. In one session, he taunted me with evidence of my supposed inadequacies. Recalling the interrogation he had conducted the previous year of Ramin Jahanbegloo, the Iranian political philosopher who in 2006 had spent four months in Evin Prison, he spat, "We used to ask Mr. Jahanbegloo one question, and he wrote seventy pages. We ask you a question and you hardly write seven lines!"

Hizbollywood

Amid the grim and grueling interrogation sessions, I had my moments of amusement. Ja'fari once asked me to tell him all I knew about the two famous "Zionist" foundations, the Ford Foundation and the Rockefeller Foundation. I burst into laughter. Clearly he had no idea that Henry Ford was no friend of the Jews. A fellowship I had been given by the John D. and Catherine T. MacArthur Foundation aroused his suspicions. "Why did General MacArthur give you a fellowship?" he asked, confusing General Douglas MacArthur with the founders of the family foundation that shared a name but nothing else, and seemingly unaware that General Douglas MacArthur had died more than forty years before. He also asked me to tell him about the Council on Foreign Relations, "where American foreign policy is made." The CFR brings together prominent American academics, journalists, officials, and former officials for a discussion of foreign-policy issues. It is a weighty organization, but it is not a secret sanctum where official U.S. policy is determined. I happened to be a member of the CFR, and for Ja'fari that was proof that I knew of the workings of the small cabal that forged American foreign policy behind closed doors. All I had to do was tell him how it was done.

One morning Ja'fari confronted me with a talk given at the Wilson Center by a Lebanese-American scholar, Marwan Kraidy, titled "Hizbollywood: Hizbollah's Information War Viewed from Lebanon." Marwan was making a play on words, combining Hizbollah, the Lebanese Shi'ite opposition group supported by Iran, with Bollywood, the term for the highly successful Indian film industry, based in Mumbai. Marwan wished to illustrate Hizbollah's skill in employing the media and publicity techniques to win adherents and support for its cause. Humor, however, was not Ja'fari's strong point. He insisted that "Hizbollywood" was derogatory, designed by the Wilson Center to ridicule Hizbollah. He lectured me for fifteen minutes on Hizbollah's military successes against the Israeli army. I waited for him to finish, then tried to explain Marwan's wordplay. Ja'fari dismissed my clarification with a cough, a smirk, and a shrug.

I never made any headway with Ja'fari. How does one persuade a man with Ja'fari's mind-set that the Ford Foundation, which had given grants to my program, is not part of a "Zionist conspiracy"? How could I convince him that my husband was not an Israeli agent? Wasn't Shaul, after all, a Jew? I could repeat ad nauseam that the Wilson Center had no secret budget; he remained certain we did. The idea that Congress could fund the Wilson Center's operating budget and not dictate its policies was alien to his mental universe. To rebut the charge that the Wilson Center was complicit with the U.S. government in trying to undermine the Islamic Republic, I pointed out that Lee Hamilton was coauthor of the Iraq Study Group report. It had recommended engagement and dialogue with Iran, not confrontation, counter to Bush administration policy. Ja'fari dismissed this inconvenient fact with a wave of his hand: "The recommendations are a sham," he said, "just a ploy to gain a foothold inside Iran."

❧ Hajj Agha

Despairing of getting me to "cooperate," Ja'fari also tried handing me over to his senior officer, Hajj Agha, who was presumably better qualified to get me to talk. I had two lengthy telephone conversations with Hajj Agha. My first conversation took place during the earliest days of my interrogation at the Intelligence Ministry headquarters. Ja'fari dialed a number on his cell phone and handed the phone to me. "Hajj Agha wants to talk to you," he said. Hajj Agha had a deep voice and was invariably courteous, although an undertone of threat was implicit in everything he said. In that first conversation, he tried to impress on me the seriousness of my situation and to disabuse me of the idea that anyone could intercede on my behalf. "You have powerful friends in this town," he said, mentioning the Iranian ambassador to the United Nations, Javad Zarif, who had tried to intercede on my behalf. "Forget about them. They can't help you. No one can help you." I felt as if he had slammed shut the door through which one last ray of light had been visible, plunging me into total darkness.

My second telephone conversation with Hajj Agha—he never showed up in person—took place near the very end of the Intelligence Ministry phase of my interrogation. Once again Ja'fari dialed his cell phone and handed it to me. Hajj Agha noted in a matter-of-fact way that he had gone over my answers carefully and was not satisfied with them. He referred again to the American plan to overthrow the Islamic Republic. "Just imagine a puzzle," he said, using the English word, for which he seemed unable to come up with a satisfactory Persian equivalent. "You have all the pieces in your head. Just put them together and give it to us. Tell us the mechanism, describe the model for us," as if there was a one-size-fits-all, do-it-yourself kit for bringing about "soft" revolutions. I found the conversation bewildering; I honestly did not understand what Hajj Agha was talking about, and I told him so. "Besides," I asked Hajj Agha in exasperation, "what does all of this have to do with me?" If there was a "model," I knew nothing of it; if there was a plan, I was not part of it. He was clearly unhappy with what he regarded as my unhelpful attitude.

He continued on this ominous tack: he invited me to "help" them save Iran from the disruptions America planned for it. "Tell us how to immunize the country from the onslaught of foreign intervention," he said. This was a line Ja'fari had used three days earlier. "You are the doctor," Ja'fari said. "How do you cure this?" It was now Hajj Agha's turn to ask me, more insistently, for suggestions. He wanted to know what I thought about the problems Iran was having with the United States and how best to handle the exchange of scholars and NGOs between the two countries. "You don't have to answer now," he said. "Go home and think about it, and put down your thoughts in writing." Before hanging up, he repeated what he had said earlier: my responses were not satisfactory. "If you cooperate, I can give you your passport in ten minutes," he said.

My passport in ten minutes! At least, I thought with grim satisfaction, Hajj Agha has unwittingly admitted that my "stolen" passport is sitting in his desk drawer.

❧ A Taxi Driver's Tale

By the time I left the Intelligence Ministry after this conversation on the evening of February 13, it was dark, and the streets were deserted. A hard rain was falling, and I didn't have an umbrella. The new "assignment" Hajj Agha had given me was troubling. It meant sitting up again into the late hours. Besides, I hardly knew what to write in response to the "your answers are not satisfactory" mantra. I needed, as always, to find a form of words that allowed me to preserve my integrity and also get me out of the clutches of my interrogators. I feared anything I wrote would only give them new material to use against me. I looked up at the sky; not a single star was visible. Where are the angels? I thought. Who is going to rescue me from these people?

I could not find a cab, not on the street, not at the taxi agency I normally used, not at a second storefront taxi service to which I was directed. All the taxi drivers had gone home, I was told, and wouldn't return because traffic was bad. As if the fates had conspired against me, I slipped in the pouring rain and bruised my legs and arm. I finally chanced on a cab at a third taxi service. In the taxi, the young man cursed his stupidity when he discovered how far he had to go. I promised him four times the usual fare.

The drive home took two and a half hours in the rain and the hopelessly snarled traffic, as the driver tried one highway, avenue, and side street after another. Eventually he stopped muttering and grumbling under his breath, settled back, and started to talk. For the next ninety minutes, he entertained me with an account of his life and work, his loves and aspirations.

He told me he held two jobs. He was a fireman by day and a cab-driver at night. He had a university degree in engineering from one of the provincial branches of Iran's Azad, or Free, University, but could not get an engineering job. A relative found him a slot in the fire department. The pay, benefits, and pension were very good, he said, and he had lots a free time. I commented that firefighting must be a dangerous job. "Living in Tehran is more dangerous," he said. "It's like living in a burning hell. You face death twenty times a day, driving a cab in this traffic, in your home, or coming face-to-face with the Revolutionary Guards, the morals police, or the *basij* [the paramilitary forces that are charged with maintaining public order and also enforce public morality]. As to work, once in a while there is a fire and we have to go and extinguish it. At least the job is rewarding, and you help people."

He told me his mother wanted to marry him off but he refused to wed any of the women his mother chose for him because they were too traditional and too religious. He also would not marry any of the girls he dated because they were too aggressive and modern. "I would rather go to Dubai or Thailand with my friends and have fun and come back to work here." He abhorred marriage. "No matter how sensible your fiancée, once you are married, she turns your life into a nightmare." All this talk about women's rights had transformed society, he said. "Women no longer know their place, and they have disoriented us men, too. They are taking our place everywhere: in the universities, the ministries, on the streets. Wherever you turn, there are aggressive women ready to push you aside. You are lucky if they don't trample you under their feet."

I laughed and asked him whether he preferred women to be invisible. He said he preferred a "segregated" society. How come, then, I asked, he approved of Dubai and Thailand? He said he went to Dubai for its nightclubs and to drink, and he went to Thailand to womanize. "I don't drink here. Why should I endanger myself? I think people who drink here are stupid. They risk being lashed or having their homes raided and searched by the *komitehs*," the neighborhood watchdog committees. What does he hope for in life? I asked. "To emigrate to Australia, marry an Iranian girl who lives there, and never to have to look back," he said. I got off at the corner of our street. I wished him luck.

No Grounds for Complaint

My mother opened the door with her usual question. “Is it over?” I shook my head. No. More than for myself, I was concerned about her. “My mother’s last year is turning into hell on earth,” I had e-mailed Shaul. She had survived the raid on her apartment; but I did not know how much longer she could bear the fear and anxiety or what would happen to her if I were arrested. Fortunately, many friends called her regularly; a few visited her. Michael Postl, the Austrian ambassador, though fifty years younger than my mother, had proved to be a very good friend. He telephoned her almost every afternoon and called on her once a week. He kept looking for ways to be of help to me.

After dinner, I sat down to write the “report” that Hajj Agha had wanted from me on the benefits of exchange of scholars and NGOs between Iran and the United States and ways of improving the Iran-U.S. relationship. What was there to say? I had consulted two friends, Baqer and Farideh. Baqer was a retired United Nations development economist who informally assisted the UN in their work with Iranian NGOs. Farideh was an academic and Iran analyst who lived in the United States but who traveled frequently to Iran and knew the country well. Both had been questioned in the past by the intelligence services about American and European think tanks and on the subject of scholarly exchanges between Iranians and Americans. Both, like me, had been asked for their views. Farideh had even spent a couple of nights in prison, when she was arrested while observing a women’s rights demonstration in which she was not taking part. When Ja’fari first pressed me about the “model” and the “mechanism” for velvet revolutions, it was to Farideh that I turned for clarification, using Shaul as an intermediary. She understood his jargon better than I.

Based on the advice of Baqer and Farideh, I wrote a few pages for Ja’fari. I once again stressed that the Wilson Center served as a forum for discussion of a broad range of views on Iran; I expressed my belief that continued exchanges between American and Iranian scholars, journalists, and institutions were the best way to calm tensions and address misunderstandings between the two countries. It was, I realized, fairly ordinary advice and certainly not the dramatic revelation or "key to the puzzle" that my interrogators were seeking. But I could think of little else to say. As I e-mailed Shaul that evening, "They want recommendations, and I don't have much to offer except to continue along the same path." I did believe dialogue between Iranians and Americans was beneficial and certainly better than no contacts at all.

At my meeting with Ja'fari the next day, February 14, I read my "report" to him, and he then read it for himself. I had imagined that Hajj Agha's request for "recommendations" meant my ordeal was at an end. But Ja'fari's facial expressions and body language told me otherwise. This was not what he had wanted. He looked up and said, "Oh, so you think conferences and inviting scholars to America should continue." His voice dripped with sarcasm, as if I were brazenly suggesting that we persist in the very activities aimed at regime change in Iran he had been accusing me of supporting. For three hours, he questioned me about my recommendations. His tone remained hostile. He ended the session by saying, "We have proof against you, and we will show it to you at the appropriate time and place."

Three days later, Ja'fari telephoned. He said Hajj Agha had reported to his superiors. "They are not satisfied with your answers. They want to know about the hidden layers." He then added: "We have warned you. There should be no grounds for complaint on your side. We will produce documents and show them to you where you will not be free to come and go."

"Do you mean you will arrest me?" I asked.

"Perhaps," he said.

That night, Haleh, Shaul, and my sister, Hayedeh, called for the latest news. I brought them up to date. I tried to sound calm, but I sensed that, across the continents, they could hear my despair.

6.

THE LULL

JA'FARI'S LAST PHONE CALL WAS followed by eleven weeks of silence. It was a period of anxious waiting, which I tried to fill in various ways. I spent most of my time with my mother. I visited older members of the family. I went for walks with one or two friends who would still be seen with me. With another friend, a publisher and historian, I started working on a series of profiles of prominent nineteenth-century Iranian women. But I knew the lull was not a good omen. I feared a sudden arrest and show trial on false charges. I feared imprisonment at Evin. I spent my days in a figurative crouch, my head hunched down between my shoulders, waiting for the blow to fall.

My e-mails to Shaul and Haleh mirrored my mood. At times I seemed to be saying good-bye for good. "I want you both to be strong and get on with your lives. I had a good life, thanks to Dad and a wonderful supportive family," I wrote on February 18; and then again, in early March, "I sometimes think I will never see either of you again; just lingering away here. I am petrified of this." I wrote to Hayedeh, telling her to look after Haleh and Mother.

Shaul tried to boost my morale. "They will never dare

arrest you," he told me on the phone and added in an early-February e-mail: "I know that you are tired; but you have been magnificent in handling this, including the interrogations. I'm really proud of you." But in an e-mail to Hayedeh, he conveyed his anxieties about me. "She is very down. I don't blame her. She wants finality, and all she gets is more uncertainty and waiting. . . . She feels alone and abandoned."

Mother and I often spent evenings looking for some step or misstep on my part that could explain my predicament. But nothing I had done during my weeklong visit prior to the "robbery" had been even slightly out of the ordinary.

Taming the Revolutionary Turmoil

For fourteen years after the revolution, I had avoided returning to Iran. In the immediate aftermath, the country was in turmoil, as the revolutionaries dismantled and replaced the old regime. Revolutionary committees roamed the streets and neighborhoods, entering homes, arresting people. Power was fragmented, and various agencies—the regular government, the Revolutionary Council, the Revolutionary Committees, the revolutionary courts, Khomeini's lieutenants, clerics in the provinces—vied for power. The Islamic Republic's first prime minister compared the country to "a city with a hundred sheriffs."

The headlines were dominated by random arrests, trials, and executions. A fierce power struggle erupted, first between Khomeini's men and their rivals for political power, such as the old National Front and radical left-wing movements, then among Khomeini's own lieutenants. In 1982, the first president of the Islamic Republic, Abol Hassan Bani-Sadr, was impeached and fled the country. When his supporters took to the streets, pitched battles ensued and thousands were killed, many executed in prisons, but others executed on the streets, in full public view.

In the meantime, Saddam Hussein, trying to take advantage of what he thought was a prostrate country, invaded Iran in September 1980. In the eight-year war that ensued, much of southern Iran was devastated, leaving the cities of Khorramshahr and Abadan, where I had spent a part of my childhood, and towns along the border in partial or total ruin. Refugees from the war zone flocked to cities farther north. Large slices of the south were occupied before Iraqi forces were driven back by counteroffensives and expelled from Iranian territory. In 1985 "the war of the cities" began, as Saddam Hussein rained down missiles on Tehran and some thirty other urban centers. Shaul and I were sick at heart at the destruction visited on our country. I stayed in touch with my parents by mail and phone, writing three times a week, telephoning at least once a week. Fortunately, Tehran Airport remained open and my mother and father were able to travel. They visited us in Princeton and later in Washington, and were in Princeton during our daughter's graduation from high school. I worried about them, especially when Iraqi missiles began to hit Tehran. But my father was rooted in Iran; nothing could make him leave. For ten years, there was never a period of calm durable enough for me seriously to consider going back.

In 1992, however, my father fell seriously ill and the decision to return was more or less forced on me and Hayedeh. By then, the internecine fighting was long over, and the clerical party closest to Khomeini had triumphed. The Iran-Iraq War had ended in 1988. Khomeini died the following year, and the transition to the new order took place without a hitch. Ali Khamenei, then president, replaced Khomeini as supreme leader. Ali Akbar Hashemi-Rafsanjani, the speaker of the Majlis, or parliament, became president. Khamenei lacked Khomeini's immense prestige, scholarly standing, and charisma; but the constitution vests ultimate authority and vast powers in the supreme leader. Khamenei gradually came to exercise these powers in his own right.

Initially, however, Rafsanjani, wily and worldly, shaped the character of the post-Khomeini regime. He was relatively pragmatic. He took steps to reduce state involvement in the economy and to encourage the private sector. He showed little interest in opening up the political arena, but he eased social controls. The Islamic *hijab*, an ample headscarf that covered head, hair, and neck, along with a robe, invariably black, that covered a woman from shoulders to ankles, was less strictly enforced; women started wearing loose head covers and robes in pastels and brighter colors. Young men and women could mix more easily in public. Iranians could listen to Western music without fearing consequences—most of the time. Rafsanjani's first minister of culture, Mohammad Khatami, took a more liberal attitude toward the non-political press, cinema, theater, and book publishing. Imaginative directors skirted the censors and made films that went on to win international prizes. Publications carried out spirited discussions of literary and broad political issues.

In all this, Rafsanjani was yielding to the inevitable. The middle class and especially the young, weary of restrictions, were pushing back. Pirate tapes and CDs of Western music and Hollywood films circulated semi-clandestinely. Young men and women could not openly mix on university campuses, but they did so during popular Friday-morning walks along the foothills of northern Tehran. Young girls and women were already challenging the dress and social code in subtle ways, entering universities in record numbers, and pushing to return to the workplace. The intellectually restless were using pen and speech to push against the parameters of the permissible.

Abroad, Rafsanjani resumed diplomatic relations with Saudi Arabia and also with Jordan and Morocco, monarchies with whom Iran had not had relations for a decade. He reached out to the United States by using Iranian influence to secure the release of American hostages held by Iranian-supported groups in Lebanon.

These developments were already under way when I chose to make my first trip back to Iran in the summer of 1992; but from abroad I did not have a full sense of the changes that were stirring in the country. I returned with both trepidation and anticipation. Arbitrary arrests were still common. At the same time, I was eager to see my parents and family, and I ached to return to the country of my birth.

Return of the Native

Tehran had changed dramatically. The *hijab* in its various forms, even if under siege, was prevalent everywhere, and I had to conform to it myself. I had to get used to the bearded men and a certain scruffiness on the streets and to an erosion of public civility. But much else was achingly familiar. My parents still lived in the same house where I had grown up. On a clear day, the sky was still the brilliant blue I remembered. Looking north from my parents' house, I could see the brown hills that I loved, and Mount Damavand, snow-capped, magical, and majestic in the distance. Despite the political uncertainty, I felt secure in these familiar surroundings, among friends and family; the skeins that tied me to Iran seemed as strong and reliable as ever. I felt, as we say in Persian, that "the ground under my feet was firm."

Other trips home followed in short order. I was excited by what I saw. On the streets, young women, beginning to show a bit of hair, daring to wear tighter clothes and some makeup, seemed self-confident, uncowed by the morals police; and they were visible everywhere: in the workplace, on university campuses, hiking in the hills above Tehran, in cafes and restaurants. I attended a university class with the literature professor Azar Nafisi, and another class with the sociologist Changiz Pahlavan, and was taken with the articulateness of their young students, their familiarity with Western literature and socio-political concepts, their eagerness to learn and explore new ideas, their easy interaction with their professors.

I met a number of professional women who were breaking new ground in their fields. Shahla Sherkat, then in her mid-thirties, was the plucky founder and editor of the women's magazine *Zanan*. She had turned the monthly into a forum for the discussion of issues relevant to women: legal equality, problems with the Islamic laws of divorce, spousal violence, child marriage, and the like. Mehrangiz Kar, whom I knew from my work at the Women's Organization before the revolution, was a lawyer. She had become an expert on women's rights under Islamic law, and spoke with great courage about expanding those rights. Shahla Lahiji had started her own publishing firm and specialized in feminist literature.

In journals like *Kiyan* and *Goft-o-Gou* intellectuals were exploring broader ideas about civil society, individual rights, and limits on the authority of the state. The ideas of the Islamic thinker Abdol-Karim Soroush, who argued for an Islam that was open to change and reinterpretation and that engaged with the problems of modernity, were gaining wide currency with university students. I did not know it then, but I was witnessing the early stirrings of the reform movement that would propel Mohammad Khatami to the presidency a few years later.

I happened to be in Tehran during the presidential elections of 1997, when Khatami scored his first, stunning victory, and again during the legislative elections of 2000, when his supporters won a respectable majority in the Majlis, shutting out dozens of prominent figures associated with the conservatives. These elections fascinated me; understanding them dovetailed with my work at the Wilson Center. In that first campaign, the excitement Khatami generated was palpable. Friends of mine who had never before voted under the Islamic Republic went to the polls in that election. In the house of a friend, I discovered all the teenage children in the family had campaigned for Khatami. The eleven-year-old younger daughter told me she had campaigned, too. "I went round defacing Nateq-Nuri's posters," she said, referring to the cleric who was running against Khatami. Khatami won the election on a huge turnout with a resounding majority.

In the 2000 parliamentary election, in a cab with Modarress at the wheel, I toured the polling stations all over Tehran. I saw long lines of men and women, many in chadors, waiting patiently to vote. I found myself devouring four and five newspapers a day and reading thoughtful and intelligent discussions of the political issues before the country. In the editorial offices of the journal *Kiyan* I ran across Akbar Ganji, already prominent as an intrepid, reformist journalist, who told me excitedly of the election slogan that the reformists had agreed on. "Iran for all Iranians" was meant to convey the idea of an Iran that included men and women of all political persuasions and ethnic groups and that would bridge the chasm that had opened up between Iranians in the country and those living abroad.

In the end, Khatami did not prove the man of the hour; he lacked the means and the will to withstand the ferocious right-wing backlash that followed these electoral mandates. The hard-liners, who opposed easing up on press and political restrictions and argued for a crackdown on the reformers, had retained control of the instruments of repression: the security services, the secret police, the Revolutionary Guards, and the judiciary. They dominated the Council of Guardians, a body of mostly senior clerics who could veto parliamentary legislation. They enjoyed the support of the supreme leader. They used these instruments to close reformist newspapers, arrest journalists, clamp down on university students, tamper with elections, and block legislation to free up the press or uphold constitutionally mandated liberties. These were years when the possibility of fundamental change seemed real and when Iranians believed, for a brief moment, that they could take charge of their own lives and government. It was not to be, and it was heartbreaking to me to witness the snuffing out of so much promise and hope.

☙ A Death in the Family

Back in August 1995, when these seeds of reform where beginning to take root, Shaul, Haleh, and I were vacationing on the island of St. Martin. I received a phone call that my father had suffered a stroke and was in a coma. Both my sister, Hayedeh, and I rushed back to Tehran. We arrived in time to join Mutti at my father's bedside, but he never regained consciousness to know we were there. I was at least grateful that he passed away quietly and without pain.

As a young bride, Mutti had accompanied Father on his travels through the Iranian countryside to gather plant specimens for his botanical studies. In some ways, Mutti came to know Iran, the hills and mountains, the northern forests, the desertlike areas of the eastern Kavir, and the small, green valleys that seemed to spring up magically among the brown aridity better than most natives. My father helped create a collection of Iranian plant life that is still used for research and study, and that formed the basis for the multivolume *Flora Iranica*, which he co-edited with his former Vienna colleague, Professor Karl Heinz Rechinger. A rare, previously unknown plant Father discovered bears his name.

My father never once considered leaving Iran after the revolution, even though several of his friends landed in jail and many others emigrated. When Saddam Hussein sent missiles over Tehran and many of the capital's residents relocated temporarily to nearby villages, to the homes of relatives in the provinces, or to their summer homes along the Caspian, Father chose to remain with Mutti in their small house in Tehran. I never asked my father why, but he must have thought it unpatriotic to leave when the majority could not.

It was satisfying to him, I think, that even the Islamic Republic, which was dismissive of practically everything and everyone connected to the old regime, came to recognize his services to Iranian botany. Before his death, he was honored at a special ceremony, a hall in the research institute he helped create was named after him, and he was given a plaque for his long years of service to the country. This was the plaque that Ja'fari chose to ignore when he raided my mother's apartment, looking for "incriminating evidence." The minister of agriculture, along with several of his deputies, had even stopped to pay their respects at my father's memorial service.

After Father's death, I came back to Iran more frequently to look after Mutti. But with the election of Ahmadinejad in 2005, I made it a point on these trips to stay away from even mildly "political" people. I avoided journalists, politically involved intellectuals, publishers, women activists, and the like. My work in Washington no longer allowed long stays in Iran, and on such brief trips I wanted to spend as much time as possible with Mutti. She was growing frail and needed attention. Aware of the paranoia of the re-empowered security services under Ahmadinejad's administration, I wanted to be extra careful. I couldn't afford to jeopardize my ability to take care of my mother.

On this last trip, I had planned to be in Iran for only a week, and I spent almost all of my time with Mutti. On the night of my arrival, December 23, we went for Christmas dinner to the home of a friend, Shabnam. As a child, we celebrated Christmas at home, and Mutti and my father always threw a party for their closest friends, as they also did to mark the Iranian and Christian new years. A superb hostess, Mutti would lay out a great feast and open up all the rooms of the house to her guests. After my father died, she stopped putting up a Christmas tree; "not in your father's absence," she would say. She eventually stopped giving her Christmas party, too. But she loved Christmas, and she still liked me to take her to Churchill Street, behind the British embassy, where Christmas trees continue to be sold, as they had been ever since my childhood.

Shabnam didn't observe Christmas herself, but she knew how much Christmas mattered to Mutti, and for the past few years it had become a tradition for us to spend Christmas at her house. She always asked three or four people to join us, and on that evening she had asked her sister-in-law and her two sons, who were visiting from the United States. Shabnam had put together a sumptuous dinner for the eight of us. She had decorated her table with pine branches and flowers. Christmas carols played on her CD player as we sat down to eat. Her cream of asparagus soup glistened in the candlelight like the white snow on the lit terrace. She served turkey stuffed with fresh fruits and Persian rice, without which no Iranian meal is complete. Dinner was followed by a selection of desserts: chocolate mousse, pomegranate jelly, and persimmon tart. We exchanged stories, laughed together, and stayed up quite late.

Mother and I went home by cab. It was a brightly lit, cold night; the reflections from the streetlights sparkled on the icy roads and sidewalks. I felt content, and so did Mutti; everything seemed so calm and lovely. As we entered the apartment, Mutti looked around and said to me in German, "*So eine schöne Wohnung.* Such a beautiful apartment. I wouldn't trade it for anywhere else in the world."

Behesht-e Zahra

I spent the next few days tending to Mutti's affairs. I made sure everything in the apartment was working properly. I did some shopping for her. I took her to visit family and friends. I also accompanied Mutti to Behesht-e Zahra cemetery to visit my father's grave.

Behesht-e Zahra is Tehran's main cemetery. Already large before the revolution, it had grown huge since 1979. The population of Tehran had nearly tripled in this twenty-seven-year period. In addition, the Iran-Iraq War left hundreds of thousands dead. The large majority were buried here, in a special section of the cemetery set aside for the martyrs of the war. Other parts of cemetery were reserved for martyrs of the revolution, high officials of the Islamic Republic, athletes, and writers and artists. In a corner of the main cemetery is a section allocated to members of opposition groups, such as the Mujahedin-e Khalq (MEK) and the Fadayan-e Khalq, who had taken up arms against the Islamic Republic and died either by execution or in street fighting. Considered apostates, they were not allowed a proper Muslim burial. (In 1988, in the last weeks of the Iran-Iraq War, the MEK, armed and supported by Saddam Hussein, sent military contingents across the Iraqi border into Iran. The raid was quickly squashed, but in fear and fury, the regime executed at least 2,000 members of militant groups already serving sentences in Evin and other prisons. The government never admitted to these mass killings and, according to widespread reports, buried the dead in unmarked graves.)

Behesht-e Zahra was known for its "fountain of blood," a pool with a fountain spraying red-dyed water to symbolize the blood shed by martyrs of the Iran-Iraq War. In general, though, the cemetery is well tended and pleasant, the long rows of graves separated by walkways, streams, and green spaces. As is the Iranian habit, families come here to place flowers or strew petals on tombs, to distribute sweets and feed the poor in honor of their dead, and to picnic among their loved ones.

Just before Behesht-e Zahra, but part of the cemetery complex, stands the huge mausoleum built as a memorial to Ayatollah Khomeini. The grandiose mausoleum, utterly at odds with the stark simplicity of Khomeini's lifestyle, was built to resemble a mosque; four minarets flank a great hall topped by a massive golden dome. Inside are a marble floor, crystal chandeliers, and expensive carpets. The compound is surrounded by shops, restaurants, a cultural complex, a religious seminary, and resting places for visitors. The authorities hoped the mausoleum would become a center of pilgrimage for millions of visitors, on par with the great Shi'ite shrines at Qom, Mashhad, and Shiraz. Foreign dignitaries are taken there to pay their respects. The Iranian president customarily holds a rally once a year at the tomb of the Imam, as he is known in Iran. In reality, however, the mausoleum cannot compete with the older, traditional shrines that resonate with religious meaning for Shi'ites. But people do visit in large numbers. Families picnic on the grounds, and buses to and from the provinces stop to give passengers the chance to rest and pay homage to Khomeini.

Mother at the Cemetery

Mutti visited my father's grave once a month, with Modarress serving as her driver. I always accompanied her when I was in Tehran. We stopped at the flower market just outside the gates of Behesht-e Zahra. I walked with Modarress among the hundreds of buckets of flowers sitting on the ground, and we picked the white and pink gladiolas Mutti loved. We drove off with the trunk full of fresh flowers, enough for the grave of every family member, the car redolent with their perfume.

Many decades ago, my late uncle, Gholam Hossein, had purchased a small mausoleum to house the family graves. My father, my paternal grandmother, two of my aunts, my uncle Gholam Hossein, and a cousin all were buried here. For my father's grave, Mutti had chosen a plain black marble stone engraved with four words in German: *In Treue und Liebe*—in faithfulness and love. She had designated a space right next to my father for herself.

Modarress took the key from Mutti, unlocked the iron door, opened the windows to air the room, swept the floor, removed the old flowers and, as is customary, poured water and rose water on the graves. He helped Mother up the steps to the main landing, handed Mutti and me the flowers, and waited outside. Mutti stood before Father's grave and whispered a prayer; I could hear her telling my father in German how much she missed him, asking him why he had left her, her folded hands reminding me of Dürer's *Praying Hands*. It was one of Mutti's favorite paintings, and whenever we were in Vienna together we went to the Albertina Museum to view it. Having covered Father's grave with flowers, Mutti placed one more flower on each of the family graves, and stopped to say a short prayer in front of my grandmother's resting place.

As always when at Behesht-e Zahra, I stopped briefly at the artists' section of the cemetery, where I walked to the resting place of two people I loved, Karim Emami, who, along with his wife, Goli, were among our dearest friends. Karim had been especially close to Shaul, since they had both worked for the same newspaper organization early in their career. At the time of his death in 2005, Karim was one of Iran's foremost lexicographers, editors, and translators. He had translated into Persian F. Scott Fitzgerald's *The Great Gatsby*, John Osborne's pathbreaking play *Look Back in Anger*, the Sherlock Holmes mysteries of Sir Arthur Conan Doyle, and much else. Just before his death he had completed work on a one-volume Persian-English dictionary.

Even Karim did not escape Ja'fari's attention. At one point during my interrogation, Ja'fari asked me how I knew Karim and what I knew about him. "But he is deceased," I said. Besides, Karim, though interested in politics, was one of the most unpolitical of men. His life was devoted to his books, his translations, his fascination with words and their meanings. "Just write," Ja'fari replied, paying no attention to my protest. As if it were not enough to pile up fat files of information about the living, the Ministry of Intelligence was also piling up fat files about the dead.

Waiting

My entanglement with the Intelligence Ministry meant I would never again feel safe in Iran, even at home. I could no longer carry out an unguarded conversation over the telephone. I believed the intelligence people were reading my e-mail. My nerves were always on edge. One evening, the doorbell rang and Mutti and I panicked at the sight of two men with bulky bags standing by the door. Mercifully, they turned out to be repairmen who had rung the wrong doorbell. After the raid, fearing microphones had been planted in the apartment, Mutti and I took to going to the bathroom and turning on the shower if we had something important to say to each other. I hated being cooped up in the apartment, but I was uncomfortable going out. Taxis made me claustrophobic. I could not shake off the feeling of being watched and followed. I found myself looking over my shoulder on the street and constantly checking the rear window of taxis in case I was being tailed.

Mutti and I became increasingly isolated. The small group of academic "insiders" who had generously tried to help me began to disappear from my life. Our Tehran University friend Nasser's calls grew infrequent and then stopped altogether. Hadi, the academic who had selflessly spent the best part of two months trying to do something for me, returned to Tehran from Washington, D.C., but never telephoned. When I called Mostafa at his think tank to offer condolences on the death of his father, he hastily hung up. These people understandably feared they would come under suspicion themselves. A very old and politically savvy friend turned visibly ashen when I told him of my interrogation. An acquaintance who had boasted of his excellent connections in the Intelligence Ministry disappeared once he learned of my case. When I ran across him at a memorial service, he said, "Please don't ever mention you know me. There is nothing I can do for you."

Family members seemed full of undeserved reprimands. A distant cousin took me to task for my too-frequent trips to Iran. "You shouldn't have come so often," she snapped. Another cousin wondered why I hadn't moved Mutti to the United States years ago, as if my mother were baggage I could just carry away and who had no will or preferences of her own.

Ahmadinejad's Tehran

I could no longer see the beauty of the landscape I had always loved. I saw only the gray ugliness of the streets, the piles of uncollected garbage, the potholes, the dirty water in the canals, the smog and the snarled traffic. I also could not help but contrast the elegance in which some of the city's residents, including friends, lived with the rampant poverty and economic hardship evident everywhere. Life in Tehran was expensive, and prices were going up every day. I saw an old man walk into a dairy store to buy a single egg and shoppers who waited till late in the evening to buy the battered fruits and leftover bits of fatty meat. I often witnessed the morals police stopping young boys and girls on the streets and hauling them away. Not for the first time, I heard of vigilantes barging into a wedding party, leaving the bride and groom in tears at the wreckage of a celebration they had planned for months. The sense of excitement, the possibility of freedom I had sensed in the early years of the Khatami presidency were gone. Ahmadinejad's morose shadow had fallen over the country.

Noting my despair, my cousin Elli suggested I leave the country illegally. Someone could be found to take me across the Persian Gulf in a boat. After the revolution, large numbers of people left the country illegally, crossing over into Turkey or Pakistan or traveling by boat and dhow to one of the Persian Gulf sheikhdoms. Initially the exodus was of people escaping the uncertain mercies of the revolutionary courts. Later, mostly young men made the crossing to escape military service during the Iran-Iraq War. These networks continued to operate, but they had shrunk dramatically.

I considered this option—but never seriously. I was being watched. The dangers of an illegal crossing were considerable. I could not picture myself trekking across mountain passes or crossing the Persian Gulf in a creaking boat. At bottom, I simply didn't want to leave my own country like a fugitive. When I left, it would have to be on a proper passport, through a proper port.

❧ Getting a Lawyer—and a Passport

The most difficult time for me in this period of waiting came as Nowruz, the Iranian new year, approached. Nowruz coincides with the spring equinox. It is a moment of rebirth, and a time for family reunions, visits, and exchanging gifts. For a child, Nowruz was always a magical moment, and it never lost its special meaning for me. But this year, I only went through the mechanics of the festivities. "I can't share in the joy and happiness around me," I wrote Shaul. Our wedding anniversary also fell in the Nowruz period. It was hard to be away from Shaul. I e-mailed him on March 16: "Tomorrow is our anniversary. Forty-two years! I miss you very much and love you so very much. I thank you for the wonderful life you gave me. I learned so much from you. Every day has been a wonderful experience for me."

There was also the now-vital precaution of getting a lawyer. My preference was for Shirin Ebadi. I had met Shirin before the revolution, visited her on some of my trips to Iran, and interviewed her for my book *Reconstructed Lives: Women and Iran's Islamic Revolution*. Persistent, outspoken, feisty, and enjoying a degree of immunity from arrest due to her high international profile, she was not popular with the Intelligence Ministry or the revolutionary courts. I knew her and admired her down-to-earth, plainspoken style, but I still hesitated to ask her to take my case. She had made a name for herself defending high-profile political dissidents in court. I had not been arrested or put on trial—yet. My retaining a lawyer like Ebadi might force the ministry's hand, giving it even more incentive to manufacture a case against me and ram it through the court system. Furthermore, Ebadi had become an international figure when she was awarded the Nobel Peace Prize in 2003, the only Muslim woman ever to receive such an honor for her work on human rights and women's rights. By taking her as my lawyer, I might have alerted some of the foreign press, which we had thus far so carefully avoided as well as the U.S. State Department or prominent American officials. The Intelligence Ministry was trying to implicate me in a supposed American plot to overthrow the regime; it hardly made sense to provide fodder for their false allegations by involving the American government, which had precious little clout in Tehran. Reluctantly, I decided against contacting Ebadi for the time being.

Friends had recommended a couple of other lawyers. One of them was a woman in her fifties who had built up a lucrative practice before the revolution representing foreign companies. She agreed to see me, on the condition that I told no one. I took extra precautions for our meeting. Rather than calling for a cab, I picked up a taxi on the street and paid the driver not to take on additional passengers. I got off several blocks away from the law office and walked in and out of several stores. Once at the lawyer's building, I pushed the elevator button for the wrong floor, then took the stairs to her office.

She believed that once I was milked for information, my case would be closed and I would be sent home. She advised me to keep a low profile, not to talk to the press, and not to go public, since this would only provoke the Intelligence Ministry. She promised to check with the passport office regarding my case, and we parted. I never heard from her again, except for a message assuring me (wrongly) that I would not be arrested and my case would be wrapped up in a matter of days, rather than weeks.

The second lawyer had been a member of the revolutionary courts and was now in private practice. He had handled political cases like mine, and his contacts in the judiciary and revolutionary courts were reputed to be good. He listened to my account of the robbery and the interrogation and concluded that my case was being handled at the highest levels of the Intelligence Ministry, possibly by the minister himself. He promised to inquire about my file. He assured me that there remained fair-minded judges who would throw out a case based on unfounded charges. I also never heard from him. I assumed that, like some of my friends, he had been warned off once he started making inquiries.

I tried to make the best of my time, despite the grueling uncertainty of not knowing what the ministry was planning next. I had, of course, already applied for a replacement Iranian birth certificate and identity card, but knew processing would take months. My Iranian passport remained hostage to the whims of my interrogators, but I hoped to get my "stolen" American passport replaced. A few days after the robbery I had gone to the Swiss embassy in Tehran to report the theft and request a new passport. (The Swiss embassy represents American interests in Iran.) I was told that replacing an American passport would take several weeks, and having been denied a meeting with the ambassador or his deputy, I concluded the visit to the Swiss embassy was nothing but an exercise in futility.

Now I turned to Shaul and the Wilson Center for my American passport. Joseph Gildenhorn, the chairman of the board of the Wilson Center, spoke to former secretary of state Colin Powell, who called the State Department. The Wilson Center found in its files a stock photograph that could be cropped to serve as a passport photo, and the State Department arranged for a passport to be issued in record time. Within three weeks of the robbery I had an American passport, but we left it with the State Department, fearing that once in my hands in Tehran, the passport could be seized again.

I had always thought of my dual Iranian-American nationality as an accurate reflection of the two worlds and two cultures between which I shuttled, and my two passports as a token of the globalized world in which we lived. But now that I was trapped in Tehran, things looked different. I had two passports; but one had been seized and I could not use the other. My adopted country and the country of my birth were engaged in a dangerous, undeclared war; and I, and many others like me, were caught in their cross fire.

Iran and America

It was not always this way. For decades, Iran and America had enjoyed excellent relations. The shah had allied Iran closely with the United States and the West after his accession to the throne in 1941. A succession of American presidents had supported the shah. When the Soviet Union and Britain occupied Iran in World War II, the United States joined them in using Iran's overland routes to supply Russia against Hitler's armies. Yet while history taught the shah to be suspicious of British and Soviet intentions, he looked to the United States to protect Iran and to ensure withdrawal of British and Russian forces once Hitler was defeated. During the cold war, the shah relied on the United States to support him against what appeared to be a threatening Soviet Union, with its 1,200-mile shared border with Iran, its historical designs on Iranian territory, and its Communist ideology.

In 1953, during Iran's oil nationalization crisis, when Prime Minister Mohammad Mossadegh soared in popularity and the shah nearly lost his throne, a coup hatched by the CIA and British intelligence restored his rule. Over the next two decades the United States and Europe became Iran's principal trading partners. Western companies operated Iran's petroleum industry and were the almost exclusive purchasers of its oil. Iran's military was trained and supplied by the United States. Ties remained close in other fields. By the 1970s, tens of thousands of Iranians were studying at American universities. President Carter and his wife, Rosalynn, chose to celebrate New Year's Eve in 1977 with the shah and the queen in Tehran, and Carter toasted the shah's Iran as an island of stability in a turbulent region.

For the United States, the shah was an ally against the Soviet Union during the cold war, a partner in ensuring Persian Gulf security in the 1970s, and a reliable source of oil. Iran provided a substantial market for American weaponry and industrial and commercial goods. For the shah, the close relationship he developed with America was a mixed blessing. America provided him with great power patronage, access to weaponry and technology, diplomatic support, and, when he needed it, an additional level of security. But the shah never overcame the stigma of having been restored to power in 1953 in a CIA-engineered coup, and with segments of the Iranian population, the alliance with the United States was not popular.

In these years, the shah also developed close if not always publicly acknowledged relations with Israel. The wave of revolutions that swept the Arab world in the 1950s and early 1960s toppled monarchies in Egypt, Iraq, and Libya. In this clutch of Arab states, military officers embracing a heady ideology of Arab and pan-Arab nationalism and socialism came to power. They pursued policies hostile to Israel, the West, and the region's remaining monarchies, and turned to the Soviet Union for military and economic assistance. Israel and Iran seemed natural allies against this wave of Arab radicalism. The Iranians were not Arabs, and an age-old sense of difference reinforced these divergent political orientations. The shah admired the deadly effectiveness of Israel's military. The two countries shared intelligence; Iran supplied Israel with oil; trade, never very large, expanded; and Israeli companies carried out agricultural projects in Iran.

The shah was not the pliant junior partner in the U.S.-Iranian alliance that his critics painted him to be. He had relied heavily on American support in the early years of his reign, when he was weak, inexperienced, fearful of Soviet intentions, and recovering from the scars inflicted by Mossadegh and the oil nationalization crisis. But he chafed at American tutelage and broke free of it as soon as the easing of international tensions and Iran's growing financial independence allowed. He ignored the admonitions of President Nixon to lower oil prices, putting his country's interests first, and was the principal architect of the decision by the Organization of Petroleum Exporting Countries (OPEC) to quadruple oil prices in 1973. Earlier, much to Washington's consternation, he purchased from the Soviet Union the steel mill he could not obtain from the West, allowed the USSR to build a machine tools plant in Iran, supplied the Soviet Union with gas, and even bought light arms from the Russians. When the British announced their decision to withdraw their military forces from the Persian Gulf in 1971, he made sure three disputed islands he regarded as strategically important fell under Iranian control. He expanded Iran's naval forces and embraced the idea that he would now serve as the guarantor of Persian Gulf security.

Nevertheless, the shah's close alliance and identification with America and Israel did not sit well with his opponents, who tried to portray him as a lackey of the United States. Ayatollah Khomeini played on this theme with particular skill. In 1963, he chose one of the holiest mourning days in Shi'ite Islam to preach a sermon harshly critical of the shah's policies and his close relations with Israel, warning the shah that the people would "throw you out of Iran." His arrest led to severe riots in Tehran and other cities. The following year, he delivered a sermon attacking the status-of-forces agreement that Iran had signed with the United States. The agreement reminded Iranians of the humiliating nineteenth-century "capitulations," which made all Europeans resident and working in Iran subject to their own consular courts rather than to the jurisdiction of Iranian courts. Khomeini described the SOFA as a document "for the enslavement of Iran."

Sent into exile, first to Turkey, then, in 1965, to Iraq, Khomeini continued to depict the shah as subservient to American and Israeli interests, a theme he pursued during the year of protests and demonstrations in 1978 that led to the overthrow of the monarchy in 1979. He and his supporters noted that America stood by the shah even as his troops were killing protesters on the streets of Iranian cities. By

December 1978, the Carter administration, which had strongly supported the shah, concluded he could not survive. Khomeini's lieutenants had already entered into discussions with American diplomats in Paris, hoping to persuade Washington to ease the shah out of office. Washington eventually did so, but when the revolution triumphed in February 1979, a strong strain of hostility to the United States remained part of the revolutionary ideology, and Khomeini used and encouraged it.

Even so, the Islamic Republic's first prime minister, Mehdi Bazargan, quietly sought to repair relations with Washington. But it was not to be. On November 4, 1979, just days after Bazargan met with U.S. national security adviser Zbigniew Brzezinski in Algiers, students from Tehran's universities seized the American embassy in Tehran and took more than sixty diplomats hostage. They wanted to sabotage normalization of relations between Iran and the United States, and they were protesting the U.S. decision to allow the shah, by now very ill from cancer, into the United States for medical treatment.

The embassy seizure proved a seminal event in the history of the revolution and in Iran-U.S. relations. Diplomatic relations were ruptured and remained unrepaired thirty years later. The images of blindfolded, handcuffed, and disheveled American diplomats paraded before television cameras were seared into the American conscience. In Iran, the embassy seizure was hugely popular. It gave the faltering revolution a new lease on life, strengthened the radicals, and weakened the moderates in the internal struggle for power. Khomeini, after wavering for a couple of days, came out in support of the students, recognizing that the students had managed to galvanize the population. He capitalized on the anti-American sentiment sweeping the country. He termed the United States "the great Satan" and the embassy itself "a den of spies," labels that remained part of the revolutionary lexicon for three decades. Some of the hostages were released because they were women, African Americans, or ill. But fifty-two Americans spent 444 days in the embassy and makeshift places of incarceration. Their release was negotiated by the Carter administration, but in a final humiliating snub to the sitting president, the aircraft flying them out of Tehran was not allowed to leave until President Reagan was sworn in.

In the decade that followed, the estrangement between the two countries grew deeper. When Iraq's Saddam Hussein invaded Iran in 1980, the United States did not condemn the aggression and even took quiet satisfaction at seeing the Islamic Republic in dire straits. Initially, Washington hoped two unsavory regimes would simply wear each other down. But when the tide of the war turned in Iran's favor and the Iraqi regime appeared threatened, the Reagan administration tilted toward Iraq. An Iranian victory over Iraq could destabilize the region and threaten America's Arab allies in the Persian Gulf.

The administration took Iraq off the terrorism list, provided Saddam Hussein with economic aid, and allowed Iraq to purchase helicopters and high-tech equipment from the United States. It lent Iraq diplomatic support and supplied it with crucial military intelligence. It successfully pushed for an embargo on west European arms sales to Iran, but raised no objection to significant arms deliveries to Iraq. When Iraq used poison gas against Iranian forces, the Reagan administration issued a very mild reprimand. At one point during the war, the United States had information that Iraq was using chemical weapons on "a daily basis" against Iranian troops, yet Donald Rumsfeld was dispatched to Baghdad in December 1983 to lay the grounds for resumption of full diplomatic relations between the two countries. In 1987–88, the United States pushed for resolutions in the UN Security Council to end the fighting, but on terms favorable to Iraq.

The war inflicted enormous physical damage on Iran, cost over 200,000 lives, and left deep scars on the Iranian psyche. American support for Saddam Hussein was not easily forgotten by Iranians.

Iran responded by seeking to make trouble for America's friends and to strengthen America's enemies. It sought to destabilize Saudi Arabia and Bahrain. When Israel invaded Lebanon in 1982, in a war aimed at uprooting the PLO's strongholds in the country, Iran sent "volunteers" and Revolutionary Guards to the Bekaa Valley to assist the Lebanese resistance. Iran was also instrumental in creating, then funding and equipping, the Shi'ite resistance movement, Hizbollah. It helped Hizbollah create a network of mosques, medical clinics, and schools for Lebanon's Shi'ites. It also provided the movement's military wing with money, training, and equipment. Hizbollah harassed Israeli forces and their surrogates in the buffer zone that Israel occupied in southern Lebanon. It took a number of Americans hostage. Both America and France had sent troops to Lebanon to maintain peace after the Israeli withdrawal. In October 1983 suicide bombers linked to Hizbollah drove trucks into the United States Marine compound near Beirut Airport, killing 241 Marines, and into the French military compound, killing 57.

The one exception to almost unmitigated Iran-American hostility in the Reagan years came during the mid-1980s, in what came to be known as the Iran-Contra affair. President Reagan was keen to secure the release of seven American hostages in Lebanon. Iran badly needed arms for its war with Iraq. Iranian intermediaries using Israeli contacts suggested an arms-for-hostages swap. The United States agreed and a clandestine but clumsily handled series of arms deliveries took place; 2,000 TOW antitank missiles and smaller amounts of HAWK surface-to-surface missiles and missile parts were sold to Iran. For some members of the Reagan administration, an added attraction of this arms-for-hostages deal was that money generated by the arms sales could secretly be funneled to the Contra guerrillas fighting the Sandinista government in Nicaragua. But, as an indication that the Iranians and Lebanese were feuding among themselves, only a few hostages were released while additional ones were taken. In November 1986, Iranian hard-liners opposed to any Iran-U.S. reconciliation leaked a few details of the deal to a Lebanese weekly. Exposure created an uproar in both Tehran and Washington. The arms deliveries abruptly stopped, and the Reagan administration reverted to a policy of steady support for the Iraqi war effort.

A "Quid without the 'Quo' ": Bush I

The end of the Iran-Iraq War in 1988—when both countries, exhausted by a conflict neither could win, accepted a cease-fire in place—and the election as president of George H. W. Bush in the United States and of Hashemi-Rafsanjani in Iran the following year appeared to provide the opportunity for some understanding between the two countries. In Iran, Rafsanjani was focused on postwar reconstruction and was eager for foreign investment; he believed a deal could be struck between Tehran and Washington. The Bush administration was looking for ways to open a dialogue with Tehran. But while there was some reaching out, little was accomplished.

In remarks directed at the Iranians in his inaugural address in January 1989, Bush remarked that "goodwill begets goodwill," indicating that Iranian help in obtaining the release of the remaining American hostages in Lebanon would be reciprocated. Rafsanjani helped secure the release of a number of American hostages, but there was no American quid pro quo. Still, when Saddam Hussein invaded, occupied, and annexed Kuwait in 1991 and President Bush led an international coalition to force him to withdraw, Iran effectively sided with America and its allies. It did not join the coalition, but it did not obstruct the war effort, either. Moreover, Saddam Hussein sent almost his entire fleet of fighter aircraft to Iran, somehow believing Iran would help him keep them secure from U.S. attack. Iran pretended the aircraft never arrived and held on to them, denying their use by Iraq during the fighting. Yet Tehran felt it was little rewarded for its good behavior.

In exchange for an American-sponsored Security Council resolution finally recognizing Iraq as the aggressor in the Iran-Iraq War, Iran secured the release of the remaining American hostages in Lebanon. But feelers from the American side never resulted in direct talks. Rafsanjani could not show sufficient dividends for his indirect engagement with the United States to overcome the opposition of hardliners at home, who were unenthusiastic about a rapprochement with

America. It did not help that Iran, hostile to Israel and concerned lest an Israeli-Syrian agreement would lure away Syria, its principal regional ally, opposed a new effort at Arab-Israeli peace launched by President Bush in 1991 in Madrid. A spate of killings of Iranian dissidents in Europe in the early 1990s persuaded the U. S. administration that the security services and those willing to resort to assassination were still setting the agenda in Tehran.

Lost Opportunities: Clinton and Khatami

Rafsanjani, ever the optimistic deal maker, reached out to the United States during the first Clinton administration as well. In 1995 he offered a multibillion-dollar deal to the American oil company Conoco. It turned out to be an ill-timed gesture. Concern had been rising in the United States over Iran's nuclear and long-range missile program. Members of Congress were calling for stronger economic sanctions against Iran. Israel's friends were concerned about Iran's active opposition to the Arab-Israeli peace process. President Clinton had been urging Russia and other countries not to transfer nuclear and missile technology to Iran. He had similarly urged Japan and the Europeans to curtail trade with Iran. He could hardly allow an American oil company to invest in developing Iran's oil industry.

In March 1995, Clinton signed an executive order banning investment by American firms in the Iranian oil industry. In May, he went further and signed a second order banning all trade with Iran. In the following year, he signed into law the Iran-Libya Sanctions Act (ILSA). The law, principally the brainchild of Senator Alphonse D'Amato of New York, penalized any country that invested more than $40 million (later lowered to $20 million) in Iran's or Libya's energy industry. ILSA was never strictly enforced. The law allowed for a presidential waiver, which Clinton often used; it probably was illegal under World Trade Organization (WTO) rules, and European and other states bristled at the suggestion that America would dictate trade policy to them. However, ILSA was indicative of the hardening mood in Washington.

Iran hardened its position, too. It intensified obstruction of the Arab-Israeli peace process, increased its support for Hizbollah, and began to support two other Palestinian rejectionist groups, Hamas and Palestinian Islamic Jihad (PIJ). Hizbollah fired rockets into northern Israel, and in February 1996 Hamas and PIJ carried out four bombings in Israel in nine days, killing 59 Israelis. The bombings had a direct impact on the Palestinian-Israeli peace process, which had progressed rapidly under the direction of Prime Minister Yitzhak Rabin and his foreign minister, Shimon Peres. In November 1995, Rabin was assassinated by one of his own countrymen, and elections in the spring were contested by Peres, who had succeeded Rabin, and Likud Party leader Benjamin Netanyahu, a strong critic of the agreements already reached between Israel and the Palestinians. The bombings ensured Peres's defeat.

In June 1996, a truck bomb killed 19 Americans and wounded 372 others at the Khobar Towers housing complex in Saudi Arabia. There were claims of Iranian complicity in the bombing. Hopes for better ties between the two countries were, for the moment at least, buried beneath the rubble.

Nevertheless, the election of Mohammad Khatami as Iran's president in 1997 offered a new opportunity for a rapprochement between the two countries. Khatami came to office as a reformer. He moved quickly to improve relations with Saudi Arabia, and the Saudi crown prince indicated trust in Khatami's intentions by attending the Islamic summit in Tehran in December 1997. At the summit, Khatami assured the PLO leader Yasser Arafat that Iran would abide by any solution to the Palestinian-Israeli conflict that was acceptable to the Palestinian people. Since Arafat was already committed to a two-state solution, this was a far cry from Iran's call for the destruction of Israel. In January 1998, in an interview on CNN, Khatami called for a dialogue between the people of Iran and the people of the United States to remove the "wall of mistrust" between them, and for an exchange of writers, artists, journalists, academics, and tourists. It seemed fairly clear that he saw these exchanges as preliminaries to an eventual dialogue between the two governments.

President Clinton responded cautiously but enthusiastically. He encouraged an American wrestling team to participate in a tournament in Iran, and the American athletes were warmly received. In a series of steps over the next four years, the United States eased visa restrictions on Iranians; facilitated visits by Iranian academics, artists, and tourists; added the MEK, the Iranian opposition movement based in Iraq, to the list of outlawed terrorist groups; eased sanctions to allow the purchase by Iran of medicines and humanitarian supplies as well as spare parts for Iran's aging fleet of Boeing aircraft; and allowed the import of Iranian pistachios, carpets, and caviar. These were small steps, but intended to signal a readiness to do more.

Clinton also reached out to the Iranians directly. He sent a message via the Swiss that the United States was ready for direct talks on all relevant issues. In May 1998, Vice President Gore handed a message from Clinton for Khatami to Crown Prince Abdallah of Saudi Arabia expressing a desire for better relations and direct discussions. In April of the following year Clinton added remarks to a dinner speech at the White House recognizing Iranian grievances against the West going back many decades. In June 1999, two high-ranking administration officials handed a letter from Clinton for Khatami to Sultan Qaboos of Oman. It stressed the American desire for better relations with Iran, but cited the possible involvement of Iran's Revolutionary Guards and Lebanese Hizbollah in the Khobar Towers bombing as an obstacle. It was important that this matter be cleared up first, the message said. The letter was delivered to Khatami in Tehran. The reply came a few days later, not from Khatami but in a statement by a government spokesman, denying any Iranian involvement in the Khobar Towers bombing.

In a June 1998 speech, Secretary of State Madeleine Albright had already invited Iran to join the United States in drawing up "a road map leading to normal relations." In a major speech in March 2000, she renewed this offer and, in a gesture thought to be important to the Iranians, expressed regret for the American role in the overthrow of Mossadegh in 1953. But the speech also noted that in Iran "control over the military, courts, and police remain in unelected hands." That sentence caused offense to Iran's supreme leader, Khamenei. He replied three days later, again not directly but in a public speech, and his response was uniformly negative. Once again, an attempt to reach out had failed.

The Clinton-Khatami years had presented the most promising opportunity since the 1979 revolution for dialogue between Iran and the United States. Both Clinton and Khatami were eager for an understanding; and both, in word and action, sought to open the door for talks. But Khatami was almost certainly prevented from taking up Clinton's advances by Iran's supreme leader, Ayatollah Khamenei, who had deep reservations about the utility for Iran of negotiations with the United States. America was the stronger power, and he did not want to negotiate from a position of weakness. He knew that in negotiations he would have to compromise on issues central to his regional policy, such as Iran's unflinching hostility to the state of Israel. He believed that Iran's search for regional and Islamic leadership and its claim to be the one country that dared stand up to the United States would be jeopardized if Iran sat at the negotiating table with America. He relied on powerful constituencies in Iran, including the Revolutionary Guards and the security services, that opposed a rapprochement with the United States.

President Clinton could not make the "grand gesture"—for example, the lifting of sanctions—that might have strengthened Khatami's hand at home until Iranian policy on key issues, such as opposition to the Palestinian-Israeli peace process or support for groups such as Hizbollah and Hamas, changed. Yet Khatami could not act unilaterally on these key issues or soften Iran's opposition to Israel and support for Israel's enemies because they had become pillars of Iran's foreign policy. The Clinton-Khatami years offered glimpses of tantalizing possibilities but tragically devolved into a stark reminder of the serious obstacles to an Iranian-American understanding.

❧ The Barren Years: Bush II

These obstacles only multiplied during the presidency of George W. Bush. The new administration came to office believing that, as the world's sole superpower, it could set the international agenda and need pay little heed to governments that disagreed with America's policies and priorities. This view became entrenched after 9/11 and America's overthrow of the Taliban in Afghanistan. The administration saw no need to compromise with countries like Iran and Syria that pursued policies in the Middle East opposed to U.S. interests. In Iran, President Khatami was much weaker than he had been during the Clinton years and his reform movement was in retreat. His successor, Mahmoud Ahmadinejad, elected president in 2005, adopted a populist style at home and a confrontational style abroad, which exacerbated long-standing issues between Tehran and Washington. The American invasion of Iraq and the collapse of the regime of Saddam Hussein found Iran and the United States competing for influence in that country.

Mistrust of Iran and a disregard for serious negotiations with Tehran characterized the attitude of the administration. This was illustrated during Bush's first term by the response to an Iranian proposal for what some observers described as a "grand bargain" between the two countries. In May 2003, using the Swiss as intermediaries, Iran submitted in writing a proposal for comprehensive talks on all outstanding issues. In exchange for recognition of Iran's legitimate security interests in the region and an end to U.S. sanctions and attempts to isolate Iran, the Islamic Republic expressed readiness to discuss its nuclear program, its policy in Iraq, its support for rejectionist Palestinian groups, and possible recognition of Israel within its 1967 borders. The Bush administration, however, did not give the initiative serious consideration or respond to it, and as a result no effort was made to test Iran's sincerity in making these proposals. Other attempts by Iran to initiate bilateral talks in 2005 and 2006 were also rebuffed.

Initially, prospects for improved relations looked promising. The so-called six-plus-two talks on Afghanistan, initiated in 1997 among Afghanistan's six immediate neighbors and representatives of the United States and the European community, continued under the Bush administration; and Iranian and American representatives met regularly around the same table. In 2001, these talks evolved into one-on-one talks, and representatives of Iran and the United States continued to meet in Paris and Geneva until 2003. Iran quietly assisted the American war in Afghanistan and was instrumental in helping the United States put together an interim government to run the country after the fall of the Taliban in 2001. Eager to see Saddam Hussein overthrown, Iran raised no objection when the United States invaded Iraq in the following year.

But perennial problems soon resurfaced. In January 2002, the Israelis captured a ship, the *Karine A*, which they said was carrying Iranian arms for the Palestinian Authority. The Iranians denied any connection, but the Bush administration saw the incident as evidence that Iran was continuing to play the spoiler in the Middle East. In his State of the Union address later that month, President Bush included Iran, along with Iraq and North Korea, in what he described as "an axis of evil." His remarks undercut moderates in Tehran who had argued that cooperation with the United States in Afghanistan would be reciprocated by Washington.

Iraq proved a particularly contentious issue. Iran believed it had legitimate security interests in Iraq, but after the overthrow of Saddam Hussein, the United States saw no reason to accommodate Iran or to allow it any role in Iraq. This exclusion proved impossible to accomplish. Iran had its hands on many levers of influence in Iraq. The two countries shared a long and porous border. More than half the Iraqi population were Shi'ites, with ties to their coreligionists in Iran. Many of the senior Shi'ite clergy in Iraq, including Grand Ayatollah Ali Sistani, were of Iranian origin. Iran had supported the Iraqi opposition during the years when the United States was supporting Saddam Hussein. Iran's protégés were now in power. Iranian agents and officials could meld easily into the local population; trucks and buses moved in large numbers across the border; each month, tens of thousands of Iranian pilgrims visited the shrines in Najaf and Karbala.

As order broke down and chaos ensued in postwar Iraq, Iran sent in agents, funded Iraqi political parties and militias, built schools and roads, and invested in social welfare projects. The United States and Iran were soon locked in a struggle for power and influence in Iraq. Before long, Washington was blaming Iran for the mayhem in Iraq, including roadside bombings and attacks on American troops. These allegations could not be independently verified; but Iran, fearing American intentions and the consolidation of an American military presence in Iraq, supported various Iraqi militia groups, including those hostile to the United States.

Iran's nuclear ambitions emerged as another major source of friction. By 2002, it was obvious that Iran's nuclear program had progressed further than previously assumed. Beginning in 2003, Britain, France, and Germany, representing the European Union (and later joined by Russia and China), entered into negotiations with Iran, hoping to induce Iran to give up uranium enrichment (and a possible weapons program) in exchange for a range of incentives, including expanded trade and diplomatic ties, a guaranteed supply of nuclear fuel for peaceful purposes, and consultation on regional security issues. For two years, the Bush administration remained dismissive of these negotiations and kept its distance from them, expecting they would fail. In March 2005, mired in Iraq and finally persuaded that it had to come on board if the Europeans were to have any chance of success, the Bush administration changed course, and offered Iran small incentives if it gave up uranium enrichment. It agreed to allow Iran to purchase spare parts for its aircraft and to end obstruction of Iran's application to join the World Trade Organization. In May 2006, Secretary Condoleezza Rice announced with much fanfare Washington's endorsement of the incentives the Europeans had offered Iran and her readiness to participate personally in the negotiations with Iran.

These offers proved unpersuasive to the Iranians. Tehran continued to insist on Iran's right to enrich uranium on Iranian soil. The incentives were deemed inadequate and vague. The United States continued to hint at the possibility of the use of force against the Islamic Republic. In regard to Iran, the president repeatedly said, "All options are on the table." This threat, taken to mean air strikes against Iran's nuclear facilities, created uncertainty about ultimate American intentions and only deepened Iranian skepticism about the utility of talks.

The administration's "democracy promotion" program further exacerbated tensions between the two countries. After the fall of Saddam Hussein, having discovered no nuclear weapons in Iraq—the original reason for invading the country—the administration increasingly cited democratization in Iraq and sweeping democratization across the Middle East as a rationale for the war. "Democracy promotion" became a pillar in the administration's Iran policy as well. In 2005, the State Department announced the allocation of funds to this end, and invited applications from groups and individuals working to advance democracy in Iran. The amounts—$3 million to $10 million—were modest. But the State Department asked Congress for $75 million for democracy promotion in Iran the next year; Congress offered up to $66 million. In 2008, Congress voted a further $60 million for democracy promotion in Iran.

The program was ill conceived from its inception; it probably ended up harming rather than helping Iran's democracy advocates. A large share of the money paid for expanded Persian-language broadcasts to Iran, but money also went to Iranian dissident groups in the United States; the lack of transparency regarding the recipients only fed Iranian suspicions. The Tehran government cracked down more severely on intellectuals, political activists, and NGOs—the very people the democracy fund was presumably intended to assist—accusing them of accepting American financial help to undermine the government. The Bush administration said it sought to change Iranian behavior rather than its regime, but senior officials, including the president, often blurred the lines by seeming to call on the Iranian people to change or overthrow their own government. In his January 2005 inaugural address, President Bush said, "America will . . . support democratic movements in the Middle East and beyond, with the ultimate goal of ending tyranny in our world," and, directly addressing the Iranian people, added, "As you stand for your own liberty, America stands with you." On the eve of the Iranian presidential elections in June, he issued a statement noting that "today Iran is ruled by men who suppress liberty at home and spread terror across the world," and said that an "unelected few" held power in Iran through "an electoral process that ignores the basic requirements of democracy."

There was not the remotest possibility that any significant NGO, publication, association, or political organization in Iran would risk accepting American government money, anyway. Shirin Ebadi noted that the democracy fund had "created immense problems for Iranian reformists, democratic groups, and human rights activists" and had made it "more difficult for the more moderate factions in Iran's power hierarchy to argue for an accommodation with the West." Echoing the same views, the dissident journalist Emadeddin Baghi described a policy of promoting regime change by trying to give money to dissidents as "neither wise nor morally justifiable." At the Wilson Center, almost every speaker from Iran criticized the "democracy promotion" funding as ineffective and unwelcome to Iran's political activists and NGOs. These criticisms fell on deaf ears in Washington.

When I returned to Iran in December 2006, I did not realize I was walking into the heart of a storm. It was fueled by long-standing animosity between Tehran and Washington, an ineffective and ultimately harmful program of democracy promotion that contributed to my detention and that of many others, and an iron determination by Iran's security services to squash all American plans regarding the Islamic Republic.

7.

THE ARREST

ON MAY 2, THE LULL finally ended. Ja'fari called and invited me to "cooperate." The Islamic Republic is compassionate and pardons those who cooperate, he said. What they wanted from me was not the "old stuff' but "the plan," "the program" for the future, alluding to what the Intelligence Ministry still clearly believed was an American blueprint for regime change in Iran, about which they presumed I had inside information. When I told him I had expected him to call with the good news that I could go home, he replied, "I didn't call for good news. I was asked to pass on a message so that there should be no grounds for complaint."

On May 7, Ja'fari called the house several times while I was out. Mutti said he sounded irritable and was upset when he could not find me, banging the phone down on the last occasion. He finally reached me in the afternoon and summoned me to the Intelligence Ministry the next day at nine a.m.

That evening I went to dinner at a friend's house, and when I returned home, Mutti was awake and excited. A friend whose contacts we thought good had called and left a message for me. "Tell her it is all over; she will be going home soon." We received a similar prognosis from a second contact. The next day's "interview" would be the last, he said. But I continued to feel uneasy. "I think they will take me in," I e-mailed Shaul, who insisted I was being overly pessimistic. If they had wanted to arrest you, he reassured me, they had had ample opportunity to do so. I tried to share his certainty, but my gut instinct told me otherwise. Shaul was my tower of strength; he had always protected me. I knew he would do everything in his power to get me out of this predicament, but now he was far away. "Look after Haleh," I e-mailed Shaul. "Give her a lot of love and support. We had a wonderful life together." The tone of farewell in the message reflected my deepest misgivings.

I left the apartment early and took a taxi to the house of a friend who would drive me to the Intelligence Ministry. I was nervous; cramps clawed at my stomach. To cheer me up, my friend tried to joke when he dropped me off: "Don't worry," he said. "I will visit you at Evin and bring you lots of parcels."

I hadn't been in this grim neighborhood for nearly three months. The streets looked the same, except that the trees were full of fresh green leaves. Inside the building, the security belt still was not working. I passed through the metal detector with my book under my arm and was directed to a room. Ja'fari walked in. He was wearing a checkered shirt and the same parka he had worn throughout the cold winter months. I noticed that he wasn't carrying his laptop and seemed unusually edgy. He sat on an easy chair facing me, pulled a clutch of papers from his shirt pocket, selected one, and handed it to me. He said, "This is your arrest warrant and we are taking you to Evin."

I was stunned. For a moment I felt nothing at all. Then fear, like a wave of nausea, washed over me. Evin Prison had a fearsome reputation. It had been built under the monarchy to house both political and ordinary prisoners. After the Islamic revolution, the thousands of officials of the old regime swept up in the first wave of arrests were incarcerated here, soon to be joined by thousands more arrested in the factional infighting that followed. Men and women had been executed here following midnight trials before hooded judges. Torture to extract information was common. The notorious warden of Evin Prison, Asadollah Lajevardi, had instituted ideological "reeducation" classes for prisoners from left-wing guerrilla organizations, demanding public recantations of their previously held beliefs. It was at Evin and a second prison that some 2,000 inmates were murdered in 1988 in an extended "night of the long knives."

I asked to call my mother. Ja'fari allowed me the one phone call. Mother picked up the phone. I took a deep breath and said in German: "Don't be upset. Please listen carefully. They are taking me to Evin. Notify my family and get me a lawyer."

I said good-bye to Mutti and walked with Ja'fari to the front door. A dark green Peugeot was waiting for us. The bright sunlight blurred my vision, but I took in three people: the vaguely familiar face belonged to the man from the judiciary who had led the raid on my mother's apartment and had tried, absurdly, to engage her in small talk as his men rifled through her things; beside him, a sinister-looking man with a pistol strapped to his belt who served as the driver, and, third, a chador-clad woman who sat with me in the backseat. We drove off, and Ja'fari followed in his own car.

The two men in the front spoke into a walkie-talkie, reporting our progress, which seemed pointless since we barely crawled in the bumper-to-bumper traffic. I tried not to think of what they might do to me: would I be subjected to torture, beatings, verbal abuse, humiliation? After an hour, the high walls of Evin Prison rose before us. Two large iron doors swung open; guards peered into the car and waved us through; the car drove into the courtyard and stopped before the door of a building. "Let's go," the woman said to me. Here, I was handed over to a man in wrinkled gray trousers and a checkered shirt who took me inside and told me to stand facing the wall. I joined others already there, all men, each of us standing barely six inches from the wall in the narrow corridor, staring at nothing.

After a wait that seemed like an eternity, a woman tapped me on the shoulder. She was short and chubby. Beneath her tight black hood and black chador, I saw a round face, very white skin, and glasses with gold rims. Her voice was comfortingly gentle. She gave me a blindfold. "Wear this," she said. She took me by the hand and walked me through the building. Walking blindfolded is not only disorientating but humiliating. You hear voices, footsteps, and sounds but cannot quite place them. You worry that you will crack your head on a low beam or break your leg falling down unseen stairs. You are dependent on others to navigate the unfamiliar corridors and stairways, hanging on to the guard as if you were a helpless child.

The process of booking me into Evin was under way.

Blindly into Evin

Our first stop was a small office, where a man with a bored look took down my particulars—name, family name, age, place of birth. I was fingerprinted and photographed without the blindfold. We stopped next at the dispensary. My blindfold was removed once again, and I faced a morose doctor who instructed one of two male nurses to take my weight and blood pressure, and then asked me about my medical history and the medications I was taking. I gave him the particulars: over-the-counter eye drops for a chronic eye condition, pills for my arthritis and vitamins for my bones, and a skin condition that required regular attention. He said the prison dispensary would provide me with the necessary vitamins and pills. I said I would rather take my own medication. We left the issue unresolved.

We stopped at what appeared to be a door—the entrance to ward 209. I could hear the guard ring a doorbell, push open the door, then pull back a curtain. We stepped inside. The guard told me to remove the blindfold. I was standing in a corridor roughly fifty feet long and barely five feet wide, with windows on my right and iron cell doors, painted white, on my left. The guard walked me to the last of the doors, which was open. This was the entrance to my cell. She motioned me to go in. She emptied my bag, made a list of the contents, and took away everything, even my watch and hand cream, leaving me only my reading glasses and my hairbrush. Two other female guards had come to the door for a look at the new arrival. One was in her twenties, the other in her mid-forties.

They soon left. I heard the door swing shut, then heard the click of the lock as it fell into place—a quiet click that echoed in my head like thunder. I looked at my new "home." The room was bare but clean. The walls were painted a greenish yellow, with patches of white where the paint had peeled off. Against one wall stood a dirty iron sink. Well-worn, brown, wall-to-wall carpet covered the floor. In one corner there was a single folded blanket and a copy of the Quran. There was no bed or toilet. About eight feet up one of the walls were two rectangular windows that looked out onto a flat roof. They were open to let in fresh air, screened to keep out flies, and barred to keep in prisoners. Fixed to the high ceiling were two sets of bright fluorescent lights. They remained turned on, day and night.

A female guard with disheveled hair and a wrinkled shirt and skirt came to tell me shoes were not allowed inside the cells (which I ignored) and to admonish me not to "sit or sleep with your feet stretched toward the Quran." Later she brought me lunch—a plastic container of rice and stew and a plastic spoon. But I could not eat. The chubby-faced guard came by with a hand towel, a bar of soap, a toothbrush, and toothpaste—the standard toilet kit for every prisoner—and later with a chador, which she asked me to please wear whenever I was summoned out of the cell. She showed me the location of the inmates' bathroom and an outdoor terrace where prisoners were allowed for air one hour each day. Each time I wanted to use the bathroom, I had to knock on the door and be escorted to the facility and then escorted back.

Ja'fari showed up that very afternoon and subjected me to a lengthy and angry interrogation, which lasted into the late evening. I had not cooperated, he said, and I was therefore brought to Evin. Now I was in their hands and could go nowhere.

Back in my cell many hours later, I felt drained and exhausted. I refused dinner. I badly wanted to lie down. I undressed, wrapped myself in my chador, and, using my robe as a cover, lay down on the thin blanket on the floor and tried to sleep. But I could not. I was racked by anxiety. The floor was hard; the glare of the fluorescent lights bothered me. I had only a thin headscarf for a pillow. Every hour or so, I heard the clip-clopping of the night guard's slippers on the concrete floor of the corridor, as she checked on me and the other inmates through the little opening in the cell doors. Through the window bars high up on the wall, I could see the stars in the Tehran sky. I thought my heart would break.

It must have been around five in the morning when the birds started singing. For a moment I thought I was back home in Potomac being nudged out of sleep, as I was every morning, by the birds in our garden. I sat up and took in the reality of my prison cell. Still, I thought, these birds are my guardian angels, come from Potomac to protect me.

At six in the morning the guard with disheveled hair—I had dubbed her Sour Face—showed up with a cup of tea, a piece of bread, and a slice of cheese which she carried in her bare hands. I refused the food; disgusted and numbed, I felt no hunger. An hour later, a young guard whom I nicknamed Rashti because her accent told me she was a northerner from Rasht, came to the cell door and offered me a breakfast of milk, tea, bread, butter, honey, jam, and cheese. I was still too upset to eat; but tea, a slice of bread, and cream cheese became my standard Evin breakfast.

I was summoned for a second interrogation session soon after breakfast, this time with both Ja'fari and Hajj Agha. It lasted all morning. In the afternoon, a middle-aged guard whom everyone referred to as Hajj Khanum told me to put on my chador and blindfold and follow her. I was to appear before a revolutionary court magistrate.

The Revolutionary Court

We went down two flights and out of the building, where I was told to remove my blindfold and step into a Nissan SUV. The driver and another man, a guard, sat in the front. I sat directly behind them. One seat farther back was a male inmate in a prison uniform sitting next to a guard. The traffic, as usual, was snarled. I gazed at the familiar streets through tear-blurred eyes. Strange ideas came into my head. I hoped for an accident—an everyday occurrence in Tehran's mad traffic—and a broken arm or leg, so that I would end up in a hospital rather than back in Evin. We went up Shariati Avenue, turned into Moallem Avenue, and stopped in front of the large building housing the revolutionary court.

All five of us got out and we followed the driver and guard through a large courtyard and up to the eighth floor. A long wait ensued. The other inmate fetched me a chair and a cup of water. From a window, I could see the snow-capped peak of Mount Damavand—a calm and majestic view that I had loved both as a child and as an adult. I recalled that when things seemed to be taking a dramatic turn for the better under President Khatami, Shaul and I even thought of buying a small place at the foothills of the Alborz Mountains and retiring there.

Finally a magistrate motioned for me to sit in an easy chair, facing him. He leafed through a file, asked me a few questions about my work at the Wilson Center and about people I knew, and gave me a piece of paper to sign. I read that I was accused of "endangering national security" and that the magistrate had ordered a one-week detention and set bail at 30 million tomans, or about $30,000. The whole business took no more than fifteen minutes. I felt numbed, caught in the coils of a system I could neither understand nor challenge, facing accusations that were at once outlandish and fearsome. I did not even have the presence of mind to ask why I was charged—nor would it have made the slightest difference had I done so. I asked only that I should not be handcuffed. No, the magistrate agreed, that would not be necessary. I asked whether I could call home. "You can call from prison, not from here," he replied.

We drove back in the SUV. The driver and the guard in the backseat were idly chatting, and I wondered how they could talk so casually while my world was falling apart. "How quickly they came out," the driver commented. "The magistrate was in a hurry to get home to his wife and children," the other man replied, chuckling at his own observation. We stopped once again at the looming iron gates of Evin. Outside the gates, men and women waited, anxious, talking among themselves and to the gatemen, hoping for some news of a friend or relative. A similar scene had played out at the revolutionary court only an hour earlier. Inside, we were once again lined up, facing a wall, and I waited until a prison guard came and took me, groping in my blindfold, back to ward 209.

That evening, I was able to call Mutti. I told her I had been before the magistrate. Half believing I might be able to get out on bail, I asked her to find some way of raising the 30 million tomans. Mother said she had come to Evin for the second time that morning and with some difficulty had been able to leave a package of food, clothes, and medicine at the gate. When she had come on my first day at Evin, she had been told I was not there. I asked one of the female guards for my package; she said they needed Ja'fari's permission before they could give it to me.

The next day, when I saw Ja'fari, I spoke angrily to him about my treatment—the appearance before a revolutionary court magistrate, the absurd accusations against me. He merely shrugged. I also complained of the way my mother had been treated at the prison gate. He reluctantly agreed to speak to the prison authorities.

The Magistrate as Superman

It must have been around nine that evening when the guard I had nicknamed Sour Face announced a visitor. "Wear your chador."

Ignoring her, I wore only my robe and waited. Who would call on an inmate at night? The door opened. A tall, neatly dressed man with a trimmed beard stood there, accompanied by a short, stout assistant. He had come to inspect my room, he said, to see if I had everything I needed. You might have thought I was a guest at a five-star hotel and the manager had come to make sure I was comfortable. He saw my book lying next to the Quran and asked what I was reading. I assured him Ja'fari had okayed it. He instructed Sour Face to take me downstairs to his office. Three flights of stairs later, my blindfold off, I found myself in a large room, like the living room of a middle-class family: there were easy chairs and low tables and a glass bookcase against the wall. My visitor was now sitting behind a desk sipping tea. To Sour Face's horror, I removed the chador I had put on before leaving my cell and sat in the chair nearest to him in only my robe and scarf. I ignored her frantic signals to cover myself.

Matin-Rassekh introduced himself as the prosecuting magistrate in charge of my case. He was not in the day before, when I was first brought before the revolutionary court, he explained. His tone conveyed that he was taking over and that he meant business.

After verifying my name and particulars, he abruptly said, "You are married to a Jew. Such a marriage is not acceptable in the Islamic Republic. Do you know what the punishment is?" I knew, of course. Under strict Islamic law, a Muslim woman who marries a non-Muslim is considered to have committed adultery. The punishment is death by stoning. I recalled pictures and film clips of such stonings: a village square or an open field; a woman buried to her shoulders in the ground; a crowd of would-be participants and bystanders; the mullah casting the first stone; the flurry of stones that followed in a frenzy of vengefulness.

I tried to maintain my composure. "I have been married for over forty years, twenty-seven of them under the Islamic Republic. Both my husband and I have regularly renewed our Iranian passports and our national identity cards. Nobody has ever made this an issue. Why should it become a problem when I am sixty-seven and he seventy?" Matin-Rassekh did not answer, but he left me deeply shaken.

He also asked why our daughter was named after me—a curious question perhaps meant to single us out as people who broke all sorts of traditions. "This is very unusual for Iran," he said. "The Turks do it." Unable to think of any better explanation (we had named our daughter Haleh because Shaul liked the name and because, in our mixed marriage, it was religiously neutral), I noted that the practice was not uncommon among the Qajars, the Iranian royal house in the nineteenth century. Citing royalty as a model was perhaps not the most politically astute thing for me to do in the circumstances, but Matin-Rassekh let it pass.

Under his desk I saw that he had removed his shoes and put on slippers. He sipped tea and played with his prayer beads while I talked or wrote answers to his questions, and he leafed through one of the volumes of *Nest of Spies*, the collection of diplomatic dispatches and documents discovered by the students who had seized the American embassy in Tehran in November 1979. They had published over fifty volumes of documents under this title. One of the dispatches mentioned Shaul and me as prominent journalists in Iran. Another described a conversation between Shaul and an embassy official. More trouble for me, I thought. Matin-Rassekh repeated many of the questions Ja'fari had already asked numerous times. But he seemed hardly interested in my answers.

At one point, Hajj Khanum relieved Sour Face, who had been visibly taken aback when Matin-Rassekh spoke of my husband's religion. I later learned Sour Face raced back to the ward and told the other guards on duty the scandalous news that "she is married to a Jew! She committed *zena-ye mohseneh*—adultery!"

Matin-Rassekh, with an office in Evin Prison, worked particularly closely with the Intelligence Ministry. He had taken charge of my case for obvious reasons: the first magistrate seemed to grasp the thinness of the case against me, and consequently issued a short detention order and set "reasonable" bail by Iranian standards. Clearly, bail implied the possibility of release. From Matin-Rassekh I could expect no such fairness and objectivity. On the contrary, I could easily imagine him signing death sentences in the afternoon, saying his prayers in the early evening, and comfortably having dinner with his wife and children at night.

I was accused, he noted, of plotting against and endangering national security. He handed me a sheet of paper and asked me to sign it. He was issuing an order for my detention in solitary confinement for three months "to prevent [my] escape from the country." I had mentally prepared myself for such a detention order, which was common in political cases, but anticipation is never the same as the reality. I reread the single sheet of paper and its key sentences: "accused of plotting against national security . . . three months in solitary confinement." They still came as a shock, like hammer blows on an anvil. I was truly afraid.

I mustered whatever courage and anger I could: "If I intended to escape, I had four months outside prison to do so. I have no intention of running away, because all these charges are fabrications and false, and I will fight them." Matin-Rassekh must have taken note of my ashen face. "If you cooperate and they are satisfied with your answers, you will be released sooner," he said before ending the session.

I only saw Matin-Rassekh once more, a month later, again late at night. I was reading when a guard showed up at my cell door and told me to get ready for a "visitor." When I expressed annoyance that Matin-Rassekh came at such a late hour, the guard said, "This is not late. Sometimes they summon people at two in the morning." A few minutes later, I saw his thin silhouette by my door. He asked if I had any complaints, but I didn't bother to answer. Again I was blindfolded and guided downstairs, to his office.

Matin-Rassekh shoved a paper in front of me and asked me to sign it. It said, in effect, "I, Haleh Esfandiari, waive the right to have a lawyer." Inwardly, I felt a little emboldened, a bit triumphant. I had told Shaul that, if arrested, he should proceed immediately with the idea of having Shirin Ebadi as my lawyer. I knew Shaul would do everything to persuade her to take my case. This sheet of paper, I concluded, meant Shirin was now representing me and they wanted her off my case. "If my family decided I need a lawyer, then I need a lawyer. I will not sign this paper," I said. I took the sheet from Matin-Rassekh and wrote on it: "I waive the right to a lawyer only for the next three days. After that the lawyer hired by my family has the authority to represent me." If they were fearful of the publicity Shirin Ebadi would create in the international community, I had given them an opening, three days in which to release me. Since the next three days were holidays, when all government offices were closed, it wouldn't matter if I had legal representation in this short interval.

Matin-Rassekh moved from behind the desk and sat across from me on an easy chair. I could see he was furious. "I will never let this woman, this Shirin Ebadi, who works for foreigners, see your file." Matin-Rassekh regained his composure. He said, "Kian Tajbakhsh is wiser than you. He followed our advice and refused a lawyer." I shot back, "You people are accusing me of plotting to overthrow the regime and expect me not to have a lawyer?"

Kian Tajbakhsh was the Iranian American academic who was a consultant to George Soros's Open Society Institute and about whom I had been questioned. He was also being held at Evin. Matin-Rassekh had prepared a single document for both of us and had taken it to Kian first. He showed me Kian's signature; I had no reason to doubt it was his. Kian had waived his right to legal counsel. I handed the waiver back to him. He understood that the subject was closed. "Do you have any complaints?" he asked. He was going through the motions. His question was a mere formality. "Yes," I said. "I want to go home."

"No one is going to set you free or let you go home," he replied.

I turned my back on him, fighting my tears. "Are you done?" I asked.

His reply, dismissing me, was a hiss of suffused anger. "Yes," he said.

The next day, at an interrogation session, I told Ja'fari and Hajj Agha about the nighttime visit. "I don't want that man swooping down on my cell unannounced like Superman anymore," I said. Hajj Agha had a long chuckle, savoring the depiction of the magistrate as Superman. I never saw Matin-Rassekh again.

❧ The Rise of the Intelligence Ministry

The Ministry of Intelligence and Security, in whose hands I found myself, was heir to the shah's secret police, SAVAK. The Islamic Republic took over SAVAK's offices and buildings; it used SAVAK's files against those it chose to treat as enemies. It even appropriated SAVAK's name, except that the agency was upgraded to a full ministry. But the Intelligence Ministry was also a creation of the revolution. Its personnel came from within the revolutionary ranks. Its repressive apparatus cast a longer shadow over society; and it used methods, such as the murder of dissidents, rarely practiced by the shah's secret police.

When the monarchy was overthrown in February 1979, the revolutionaries turned with fury on the members of the old regime, including cabinet officers, members of the military and police, and, of course, officers and operatives of SAVAK, whose agents had been the interrogators, jailers, and sometimes the torturers of the men who were now in power.

In the weeks and months immediately following the victory of the Islamic revolution, widespread purges took place in the government, the army, and the security services. Hundreds and eventually thousands of men were brought before hastily convened revolutionary courts and then sent before the firing squads or sentenced to long prison terms. As a result, the shah's intelligence service unraveled.

In those chaotic early months, lines between interrogators, revolutionary court judges, and executioners were blurred. Judges were often interrogators and sometimes even executioners. The new rulers were obsessively fearful of counterrevolution, foreign intrigue, spies, and rival factions, yet had little real intelligence to guide them. Willy-nilly, the nucleus of what would become the new secret police emerged: interrogators, investigators, men who made it their business to root out anyone they believed to be plotters, agents of foreigners, or dissidents. This air of improvisation continued through the first year of revolutionary terror and prevailed even in 1981–82, when the men around Khomeini turned against some of the radical left-wing groups and thousands were executed in a second wave of terror.

However, in 1983, the Majlis, or parliament, passed a law establishing the Ministry of Intelligence and Security, formalizing what until then had been makeshift and improvised. The ministry was given wide powers of information gathering and investigation. It was charged with uncovering conspiracies; espionage; sabotage; coup plans; and incitement to unrest threatening to the political system, security, and territorial integrity of the country. It was permitted to share intelligence with approved foreign intelligence services. All government agencies were required to place their personnel and information at the disposal of the Intelligence Ministry. Provision was made for coordination of intelligence between the ministry, the Revolutionary Guards, and other security agencies. The ministry's budget was exempted from the regular government audit. The minister was to be a cleric of high rank. While, as a member of the cabinet, the minister was in theory subject to parliamentary oversight, in practice, he became the appointee of the supreme leader and answered to him, not to the Majlis. Thus was born the security apparatus of the Islamic Republic.

Ali Fallahian, a cleric and the first minister of intelligence, proved to be no slouch in silencing dissent and in the use of extralegal methods. Mistreatment and torture of political prisoners and forced public confessions were, from the beginning, features of the post-revolution repressive apparatus. They became institutionalized once the ministry was in place. In 1983, for example, two leaders of the Tudeh, Iran's Communist party, were produced on television to confess to high treason, betrayal, belief in an "irrelevant ideology," "foreign ways of thought," and serving the Soviet Union's interests.

The ministry gained greater freedom of action and expanded its scope of operations in the post-Khomeini period. Abroad, it inserted its agents into Iranian embassies under diplomatic cover and assassinated Iranian opposition figures. In 1989, Abdol-Rahman Qassemlu, leader of Iran's Democratic Party of Kurdistan (DPK), was lured to a meeting in Vienna with Iranian government emissaries and shot and killed, along with two associates. Three years later, his successor as leader of Iran's DPK, Sadeq Sharafkandi, was murdered while at dinner with associates at the Mykonos restaurant in Berlin. In March 1996, the German federal prosecutor issued a warrant for the arrest of Minister of Intelligence Fallahian for his alleged role in planning the assassination. In the following year, a German court found one Iranian, the alleged leader, and two Lebanese nationals guilty of killing Sharafkandi and his associates and implicated Iran's highest officials in the assassination. In a particularly grisly killing in 1991, Iranian agents murdered Shapour Bakhtiar, the shah's last prime minister and leader of an opposition movement, slashing his throat in his own home in a Paris suburb. Other opposition figures were killed in Paris, Geneva, Istanbul, and elsewhere.

At home, the Intelligence Ministry launched a multipronged attack on intellectuals, writers, and journalists whom it considered liberal, secular, or Western in orientation and who, along with members of the clerical establishment, advocated freedom of expression and criticized the manner in which power was exercised in the Islamic Republic. The ministry undertook an ideological campaign designed to paint Westernized intellectuals and artists as unpatriotic, un-Islamic, a threat to Iran's national and religious identity, and the willing or unwitting agents of foreigners. It sent out death squads to murder writers, journalists, and academics. It arrested others and subjected them to show trials and prison terms.

The ideological campaign was spearheaded by Supreme Leader Ali Khamenei. In a series of statements and speeches he warned against the Western "cultural onslaught" that, he said, was aimed at undermining Iran's national and Islamic values. The national Iranian television network followed up with the notorious biweekly program titled *Hoviyyat*, or *Identity*. Inspired by the Intelligence Ministry, the TV series targeted prominent liberal intellectuals, depicting them as morally corrupt, tools of Western cultural imperialism, and disloyal to Iran and Islam. On the program, the portrait of Benjamin Franklin on the American hundred-dollar bill dissolved into the face of the Iranian intellectual under attack.

Domestic killings proliferated as well. In November 1994, the well-known writer and satirist Ali Akbar Saidi-Sirjani died while in police custody. He had been arrested on trumped-up charges of spying, homosexuality, and drug use. The body of the translator Ahmad Mir-Alai was found in an Isfahan alley, far from his usual haunts, in October 1995. More deaths followed. The Intelligence Ministry seemed to be running amok. In that same year, the driver of a bus carrying twenty-one writers and intellectuals to a conference in Armenia jumped off the bus, leaving it to roll toward a cliff with its dozing passengers. Miraculously, one of the passengers, who awakened, was able to pull the brake and save the others from death or serious injury.

In November 1996, the writer and editor of the journal *Adineh*, Faraj Sarkuhi, "disappeared" before boarding a plane at Tehran Airport to visit his family in Germany. He suddenly reappeared at a press conference seven weeks later with an implausible explanation for his absence. In a letter later smuggled out of the country, Sarkuhi revealed that he had been subjected to interrogation, beatings, and intense psychological intimidation over several weeks. He was made to confess that he had been spying for France and Germany and that he had given his journal an ideological slant dictated by the French and German embassies. He also was forced to confess to illicit relations with several women. So severe was his treatment, Sarkuhi wrote, that he had begged his interrogators to kill him.

The Khatami Presidency

Mohammad Khatami sought to curb such activities by the Intelligence Ministry after he was elected president in 1997. Khatami was

Iran's unexpected president. When he ran as a candidate of the left-wing parties and of the smaller of two clerical associations in Iran, few gave him a chance against the front-runner, Ali Akbar Nateq-Nuri. Nuri was speaker of the outgoing parliament. He was the candidate of the leading clerical association in the country and the majority party in the Majlis. He was endorsed directly or indirectly by the leaders of the Revolutionary Guards, by Friday-prayer leaders in much of the country, by the influential Seminary Teachers of Qom, and, indirectly, by the supreme leader himself, who said that Iranians would not vote for "an American president."

But Khatami ran on a platform that emphasized individual freedoms, tolerance for a variety of views, and openness to the outside world. This message resonated powerfully with the electorate, particularly among young people and women. In office, Khatami greatly loosened controls on the press and political activity. Several newspapers were launched, providing a new forum for vigorous discussion of major political issues before the country. New political associations were formed. The country experienced a revival of political life.

Khatami also took on the Intelligence Ministry, insisting on the removal of the minister, Fallahian; and when a new round of assassinations took place, he succeeded in forcing the ministry to clean house. Its hard-liners, however, simply moved elsewhere, setting up a parallel intelligence operation within the Revolutionary Guards and other institutions. From their new centers, these people continued their harassment of intellectuals and their attempts to repress Khatami's nascent reform movement. They were not alone in this endeavor. They had allies within the conservative wing of the regime, eager to cripple reform, prevent meaningful change, and crush their political rivals. They enjoyed the support of the supreme leader and the active cooperation of a cluster of pliant courts, judges, and investigating magistrates within the judiciary and the revolutionary courts. The police and security services cooperated, breaking up lectures by reformist intellectuals as well as protests and student demonstrations. *Kayhan* continued to serve as the mouthpiece of the hard-liners in the intelligence community, and national television provided them with a forum when they needed it.

Khatami's first term saw a tug-of-war between the reformers and the hard-liners. The mayor of Tehran, Gholam Hossain Karbaschi, a staunch supporter of the president, was tried on trumped-up charges of corruption, sentenced to a lengthy prison term, and barred from holding public office for ten years. Khatami's interior minister, Abdollah Nuri, was forced out of office, then tried and imprisoned for the views expressed in his highly popular newspaper, *Khordad*. A nearly successful assassination attempt left Khatami's chief political strategist, Sa'id Hajjarian, physically incapacitated and with severely limited powers of speech. Several reformist newspapers were closed down, although the new government's liberal policy in issuing publishing licenses allowed them to reopen within days under new names. When Tehran University students staged rallies in July 1999 to protest the closure of one of these newspapers, club- and knife-wielding thugs broke up the protests and trashed the university dormitories where the demonstrations had taken place. The police commander and seventeen officers charged and tried for the attack on the dormitories were all acquitted.

Killings of dissidents resumed in November 1998. The leader of the small Nation of Iran Party, Dariush Foruhar, and his wife, Parvaneh, were found gruesomely murdered in their apartment. In the weeks that followed and in what Iranians called "the serial murders," half a dozen other political activists and intellectuals were found dead under mysterious circumstances. The chain of killings terrified the intellectual community—as they were intended to. The newly freed press, however, would not let the issue die, and Khatami insisted on an investigation. In the end, the Ministry of Intelligence admitted that its own agents were responsible for the killings but blamed a rogue operation. Sa'id Emami, who for years had been one of Fallahian's principle deputies, was arrested as the ringleader, along with a number of other Ministry of Intelligence agents. However, Emami was conveniently found dead in the shower of his prison block, allegedly having committed suicide by swallowing a bottle of hair remover, in effect shutting down the "investigation."

Khatami's political party and its allies went on to win a majority in the 2000 parliamentary elections, and many prominent conservative candidates were soundly defeated. Khatami himself comfortably won a second term in 2001. But by then, a full-scale onslaught on the reformist camp was under way. In April 2000, Supreme Leader Khamenei launched a sharp attack on the reformist press, which, he said, had become the "bases of the enemy" and instruments of "enemy agents," causing "discord and division" among the people and undermining Islamic sanctities. A severe crackdown on the press followed. Fourteen newspapers and weeklies were suspended in April. In a ten-week period, more than twenty publications, constituting virtually the entire reformist press, was shut down. Several prominent newspaper editors and journalists were tried and sentenced to multiyear prison terms, on charges of "undermining state security," "insulting Islam," and "confusing" public opinion. Among the journalists were Emadeddin Baghi and Akbar Ganji, whose investigative journalism implicated the Intelligence Ministry and unnamed senior officials in the 1998 "serial murders" and other assassinations.

Judiciary officials also arrested and tried several writers who had participated in a conference on Iran at the Heinrich Böll Institute in Berlin, allegedly for insulting Islamic sanctities and undermining national security in their remarks. In a clear warning to the intellectual community, six of the participants were sentenced to prison terms ranging from four to ten years. In 2003, the Iranian Canadian photographer Zahra Kazemi died while under interrogation at Evin Prison. It was a further indication of the impunity enjoyed by the security services and their judicial accomplices that, parliamentary pressure notwithstanding, no one was ever tried for Kazemi's death, nor was any serious investigation into the circumstances leading to it ever carried out.

When Ahmadinejad was elected president in 2005, the repressive apparatus of the state had easily survived Khatami's attempted reforms and was in full resurgence. The new president further strengthened the hand of the most radical hard-liners. Mostafa Pour-Mohammadi, the newly appointed minister of the interior, had served as deputy minister of intelligence during the "serial murders" and was implicated in the mass execution of dissidents in Evin Prison in 1988. Mohammad Hossein Safar-Harandi, Ahmadinejad's minister of culture and Islamic guidance, had been the managing editor of *Kayhan*, the newspaper with the closest links to the security agencies and the bane of liberal intellectuals. His new position gave him considerable say in policy toward the press, book publishing, and the arts. Gholam Hossein Mohseni-Eje'i, the new minister of intelligence, had served as a judge of the revolutionary courts, presiding over the trial of Tehran mayor Karbaschi and the trials of several reformist members of the clergy. The offices he held over the years, including a spell as the judiciary's representative to the Intelligence Ministry and membership in a high-level intelligence committee, placed him at the nexus of cooperation between the judiciary and the Intelligence Ministry. A principal proponent of the theory that the United States was plotting a "velvet revolution" in Iran, he was now in a position to act on his suspicions.

It was such men who now had me in their gun sights.

"We Know How to Handle You"

My daily routine varied little over my first weeks in Evin. The bell on the iron door separating the men's block from the women's block rang, echoing through our corridor and indicating a visitor was at the door. A minute later, one of the guards came to my cell door and told me to put on my chador and prepare for interrogation. At the door of the cell block, she told me to put on my blindfold. Ja'fari was waiting on the other side of the curtain.

He led the way to the interrogation room, calling out instructions in a monotonous loud voice, as I followed in my blindfold: "turn left," "turn right," "go straight," "watch out for the stairs." He wanted to avoid an accident. Terrified I would fall, I tried to fix the route in my memory: one floor down, then left, down a second flight of stairs, across a narrow corridor crowded with men, left into a short corridor, and into the first room on the right. I discovered that if I pushed up slightly on my blindfold, I could see Ja'fari's gray socks and sandals and follow his footsteps.

The interrogation room was very small, with just enough space for a school-type chair-and-desk, at which I sat, and a larger desk with a cushioned chair for Hajj Agha or Ja'fari. One more chair and a coatrack stood in a corner. The walls were bare. No light came from the window near the ceiling. I assumed we were in a basement.

The interview on my first day did not go well. Ja'fari started off by berating me for having been uncooperative and for withholding information. "We know how to handle you," he said. "We will get every bit of information out of you. You will stay here as long as it is necessary." He pointed to the pile of papers in front of him. He had my SAVAK files, he said, plus more recent reports. "We have a roomful of information about you."

Ja'fari again asked me to describe my past career and work in Iran: at the newspaper *Kayhan*, at the Women's Organization of Iran, and at the Shahbanou Farah Foundation—ground we had covered in detail in the pre-Evin interrogations. By now I was familiar with his tactics. He wanted to catch me in a discrepancy. He wanted to wear me down. Repetition of this kind, I learned to my surprise, is in its own way disorienting. You tire of repeating the same stories. You actually want to have something new to say. You have to remind yourself not to stray from the facts.

Ja'fari's bullying led me, in turn, to defiance. We spent the afternoon in a frustrating back-and-forth. Ja'fari wanted to know about my colleagues at *Kayhan*. I wrote down the names of several colleagues—every one already dead. He was furious. "Don't you know anyone who is alive?" he asked sarcastically. He asked me with whom we socialized in America. "We work such long hours, we don't have time to socialize," I replied. Surprisingly, he let it go. He introduced a woman whose name I did not recognize and wanted to know how well

I knew her. Ja'fari identified her as a member of the Israeli embassy in Tehran before the revolution. He claimed I had met her on a number of occasions, but I had not. We continued this barren exchange for a while, with Ja'fari insisting I knew the woman and me not having the vaguest notion whom he was talking about. The subject of Israel led Ja'fari to again make the assertion that Shaul was a Zionist. I retorted, as before, that "I don't answer any questions about my husband."

Ja'fari then handed me a sheet of paper and said, "Write everything you know about him."

Astonished, I asked, "About whom? About my husband?"

"Yes," he said, in a mocking tone and with narrowed eyes, "*Perofessor* Bakhash," adding an extra vowel to "professor," since Iranians find it difficult to pronounce two consonants together. I took the paper and pen and deliberately wrote only a few lines about Shaul's career as an author and a university professor. By late afternoon I was tired, angry, and anxious at the bad turn the interrogation had taken. Ja'fari seemed to have tired of the interrogation, too. He offered me his cell phone: "Call your mother but don't speak long," he said. I called Mutti. I managed again to convey, without ever using the word, that I needed a lawyer.

I put on my blindfold and followed Ja'fari back up the stairs and through the corridors to ward 209. "Stop!" he yelled at one point. I had almost banged my head on an overhead railing.

Back in my cell, I practiced taking steps while wearing my blindfold. I taught myself to wear the blindfold so that I could see my feet and the ground in front of me. After that, I could follow Ja'fari quite easily; I don't think he ever realized how much I could see.

In the Hands of Hajj Agha

When Hajj Agha took charge of the interrogation, as he increasingly did at Evin, I would have to sit facing the wall. I was not allowed to see him. "Under no condition are you to turn around," Ja'fari warned me.

I soon realized I was up against an interrogator very different from Ja'fari. Hajj Agha was almost always courteous—a small mercy, perhaps, but important in an environment of uncertainty and fear. Even if he was only playacting, at least he got things done. At our first session I complained that it was uncomfortable to eat and read sitting cross-legged on the ground. I was given a small desk. He saw to it that Mutti could bring me clothes, although she was never allowed to bring me medications and, except for two occasions, never food.

Unlike Ja'fari, who often lied to me, Hajj Agha almost always kept his word. He let me know by way of the guards if he could not make it to an interrogation for which he told me to prepare. He apologized if he made a promise he could not keep. When I complained I couldn't sleep with the lights on, he promised to take care of the problem, then apologized after he learned that the "lights on" prison rule could not be waived. With Hajj Agha I could sometimes make small talk, or even try a bit of humor; such exchanges were unthinkable with Ja'fari. Hajj Agha was also a more astute interrogator, aware that a gentler tone might yield better results than Ja'fari's battering-ram approach. It wasn't exactly a "good cop–bad cop" routine; I simply faced two different men, different in character, sophistication, and experience.

None of this meant that Hajj Agha was any less threatening than Ja'fari. He accused me of endangering state security. He sought to intimidate me. He tried to wear me down by going over the same material again and again, jumping without warning from subject to subject, throwing out unexpected questions and outlandish accusations. He, too, resorted to the bluff: "Tell us about the meeting the three of you—Hamilton, Soros, and yourself—had to discuss Iran," he said, as if a meeting that had never occurred was a well-known fact. Even more than Ja'fari, Hajj Agha elaborated repeatedly on the "plan" for the overthrow of the Islamic Republic of which he claimed I was a part.

Day by day, I could discern no logical progression, no overarching organization, to Hajj Agha's line of questioning. However, after several weeks, Hajj Agha appeared to me to be focused on three goals:

to build the case against me personally, to nail down what he believed to be the American "plan" for Iran, and to lay out and have me endorse his characterization of the confrontation between Iran and the United States and the role each was playing on the world stage.

Hajj Agha began his first interrogation session on a conciliatory note. The *aghayun*—the gentlemen—and the *dustan*—our friends—he said, referring to his superiors, were not satisfied with my answers. I was parsimonious with words, I wasn't forthcoming; I hadn't told them anything they did not already know. He cited the example of the more talkative Ramin Jahanbegloo, whom they had imprisoned and interrogated the previous year on similar charges.

They had many documents, Hajj Agha said, proving my complicity in plans to overthrow the regime—documents so confidential, they could not show them to me outside of prison. He returned to this theme again and again. "This is a serious matter," he said to me on one occasion. "You tried to help the enemy overthrow the Islamic Republic."

"By organizing conferences?" I asked him. I would have loved to catch the expression on his face, but all I could see was the dirty wall before me.

I gathered that the "roomful of documents" and "evidence" consisted of the pre-revolution SAVAK files; reports sent to Tehran by the Intelligence Ministry's own spooks in Washington, D.C.; and what they had gleaned from their interrogation of Ramin Jahanbegloo. I knew Jahanbegloo well and respected his intellect and his work and had invited him to speak at the Wilson Center. In the interrogation transcripts which Ja'fari showed me, Jahanbegloo had been coerced into depicting me as a major player on the Washington scene and as the link between scholars, think tanks, and American government officials. I was adamant during my interrogation in rejecting this false characterization. The SAVAK files were thirty years old and obsolete. At *Kayhan* we had all known the middle-aged journalist who doubled as SAVAK's *khabar-chin*, the derogatory Persian term for a hack informer. I was certain there was nothing even remotely incriminating in them, or in the misinformation from the Intelligence Ministry's informers in Washington. This could easily be refuted, even though facts and logic did not exactly reign supreme in the interrogation room.

I was determined to remain composed during these interrogations, and to answer calmly, even when provoked. Yet there were rough days. One morning when Hajj Agha accused me for the umpteenth time of endangering national security, my pent-up anger came spilling out.

I was not endangering Iran's national security by organizing meetings and inviting university professors, intellectuals, and members of NGOs from Iran to speak, I shot back at Hajj Agha in a deliberately angry tone. They loved their country. They opposed outside interference in Iran's internal affairs and had criticized the allocation of money by Congress and the State Department to encourage regime change in Iran. They believed that the United States had made no effort to understand Iran's vital security needs in the region.

The Iranian government, I pointed out, is seen abroad as autocratic and repressive, Iran itself thought to be a country of hostage takers and terrorists. I showed Iranians who were moderate and reasonable to an American audience, men and women who could explain the rationale behind some of Iran's foreign policies. Surely, I said, it makes more sense to have an Iranian scholar analyze the results of Iranian elections or the Iranian economy than to have an outsider who has never been to the country do so.

"If this country can be destabilized by twenty of its scholars attending conferences, then how does Iran differ from a banana republic, or Afghanistan and the Arab countries you look down on?" I asked.

Both Ja'fari and Hajj Agha were taken aback. They had never seen me talk at such great length or so angrily. After a moment's silence, Hajj Agha recovered: "Well," he said sarcastically, "you no doubt expect us to apologize and thank you for all you have done. Maybe we should award you the first prize at the Fajr Festival for the services you rendered to the Islamic Republic." His sarcasm fell somewhat flat when I had to ask what the Fajr Festival prize was. (It is awarded to the best film at the annual film festival.)

But Hajj Agha persisted with another tack. "Let's accept that you were drawn into this plot to overthrow the regime unknowingly. Let's assume you did not know what the real aim of the Wilson Center, the National Endowment for Democracy, the Soros Foundation was. You were snared into this chain of plots and plans simply because you were working for the Wilson Center; and you innocently became a tool in their hands. They used you to implement their sinister plans for undermining the regime."

I refused to go down that road, either. What plots? What plans? I demanded. Programs on other regions of the world at the Wilson Center and at hundreds of institutions around the United States were doing exactly what I was doing on the Middle East. In no other country was a single program director arrested. "You have a fixation with Iranians who work abroad and are successful at what they do," I told him. The Islamic Republic harrassed Iranians but gave foreign scholars the red carpet treatment. "*Morgh-e ham-say'e ghazeh*," I told him, using the Persian expression, The neighbor's hen looks like a goose. So we went, back and forth.

The *Kayhan* Episode

Five or six days after my incarceration, Ja'fari and Hajj Agha showed me a fresh copy of *Kayhan*. A boldface headline above a lengthy story read: "Investigative Report by *Kayhan*: Who is Haleh Esfandiari?" I skimmed the article rapidly and with mounting panic. It was a vicious concoction of false accusations, distortions, and blatant fabrications.

Claiming "documentary evidence," it accused Shaul and me of working for the Israel spy service, Mossad. It claimed that I had converted to Judaism (an act considered apostasy in Islam and punishable by death) and that I had fled to Israel after the revolution and lived there for two years.

The article went on to allege that I ran the "Iranian department" for the pro-Israel lobbying group AIPAC, on whose behalf I had organized a conference on Iran and invited President Bush, Condoleezza Rice, and Israeli prime minister Ehud Olmert. There was a great deal more in the same vein. There was information in the article, even though patently false, that could only have come from the security agencies. The article was making a case for charges of treason against me.

In the interrogation room I sat facing the wall as I read. I threw the paper back at Hajj Agha and Ja'fari: "I refuse to read such filth," I asserted. "If I am free one day, I will take *Kayhan* to court." Hajj Agha could see how upset I was and tried to calm me down. "Forget the article," he said. "We just wanted you to see the adverse environment we have to deal with." Having instigated, or possibly authored, the article, these men were now trying to pose as my protectors. I was having none of it. "This is your work," I said, addressing Ja'fari.

A few days after this incident, I was walking on the larger of two rooftop terraces available to the inmates when I saw another copy of *Kayhan*, neatly propped against the wall. Even at a distance I could make out the big black headline: "Mossad and CIA Network Uncovered." Cut off from any news of the outside world, I would normally have seized the chance to read a newspaper. But this was obviously a clumsily contrived ruse designed to frighten and intimidate me. Perhaps I was mentioned in the article. Perhaps they wanted to implicate me in a CIA-Mossad plot or drag me into a discussion of these security services. Perhaps they thought reports of spy rings uncovered and spies arrested would lead me to "confess." I continued walking, passing the newspaper every time I circled the terrace, but I pretended never to have seen it.

At that afternoon's interrogation, Hajj Agha asked me if I was pleased with my new access to the larger terrace for my daily walk. I thanked him for making the arrangement. "Did you see anything interesting on your walk?" he prodded.

"Oh, there was a newspaper there, but I didn't have my glasses and couldn't even read the headline," I said. I may have imagined his sigh of disappointment, but we all understood that they had tried a ploy, and failed.

I later learned that, for Shaul, the *Kayhan* article, with its accusations of espionage, was particularly alarming. Since the newspaper was the organ of a hard-line faction in the Intelligence Ministry, Shaul feared that this article was laying the foundation for the Intelligence Ministry's formal charges against me. Few of those victimized by *Kayhan* liked to tangle with it because it was so vicious in its tactics. But Shaul knew our hope lay in confronting *Kayhan* head-on.

In an open letter, he refuted point by point each of the falsehoods in *Kayhan*'s article. He kept his rebuttal brief, factual, and unemotional. *Kayhan*, of course, never published Shaul's open letter. But it was reported on Persian-language Web sites and one or two Iranian newspapers, by the Voice of America and the BBC, and by newspapers in the United States. After the rebuttal, *Kayhan* did not cease printing brief, snide remarks about me, but the newspaper's large-scale attacks against me stopped, even as it continued to publish such libels against others. Perhaps Shaul's pointed replies and his exposure of *Kayhan*'s sloppy reporting, distortions, and inaccuracies had had an effect. Perhaps the Intelligence Ministry itself had second thoughts about the wisdom of engaging in such blatant falsehood and anti-Semitism. In any case, Hajj Agha showed up in Evin Prison a few days after the publication of the article and said to me: "Such things are over and done with."

❧ A Compelling but Mad Logic

Outside prison, Ja'fari's and Hajj Agha's repeated references to "the triangle," "plots," and "conspiracies" seemed outlandish, even amusing. In solitary confinement, under interrogation, cut off from the outside world, accused of the most serious crimes against the state, I found these endlessly repeated assertions sinister: part of a world of secret cabals, plotters, and conspiracies in which I was supposedly involved without being aware of it. I had to be careful not to lose my grip on reality or to succumb to Hajj Agha's deceptive view of the world.

There was a simple, even compelling, but ultimately mad logic to Hajj Agha's theory. It went this way: The United States wanted regime change in Iran; American officials had repeatedly said so. Congress had allocated funds for this purpose and the administration, no doubt, had additional, secret funds at its disposal. These funds were given to think tanks and foundations, such as the National Endowment for Democracy, whose mission was to advance democratization—in effect, regime change—in targeted countries. The think tanks and foundations were run by former high administration officials who often returned to government service through a constantly revolving door. It was hardly far-fetched to conclude that these men—part of a governing elite—pursued the same policy goals in thinks tanks as they did in the government, and that the Iranian scholars—many of them unqualified—whom they identified and selected for fellowships and conference participation were selected not at random but as part of a larger scheme.

Hajj Agha's technique was to string together a series of seemingly reasonable assertions to reach a "logical" conclusion that, examined dispassionately, was simply wrong, divorced from reality. But in the isolation of prison and the interrogation room, I had to fight hard to avoid Hajj Agha's conspiratorial mind-set.

Additionally, Hajj Agha's friendlier approach was in some ways harder to handle than the long, exhausting question-and-answer sessions with Ja'fari. Hajj Agha lectured me; he tried to impose on me his (or the Intelligence Ministry's) worldview. He once went into a long disquisition on the cold war. The United States and the West, he said, had brought about the downfall of the Soviet Union by undermining the fabric of societies in Eastern Europe. It had laid a trap, and the USSR and its East European surrogates naively fell into it. "Iran will not fall into the same trap," he said.

With my mother in Tehran, 1940.

In Prague in 1946 with Mutti, Uncle Max, and his wife, Inka.

Khanum Jan, my grandmother.

All photographs courtesy of the author unless otherwise indicated.

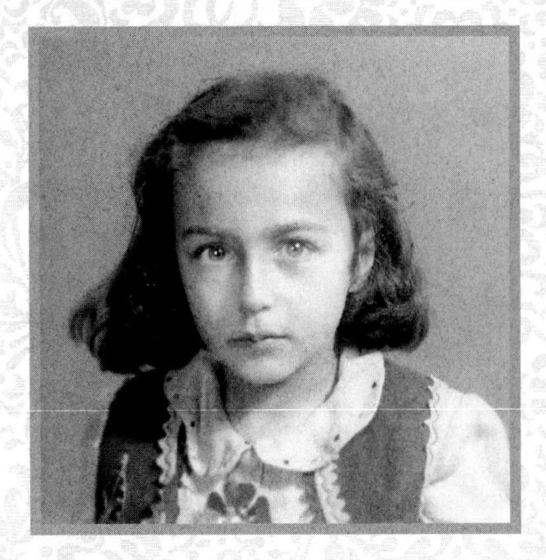

Me, at age six.

At age thirteen, with my mother.

With my husband, Shaul, on our wedding day, in Vienna.

With Shaul and our daughter, Haleh, in Tehran in the 1960s.

With my parents *(front)*; my brother, Siamack; and my sister, Hayedeh, in Vienna in the early 1980s.

One of the gates of Evin Prison through which I passed at the beginning of my 105 days in solitary confinement.

With Shirin Ebadi, my future attorney, in 2004 at the Woodrow Wilson International Center for Scholars.

(Courtesy of the Woodrow Wilson International Center for Scholars)

Speaking at a conference at Princeton in the 1980s, when I was teaching Persian language and literature.

From my televised interview from prison broadcast in July 2007 under the title *In the Name of Democracy*. The broadcast was condemned as a reprehensible attempt to make a coerced statement appear as a "confession." (Copyright © Associated Press)

31 May 2007

His Excellency Ayatollah Sayed 'Ali Khamenei
Office of the Supreme Leader
Shoahada Street
Qom, Islamic Republic of Iran

Your Excellency:

We write to you today to appeal to your humanity, sense of justice, love of learning, and love for Iran. We are all former students of Dr. Haleh Esfandiari.

For each of us, she was an inspiration. Because of her own love for Iran, she wanted us to learn about the glories of Persian history and culture, including its proud Islamic heritage, the beauty of the Persian language, and the wonderful warm-heartedness of Iran's people. By setting an example with her own courtesy and social graces, she taught us to appreciate the depth of Persian cultural traditions. She taught us all to care about a land and people very far from our own. From her we were given a lifelong love of Iran's legendary epic the *Shahnameh*, the ability to enjoy the beautiful poetry of Hafez, Rumi, and Saadi, an appreciation of modern authors like Al-i Ahmad, and a joy in seeing the glorious forms of Persian calligraphy.

Her entire career as a scholar and a teacher has been spent building bridges of understanding between Americans and Iranians. The actions of the government of Iran strain that understanding.

As her former students, we hope that you will consider the goodwill she has built for Iran and preserve that tremendous asset. We ask you to intervene for her release from Evin prison and allow her to return to her family and students in America.

Sincerely,

cc: His Excellency Mahmoud Ahmadinejad, President of Iran

The letter written to Ayatollah Khamenei by my former students at Princeton.

110th Congress
1st Session

S. Res. 214

In the Senate of the United States

May 24, 2007

Whereas *Dr. Haleh Esfandiari, Ph.D., holds dual citizenship in the United States and the Islamic Republic of Iran;*

Whereas *Dr. Esfandiari taught Persian language and literature for many years at Princeton University, where she inspired untold numbers of students to study the rich Persian language and culture;*

Whereas *Dr. Esfandiari is a resident of the State of Maryland and the Director of the Middle East Program at the Woodrow Wilson International Center for Scholars in Washington, D.C. (referred to in this preamble as the "Wilson Center");*

Whereas *for the past decade, Dr. Esfandiari has traveled to Iran twice a year to visit her ailing 93-year-old mother;*

Whereas *in December 2006, on her return to the airport during her last visit to Iran, Dr. Esfandiari was robbed by 3 masked, knife-wielding men, who stole her travel documents, luggage, and other effects;*

Whereas *when Dr. Esfandiari attempted to obtain replacement travel documents in Iran, she was invited to an interview by a representative of the Ministry of Intelligence of Iran;*

Whereas *Dr. Esfandiari was interrogated by the Ministry of Intelligence for hours on many days;*

Whereas *the questioning of the Ministry of Intelligence focused on the Middle East Program at the Wilson Center;*

Whereas *Dr. Esfandiari answered all questions to the best of her ability, and the Wilson Center also provided extensive information to the Ministry in a good faith effort to aid Dr. Esfandiari;*

Whereas *the harassment of Dr. Esfandiari increased, with her being awakened while napping to find 3 strange men standing at her bedroom door, one wielding a video camera, and later being pressured to make false confessions against herself and to falsely implicate the Wilson Center in activities in which it had no part;*

Whereas *Lee Hamilton, former United States Representative and president of the Wilson Center, has written to the President of Iran to call his attention to Dr. Esfandiari's dire situation;*

Whereas *Mr. Hamilton repeated that the Wilson Center's mission is to provide forums to exchange views and opinions and not to take positions on issues, nor try to influence specific outcomes;*

Whereas *the lengthy interrogations of Dr. Esfandiari by the Ministry of Intelligence of Iran stopped on February 14, 2007, but she heard nothing for 10 weeks and was denied her passport;*

Whereas *on May 8, 2007, Dr. Esfandiari honored a summons to appear at the Ministry of Intelligence, whereby she was taken immediately to Evin prison, where she is currently being held; and*

Whereas *the Ministry of Intelligence has implicated Dr. Esfandiari and the Wilson Center in advancing the alleged aim of the United States Government of supporting a "soft revolution" in Iran: Now, therefore, be it*

Resolved, *That—(1) the Senate calls upon the Government of the Islamic Republic of Iran to immediately release—*

Dr. Haleh Esfandiari

replace her lost travel documents, and cease its harassment tactics; and (2) it is the sense of the Senate that—(A) the United States Government, through all appropriate diplomatic means and channels, should encourage the Government of Iran to release Dr. Esfandiari and offer her an apology; and (B) the United States should coordinate its response with its allies throughout the Middle East, other governments, and all appropriate international organizations.

Attest:

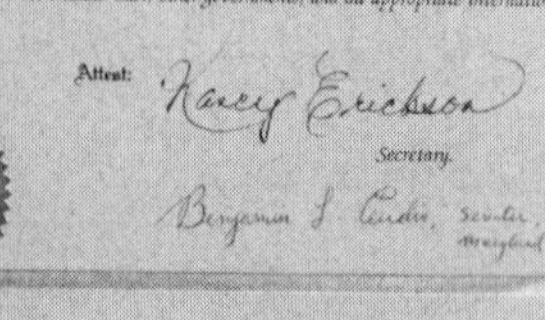

Secretary.

The resolution adopted by the U.S. Senate calling for my release. A similar resolution was adopted by the House of Representatives.

Shaul and Haleh watching my televised interview in July 2007 from the BBC studios in Washington, D.C., where the Iranian broadcast was being taped.
(Copyright © Carol Guzy/*The Washington Post*)

Leaving Evin on August 21, 2007.
(Copyright © AFP/Getty Images)

With Shaul in an interview at the Wilson Center following my release.
(Courtesy of the Woodrow Wilson International Center for Scholars/Heidi Fancher)

Reuniting with Haleh after my release.
(Copyright © Susan Biddle/*The Washington Post*)

With my granddaughters, Karenna and Ariana, on the day I arrived home, September 5, 2007.
(Copyright © Susan Biddle/*The Washington Post*)

With Haleh, Shaul, and now president Barack Obama, who gave a speech at the Wilson Center during the 2008 presidential campaign.
(Courtesy of the Woodrow Wilson International Center for Scholars/Heidi Fancher)

But things did not always work out for the West, Hajj Agha continued. The Americans were defeated in Vietnam. Fidel Castro led a revolution in Cuba, Salvador Allende in Chile, and Daniel Ortega in Nicaragua. True, the Americans had bled the Russians in Afghanistan and then supported and propped up the Taliban; but the Taliban turned against the Americans and had to be overthrown. Above all, the Iranian revolution and the Islamic Republic were "a thorn in the side of the Americans," he boasted, "and Iran will not fall apart like the Soviet Union."

For the West, he explained on another occasion, Islam is the ultimate enemy, and Iran is the the standard-bearer of Islam. The Iranian revolution restored Islam's standing in the world. Islamic countries look up to Iran because it is not the lackey of the United States. On the contrary, it is the one country that defies America. So it went with Hajj Agha. To shore up my defenses, I thought of Solzhenitsyn's Gulag novels and of the spy novels I had read. I wanted to steel myself by recalling the interrogation techniques of police states elsewhere and the lonely men and women who had managed to survive them.

Hajj Agha and Ja'fari tried another kind of intimidation. One night I was woken up at eleven o'clock and summoned for interrogation. I had heard of all-night interrogation sesions and, full of trepidation, I dressed hastily and was taken before the two men. "We had nothing important to discuss," Hajj Agha said, noticing my anger at being roused from sleep. "We were both working around the clock and thought we should continue our conversation with you. But it can wait till tomorrow."

Back in my cell, I sat on my chair. Tears ran uncontrollably down my face. I had coiled myself taut in anticipation of a rough night. Now, I went slack with relief. What had become of me, I thought, that two heedless interrogators could upset me so? I looked up at the night sky through the bars of my cell: it was overcast, and I couldn't see the moon or a single star. Even the sky was in mourning for me, I thought.

"How Do You Know Obama?"

One afternoon, in the middle of another five-hour session, Hajj Agha threw me off track with an odd question: "How do you know Obama?" he asked. Ja'fari had been grilling me about Iranians living and working in the United States, when Hajj Agha interjected Obama's name, pronouncing it as if it began with a *u*, and with the accent on the last syllable—*Oo-ba-Ma*. For a moment I thought this was another Iranian I did not know. "Who?" I said. "*Oobama*," Hajj Agha repeated. I thought for a moment. "Do you mean the senator from Illinois?" It was June 2007 and news of his run for president had reached me before I was taken to Evin.

"Yes," he said. "When did you first meet him and how often do you go see him?" With Hajj Agha, I could sometimes joke. "Oh, on a daily basis," I said. The truth was, I had never met Barack Obama. The only time I had even seen him was when I sat among several hundred people to hear him speak at the Council on Foreign Relations. I told this to Hajj Agha.

He was not convinced. He kept insisting that there must be something more, that I knew him. "He is not even my senator," I said. Finally, visibly annoyed, Hajj Agha mumbled, "Obama made a statement about you and asked for your release." I tried not to show my delight. In a conversation only two days earlier, Hajj Agha had greatly unnerved me when he said, in a mocking tone, "You have more friends in Iran than in America; and your Iranian friends are more harmful than helpful to your case. Nobody abroad really cares about you." I now knew that I was not forgotten abroad. If Senator Obama had spoken of me, then Shaul and the Wilson Center must have begun to alert people in Washington to the urgency of my predicament, some of whom must be making an effort on my behalf. Hajj Agha continued to insist I must know Obama personally. "Why would he speak of Khanum Esfandiari if he does not know her?" he asked, referring to me in the third person.

I don't think I persuaded Hajj Agha that Obama took up my case simply because I was an American citizen, but he had thrown me a lifeline. I broke my iron rule not to ask questions about myself. "Has anyone else spoken about me?" I asked. Hajj Agha reluctantly admitted that Hillary Clinton had also issued a statement regarding my incarceration, but he tried to be dismissive. "Well, you are a woman, a Democrat, and a feminist and you think she will win the election," he said. "Why shouldn't she talk about you?"

Back in my cell, I tried to factor the Obama news into my calculation of where I stood. I grasped at a thin glimmer of hope. But how much light was there? I knew that Shaul, with whom I had been allowed no contact since my arrest, would be doing everything in his power to get me released, that he would be making phone calls, seeking contacts, looking for influential international figures to intercede on my behalf, and that Lee Hamilton would do the same. But I also knew that in political cases Iran's officials could be obdurate and impervious to external pressure, publicity, or pleading, which was why we had reserved asking for outside help as an option of last resort. In July 2000, ten Iranian Jews from Shiraz were tried behind closed doors on trumped-up charges of espionage and sentenced to long prison terms, despite an international outcry, the direct intervention of the European Union, and a promise to European ambassadors that the trial would be public and they could attend. Human-rights groups protested when prominent journalists such as Ganji were put on trial; but Ganji and his colleagues were sentenced and jailed anyway. And how long could meaningful publicity be sustained? Ganji and other arrested journalists, intellectuals, and politicians had merited a story or two in the American and European press and were then forgotten. Media reports about me, I thought, would suffer a similar fate.

I could not know, of course, that the story of my arrest and incarceration had become worldwide news and that my story had captured the public imagination. I was unaware that Shaul and Hamilton had taken part in numerous interviews, that leading American papers had condemned my arrest in their editorials, that I was the subject of commentary by columnists, and that European governments were intervening with the Iranians on my behalf.

In my isolation at Evin, I had focused all my faculties on the interrogation and was fighting desperately to avoid a trial. I could not permit myself the luxury or distraction of thinking of what Shaul and our friends were doing for me. I dared not hope because, psychologically, I feared a crushing disappointment. Hajj Agha had thrown me a lifeline, but I did not dare pull too hard on it lest it unravel in my hands—lest once gain my hopes would be shattered.

In July, the interrogations became far less frequent and were down to about two a week. Hajj Agha repeated that he was doing his best to end my ordeal. He would raise my hopes, then come back and apologize. A new "hurdle" had arisen, he would say; there was a *gereh*—"a knot"—to untie. Given all these knots, I thought, we could have woven a whole Persian carpet.

Hajj Agha once disappeared for a whole week. When he showed up again, he said he had a root canal done. "It was very painful," he said. "I thought it must be that Khanum Esfandiari laid a curse on me." I assured him this was not the case. "As long as I am in prison, Hajj Agha," I said, "I wish you a long life. I don't want to start all over again with another interrogator."

It appeared to me that Hajj Agha was marking time, but the prospect of a drawn-out stay at Evin was hardly comforting. Near the end of July and my third month in solitary, Ja'fari brought me a form to sign. It turned out to be a court order for a one-month extension of my detention—"It's just routine, don't pay any attention to it," he said. I was crushed. The prospect of months and years in prison were unbearable to me. I sometimes even half hoped for a fatal heart attack and a quick end to my misery.

In my blackest moods, the unwelcome interrogations provided me with a form of healing. In the face of bullying and false accusations, I grew angry and defiant. I knew I must not let them break me.

8.

EVIN PRISON

FOR THE NEARLY FOUR MONTHS of my solitary confinement in Evin, my only human contacts were the guards, the interrogators, and the occasional prison doctor. I never once spoke to another inmate. I had no watch, until they returned mine two months into the incarceration. I learned to tell the time of day by the early-morning chirping of the birds, the changing of the guards, mealtimes, and the daily tempo of prison life.

Ward 209 was reserved for political prisoners and run by the Intelligence Ministry. It was located on the uppermost floor of Evin's main building. The men's block was to the left of the staircase. The women's section faced the stairway and was separated from the men's block by an iron door and a curtain. Though blindfolded whenever I passed through the door, I caught occasional glimpses of the men's section when I was taken to the interrogation rooms or to the dispensary. The men's cells stood along a long corridor, punctuated by doors leading to interrogation rooms, the one-room dispensary, and an enclosed rooftop terrace. Ja'fari once had me brought to this terrace for interrogation. He was recovering from knee surgery, the interrogation rooms on the men's corridor were in use, and he wanted to avoid going up and down the stairs to the lower-level interrogation rooms. There was a similar terrace in the women's section, but the men's terrace was larger.

Along the men's corridor, guards sat behind a couple of small desks at all hours, keeping watch as inmates were moved about. Initially refused reading material, I was envious of the guards sitting at their desks reading books and newspapers or watching TV.

On the women's block, doors led in succession to the small rooftop terrace, the inmates' bathroom, the separate guards' bathroom, and a row of five or six prisoners' cells. At the end of the corridor were the guards' quarters: two rooms, one small, one large, facing each other. The rooms contained bedding, a refrigerator, a hot plate, and a television. The guards also had their own air-conditioning unit. The TV was in constant use. You could hear it all night long through the thick cell walls. We were forbidden to go near the guards' rooms. Against the far wall, between the two rooms, was a chair for the guard on duty.

The wall opposite the cells had two barred windows, one of which contained an air-conditioning unit that served the whole block. There were also hooks where the guards hung their chadors, and pictures of Ayatollah Khomeini and Ayatollah Khamenei, the current supreme leader. Khomeini was frowning and fierce; Khamenei looked meek and mellow in comparison. The same two pictures appeared virtually everywhere you turned in Evin—in the interrogation rooms and lining the corridors. During my 105 days at the prison, I managed to avoid looking at either of the men. The harsh world they created and ran had turned on me and made me a prisoner. Their ubiquitous presence was more than I could bear.

The women's bathroom consisted of a single shower and an Iranian-style toilet, a ceramic basin sunk into the ground. The inmates were supposed to clean the bathroom after use, but no one did. I couldn't bear to use a dirty bathroom, and cleaned it each time, before and after I used it. On one occasion, the toilet was so disgustingly filthy, I complained to the guard, who made the previous user clean it. She took her revenge on me by complaining that I was being allowed more than the allotted time on the rooftop terraces. For a while I was limited to the regulation one hour a day, but once she left Evin, I had longer use of the terraces.

I never saw the other prisoners in the women's block, but I could hear them—knocking on their cell doors to go to the bathroom, sometimes exchanging angry words with the guards. None of the other women inmates spent as long in solitary as I did; the usual stint was two or three weeks. I could tell when a new prisoner was brought in because the cover over the small opening in my cell door would be pulled shut. When I was in the corridor myself, a door left wide open to reveal an empty cell meant a prisoner had been released or transferred elsewhere.

❧ Prison Days

From the first day, I decided that if I were to avoid succumbing to despair, I had to impose a strict discipline on myself. I vowed not to show any weakness or slackening of will to my interrogators or the guards. The possibility of a show trial weighed heavily on my mind. I knew I had to be mentally strong, keep my wits about me, remain focused on the interrogations, and do everything in my power to thwart the fate the Intelligence Ministry was planning for me: a coerced confession, a trial on trumped-up charges, a lengthy incarceration. I avoided thinking about my husband, daughter, and grandchildren or about home—knowing the pain of missing them could cripple my ability to withstand the pressures of prison. When the traditional Iranian dish called *adas polow*—a mixture of rice, lentils, and raisins, a favorite of my granddaughters—was served, I refused to even look at it and sent it back.

At my request, a guard knocked on my door at six a.m. I got up, vigorously paced the length of my cell for an hour, and then showered and changed. I then had a breakfast of tea, bread, and cheese, or tea and a piece of fruit. After breakfast, I resumed stretching exercises, push-ups, and pacing until it was time to go out on one of the two rooftop terraces available to the inmates. While I exercised, I composed two books—not on paper but in my head. One was a biography of my paternal grandmother. As I paced and stretched, I rewrote, edited, transposed paragraphs, and tried out different chapter titles. The other book was a children's story for my granddaughters. It was a fairy tale about a little Iranian girl, named Haleh, after me and their own mother. I sometimes imagined Ariana and Karenna, sitting on the beige couch in the library of their home, listening to my story, but I brushed the thought away. Thinking about my granddaughters could quickly drive me to despair.

After a lunch of yogurt and salad or fruit, and occasionally white rice and chicken, I would continue with aerobics and Pilates. Two large, water-filled plastic bottles served as my dumbbells. Counting repetitions helped me avoid brooding over the long imprisonment that stretched before me. Some days I would exercise for six hours or more. My persistent activity astonished my guards. Nothing in my previous experience had prepared me for Evin, but knew I had to avoid the listlessness that overtakes prisoners and to stave off depression, which lurked like a dark shadow in every corner of my cell.

At six I would shower again and change. I remembered a friend telling me that at her boarding school in England, everyone "dressed" for dinner. I also remembered in the film *Out of Africa*, Meryl Streep had even worn an evening dress and Robert Redford a tuxedo while on a safari in the African jungle. So, in grand style, I would put on an unironed but clean T-shirt and a fresh pair of wrinkled cotton pants and sit down and read between six and ten, taking time off only to eat a small meal of vegetables and yogurt.

For reading, I initially had only the Quran that was already in my cell and the one book I had with me when arrested, a recently published collection of letters written by a royal princess in the late nineteenth century—an interesting window into changing female sensibility. In the second week of my incarceration, one of the guards began to bring me books from the prison library, mostly on Shi'ism. I thought I might as well educate myself on the subject, but the books were dull, full of Sunni-bashing, written in a convoluted, heavily Arabized Persian, and often the work of semiliterate clerics. I begged for something more interesting, and received a hodgepodge of books: Kahlil Gibran's collection of mystical poems, *The Prophet*, which I had read as a teenager; a Persian translation of *Nostradamus*; and several novels and travel books by the Greek author Nikos Kazantzakis, also in Persian translation. I was bemused by the thought that the left-wing author of *Zorba the Greek* had fans in Evin Prison.

Later, Kian Tajbakhsh, the other Iranian American inmate, was allowed to share his books with me. He lived in Iran and had access to books from home. I was so pleased to read fiction in English again that I spent many minutes simply luxuriating in the feel of the first of his books, Dostoyevsky's *The Idiot*, in my hands before giving myself the pleasure of reading it. Tajbakhsh also sent me Dostoyevsky's *The Gambler*, John Le Carré's *The Honorable Schoolboy*, Kazantzakis's *England*, and Ann Radcliffe's *The Mysteries of Udolpho*, a dark gothic novel, which mirrored my own black mood.

My only contact with nature came from the potted plants on the enclosed rooftop terrace I was allowed to use daily. No other inmate was allowed on the seven-foot-long terrace while I used it; no two inmates were even allowed to see each other. One day as I followed my habit of pacing its length, over and over, as fast as I could, I saw a white butterfly and I thought: I am compelled to be here; but what are you doing in this place? Another time, I caught a dandelion in the palm of my hand. "Take my love to Shaul and tell him to rescue me from this misery," I whispered to it as I blew it away.

Three cats—one black, one gray, and one golden brown—perennially prowled the top of the wall. I could see them through the glass roof. I dubbed them the "killer cats" because they looked so ferocious. There were two faucets and a clothesline on the terrace and detergent was available from the prison guards. There was a small washing machine too, but it dated back to the 1960s, and was reserved for the guards. I washed my clothes by hand every day, sometimes twice a day. The clothes dried quickly in the sun. A fresh change of clothes was important to me as yet another small way to stave off the indignities and dehumanizing effects of prison and remain the same Haleh.

The larger of the two terraces was accessible through a hallway. It was about the size of a volleyball court and a far superior place for walking. It too was surrounded by high walls topped by barbed wire, but open to the sky. The killer cats prowled the top of the walls here as well. The smaller terrace was reserved for the women inmates, but the larger terrace was used by both the men and the women in ward 209. A member of the prison staff would telephone and specify, by name, whose turn it was to be out. Inmates were allowed one hour a day for what was called *hava-khori*, or taking the air. But since none of the other women inmates wanted to be outside, the guards allowed me more time on the terraces.

Because I liked to be outside without my headscarf and in short sleeves, the guards arranged for the security camera to be turned off when I was there, or so I was told. I continued to walk outside even when it rained, much to the surprise of the guards. I sometimes was able to stay on the small terrace until darkness fell.

After my first night at Evin, when I slept uncomfortably on the floor on a single blanket, I was offered a cot. I knew the thin mattress would not be good for my back, and I worried about lice and disease. Plus, a cot would take up too much space in my small cell and I wouldn't be able to keep up with my exercises. I asked for eight blankets instead. Six blankets folded in half became my bed. I used one blanket, folded into a rectangle, as a makeshift stand for my books and another for my clothes so that I wouldn't have to leave them on the dirty floor. In the morning, I gathered up my "bed" to give myself room to move around.

The two fluorescent lights in my room were left on all night and made it difficult to sleep. When Hajj Agha was unable to have them turned off for me, he offered me a pair of aeronautic goggles. I smiled to myself, thinking I would look like Snoopy, in his imaginary role as a World War I flying ace, and I declined. I began sleeping in my blindfold.

The Guards

The women's section of ward 209 was the kingdom of six female guards. Three of them were women in their forties, and three were in their twenties. I never learned any of the guards' names, but adopted a nickname for each: Hajj Khanum, Sour Face, and Sunny Face were the three older women and Athlete, Rashti, and Twiggy were the three younger guards. The six women worked in modified twenty-four-hour shifts, so that there were always three guards on duty at any one time.

Hajj Khanum, the most senior of the guards, was a neatly dressed woman, professional in her behavior, with a manner that demanded and was accorded respect. She had studied at a *howzeh*, or religious seminary, was well versed in the religious sciences, and often walked around the ward quietly reciting verses of the Quran to herself. When the ward was quiet and the other inmates and guards were resting, she stood outside my cell door and discussed with me various Quranic verses. On one occasion I asked her why so few women appeared in the Quran. She said all the women in the Quran were *shirzan*, lionesses; no lesser women deserved mention.

I had been shocked to discover in my prison reading how harsh the Quran is toward the Jews who were living in Arabia at the time of the Prophet and who did not accept Mohammad's new dispensation. Hajj Khanum wanted to reassure me that as a believer she didn't differentiate between Christians, Jews, and Muslims. All of them are God's creatures and we have to respect and love them all, she said. Islam, she stressed, was a magnanimous, loving, and forgiving religion. According to her, the problem was that the Jews had first betrayed the trust of Moses (in Egypt) and then of Mohammad (in Arabia) and had sided with the Prophet's enemies.

Hajj Khanum was genuinely concerned about my well-being. Because I did not eat meat, she carefully removed the meat from the stews and rice dishes that we were served. When the inmates were given sweets for dessert she would bring me an extra slice. One morning, she came into my cell, quietly took out a white rose from under her chador, handed it to me, and left. It was a tiny rose, the size of my middle finger. She had picked it in the prison garden. I treasured it. The gesture, in the unkind world of Evin, moved me. The rose summoned a flood of memories—of the climbing roses in my grandmother's garden and the roses I had planted in our garden at home in Potomac. Now, in a rush, I recalled everything I was missing. I wanted to be embraced and kissed by Shaul. I wanted to hold Mother's hand, hug Haleh; I wanted to sit on the floor of our house and hold Ariana and Karenna on my knees. I put the rose in a paper cup, and when it faded, I kept it pressed between the pages of my one book.

Hajj Khanum was almost always paired on duty with Sour Face, the most disagreeable of the female guards. While the others tried to make prison conditions more bearable for the inmates, Sour Face seemed intent on making them more onerous. She groused when I or another inmate asked for tea, even if it was teatime. She was reluctant to let an inmate out, even if it was her turn to spend an hour on the terrace.

One night after having to ask her to let me go to the bathroom, she lectured me. "Everyone who comes here, including you, thinks they are innocent," she said. "None of you are innocent. Islamic justice doesn't make mistakes. All of you are here because you are guilty and you don't want to repent." She got so worked up that foam formed at the corners of her lips, and her voice turned into a hiss. I walked past her into my cell and closed the door behind me. That night I had a good cry; it was one of the few times I allowed myself the luxury.

Sunny Face was the kindest of all the guards. She was chubby, light-skinned, and brown-eyed, with an ample bosom and an ample behind. She wore her dyed blond hair in a bun. She schooled me in Evin's shopping opportunities. Every Tuesday, inmates could list the items they needed and a prison employee would make the purchases in the local market. I always ordered a week's supply of vegetables and fruit. I paid cash, as Mutti regularly sent me money.

On the three days of each week that she was on duty, Sunny Face bought fresh bread from a bakery near home and shared it with me and the other guards. Without her bread, I might have shed another five pounds on top of the twenty pounds I had lost during my incarceration.

I discovered that Sunny Face loved cooking and that her family didn't eat much meat at home, either. I was happy to talk about food or anything else with someone; it was preferable to the monosyllabic exchanges I had with the guards. Sunny Face gave me a recipe for an omelet with potato and spring onions, which I promised to try when I was home again. (But once back home, and to this day, I could not bring myself to try the dish and stir up memories of Evin.) I taught Sunny Face how to cook stuffed pepper and stuffed quince, with a filling of rice, split peas, and herbs. I also taught her to make a quiche, a vegetable lasagna, and a stew based on dried fruits.

One day she brought me a small plastic container of the rice dish with green beans and dill that I had taught her to make. I had to fight back tears at the sight and taste of food I used to cook at home.

She was the most talkative of the guards and chatted with me about social practices in Iran—marriage traditions, mixing between girls and boys, and the like. She had entered into an arranged marriage with a decent man who treated her well, she said. She had gone with him on a pilgrimage to Mecca.

Sunny Face believed in arranged marriages, but young people these days, she noted, insisted on choosing their own partners. She expected her son and daughter, both in their early twenties, would do the same. She was proud that both her children were in college.

Athlete, one of the younger guards, was six feet tall and heavily built. She had given up weight lifting after injuring her knee. Battling a perennial weight problem and a stubborn skin and scalp problem, she spent all her salary on dietitians and dermatologists. She walked around all day with a vibrating belt about her waist, hoping to lose weight and develop a flat tummy. Conscious of her looks, she chose her non-prison clothes with care and consulted me on the color of clothes she should buy.

She told me she lived with a group of friends. I assumed she was from the provinces and had no family in the capital, but it was unusual for a group of women from her social background to be living without parents, husbands, or other relatives. Social norms were changing rapidly in the Islamic Republic. Like the other guards, Athlete was religious and performed her daily prayers punctiliously.

At night, when I was enjoying my last bit of fresh air on the rooftop terrace, Athlete would come and talk to me. By an odd coincidence, she was reading Dostoyevsky's *The Idiot* in a Persian translation at the same time that I was reading it in an English translation. "See what happened to the Russian royals and upper classes?" she said, referring contemptuously to the somewhat feebleminded main character, Prince Myshkin. "They all became retarded and deranged." Her tone implied that all aristocracies, upper classes, and the wealthy are doomed to universal idiocy.

Athlete ardently believed in the Iranian revolution and the Islamic Republic. But a visit to a museum dedicated to the atrocities of SAVAK clearly shook her. The museum featured pictures of SAVAK's jailers, interrogators, and torturers. When she saw the pictures, she told me, she remarked to a friend who was with her, "Someday, they will put our pictures in this museum."

Rashti was a plump young girl from a religious family who wore long sleeves even in the heat of summer, holding them tightly in place with rubber bands to make sure no man glimpsed a millimeter of her bare wrists. She told me she hoped to move to America with her future husband. "I'll come and visit you," she said. I suggested she should put aside her chador and make do with a *maghna'eh* and robe if she comes to the United States. The suggestion seemed to upset her; she staunchly defended the chador, and I did not argue with her.

My constant exercising caused Rashti to shake her head—whether in wonder or disapproval, I never knew. "Other inmates sit in a corner or nap in the afternoons," she said. "You never sit still." Yet one day she asked me to show her a few exercises to tone up her stomach muscles and her triceps in preparation for her marriage. Rashti also had a stubborn skin problem and was constantly trying new creams and ointments, asking me to translate the literature that came with her medications.

Finally, there was Twiggy, the youngest of all the guards. Twiggy was very tall and thin. Under her black chador she wore T-shirts and tight trousers that showed off her figure. She took her showers and washed her underclothes in prison. I would see her skimpy string bikini pants and bra drying on the clothesline on the terrace, incongruously out of place alongside the size-fourteen bras and ample underpants of the other guards.

Twiggy had a university degree and knew English, although I never saw her read a book or newspaper. Sweet but uncommunicative, she simply seemed bored most of the time, almost visibly wishing to be elsewhere.

I learned a little, but not a great deal, of their personal lives. They hardly ever talked about their families. They seemed all to come from the same working-class or lower-middle-class background. They were all religious, prayed regularly, and observed a strict form of the *hijab.* They were raised in traditional homes, but their lives were in flux. All had finished secondary school; one had been to university; one had trained at a seminary and another aspired to do so. They had learned to care about their looks, their clothes, their weight, and their health. At least one aspired to go to America. Their children were striking out in new directions.

For them, their jobs represented a step up in life. As prison guards, they were government employees. They had job security, a reliable monthly income, and the prospect of a pension at retirement.

The government, I gathered, took good care of them. Three of the guards had been on pilgrimages to the shrine city Karbala in Iraq, and two had been on pilgrimages to Mecca—all on government expense. Except for Athlete's one moment of self-reflection during her visit to the SAVAK museum, I never sensed they had second thoughts about working for the intelligence services or the repressive apparatus of the state. They were just doing their job. "We don't set the rules. We follow our orders," Hajj Khanum would always say. I did not sense any discontent with the Islamic Republic from these women; they were its beneficiaries and, to my face at least, never criticized it.

Prison Cuisine

Unlike the rest of Evin Prison, where, according to Twiggy, the food was disgusting, the inmates of ward 209 ate relatively well, since they were served the same food as the Intelligence Ministry's staff.

For breakfast, each prisoner was given tea and a loaf of bread with cream cheese. Lunch always consisted of rice and a meat, chicken, or vegetable dish and, occasionally, a cucumber and tomato salad or a mixed salad, which for some inscrutable reason they called Chinese salad. For dinner the food was still substantial, but lighter.

I found I couldn't face the food. I had never had the most robust appetite, but meals at the prison made me especially uncomfortable. I didn't want to get sick; I even feared they might try and drug me. I had geared my whole being to remaining alert and on top of things for Hajj Agha's interrogations and for anything else they might throw at me. It took several weeks before I was ready to accept a bit of rice or a piece of chicken. I never ate meat.

Once I learned I could have food purchased for me outside prison, I was in control of what I was eating. Every Tuesday I would prepare a list of fruits and vegetables and also order seven small containers of yogurt to last me the whole week.

I developed a routine, especially when Rashti was on duty. She noticed I did not like to eat fruit unpeeled or uncut, but knives were not allowed in the cells. Rashti would bring a knife and stand by the door while I sliced my fruit and my vegetables to prepare a salad. Then, on the rooftop terrace, I squatted down on my haunches, opened the faucet, and washed the salad, invariably splashing water over myself and everything around me. In my heart, I cursed the people who had reduced me to such devices.

The Doctors

Every two weeks, inmates in ward 209 paid a visit to the prison doctor. The dispensary, off the men's block, was a large, windowless room with a bed at one end and shelves stacked with medicines against the walls. I was taken to the prison doctor on my first morning at Evin. After the routine measurements and questions, he told me to come and see him if I needed medical attention. Two weeks into my incarceration, around ten o'clock on a Friday night, Athlete suddenly showed up: "Let's go. The doctor wants to see you," she said. I was startled. It was late, and I had heard of the use of "truth serum" at Evin. Athlete led the way in her black chador; I followed in my robe, scarf, and blindfold.

A different doctor was sitting behind the desk. He was in his forties. He had a huge hairpiece on his head and a thick Groucho Marx moustache. His ridiculous appearance was a welcome bit of comic relief. "Why am I here?" I asked. For some reason, he wanted to check my blood pressure. I rolled up my sleeve. It was one of the oddities of life at Evin that the strictures regarding female modesty ended where inconvenience began. Male doctors could touch a woman's bare arms. Interrogators could be alone with a woman in a room, behind closed doors. No one seemed to notice the incongruity.

Until the third month of my incarceration, I was taken to the dispensary every two weeks to have my weight and blood pressure checked. My medications remained a problem, however. I used Refresh over-the-counter eye drops and took vitamins for my bone and eye conditions, but Mutti was not allowed to bring me my medication from home, and I refused the substitutes offered at Evin. My refusal grated on the prison doctor and he repeatedly brought up the issue. "You don't trust us," he said. "What is wrong with our medicine and our doctors?" I tried to avoid a discussion of the relative merits of Iranian and American medicine. "I have a one hundred percent trust in Iranian medicine," I said. "I have my bone-density tests done here. But I prefer to have my medication brought from home. Why waste it?"

The doctor said he had no objection, but that Hajj Agha had banned medicine from home. Hajj Agha alleged that Refresh eye drops came from Israel. This was the kind of official cant that is common in the Islamic Republic. My eyedrops came from America. Besides, everyone knew there were plenty of Israeli goods in the markets, imported through Cyprus with the markings disguised. One day, at the large Behjatabad fruit market in Tehran, a fruit seller had asked me in a whisper if I wanted Israeli avocados.

Late in the second month of my incarceration, the physician on duty—he happened to be the doctor who examined me on my first day—brought up the subject of my trust in Iranian medicine again. Never a big eater, and with the crushing anxieties of prison taking their toll, I had been losing weight at an alarming rate and had managed to convey this to my mother, who passed the information on to Hayedeh and Shaul. I had also managed to tell Mutti that my skin condition had visibly worsened; I genuinely feared a form of skin cancer. Shaul must have reported some of this to the press, since the doctor surprised me on this visit with the news that Web sites had begun to report my weight loss, raising concerns abroad about my health. The doctor then suggested they send me to "a four-star hospital, with the best possible doctors" for a full checkup. They could even keep me for a few days, he said, as if offering me a vacation at a luxury spa. A previous inmate was so happy in the hospital, he didn't want to leave, even to go home, he added.

I firmly refused to be hospitalized. I didn't want to be in the hands of Intelligence Ministry doctors who would have a free hand in treating me. "I know what you think of us," the doctor replied, reading my thoughts. "But I am a physician. I don't care on what charges you are here. I have taken an oath to look after the health of my patients, and I don't want to be accused of negligence." He made me write down and sign a statement attesting that I had refused hospitalization. After this, my biweekly medical checkups stopped. Perhaps they wanted to teach me a lesson, or perhaps the prison doctors wanted to avoid responsibility if my condition further deteriorated.

The next day I mentioned to Hajj Agha that I had rejected the offer to go to the hospital. "The news of my hospitalization would have created a big uproar abroad," I told him, suggesting I had done the Intelligence Ministry a favor. He was unmoved: "We are not afraid of an uproar. We weighed the consequences carefully before we arrested you. We are ready to pay any price. We have to look after our own interests."

Nevertheless, on that July evening, the doctor's passing mention that Web sites were writing about me raised my spirits—but only momentarily. I tried to imagine a major campaign on my behalf, but then quickly dismissed the idea as improbable. No Iranian political prisoner had received sustained press coverage. I didn't think my case would be any different, even with the efforts of Shaul, the Wilson Center, or Shirin Ebadi. My release was not imminent, and my isolation and solitary confinement were continuing with no end in sight. As my hopes for an early release had receded, both deliberately and unconsciously, I had constructed a protective shield around myself: by not unduly raising my hopes, I avoided the letdown that was sure to follow. I quickly put the doctor's comments out of my mind and returned to my cell.

🙞 Calling Mother

Two or three times a week, at the end of every interrogation, I was allowed to call my mother on Ja'fari's cell phone. This was Hajj Agha's idea. Ja'fari would ask me the number—even after twelve weeks, he couldn't manage to remember it—dial it, and hand me the cell phone. If his cell phone battery was low, he would use one of the many phones placed along the corridors. These were available to prisoners under fewer restrictions than I. I was instructed to be brief, to limit myself to pleasantries, and to speak to Mutti only in Persian, never in German. I adhered to these rules, not wishing to jeopardize the phone calls, which meant so much to Mutti—and to me. Mother would pick up the phone at the first ring. It was obvious she hardly left the house, lest I telephone and she miss the call. I could never call over the weekend because Ja'fari and Hajj Agha, spending time with their families, did not conduct interrogations Thursdays and Fridays. My telephone calls were always monitored, and I assumed my mother's telephone at home was tapped.

My telephone conversations with Mutti never changed and hardly ever lasted more than a minute or two. I asked after her health and she asked after mine. She would try to boost my spirits by telling me that everyone was doing their best to put an end to my ordeal; and I took note, even as I reminded myself none of this effort was doing me any good.

On one or two occasions, I told Mutti that I had dreamed of my father and my paternal grandmother. In prison I often dreamed of the dead, perhaps because I had tried so hard to push the present—home, family, friends, the prison—from my mind. As a child, my superstitious nanny used to say that if the dead talk to you in a dream, it means they want you to join them in the next world. Even as I was dreaming, I fearfully imagined that if my grandmother talked to me, it meant my death was imminent. But Mutti's reaction was strikingly different. She said, "Your father and grandmother were the kindest people in the world. They are with God and they are watching over you. It means you will get out of prison soon."

There were a number of times when I tried to convey to Mutti more important messages. One of these I dubbed the "tsunami affair." In a telephone conversation with Shaul before my arrest, I told him yet again of my certainty that I would be arrested and taken to Evin. Shaul said: "If they take you to prison, I will unleash a tsunami in the press the likes of which they have never seen." Several weeks into my incarceration, fearing I had been forgotten by the outside world, I remembered that conversation and wanted in some way to convey to Shaul that the time for the tsunami had come, that he must get the media to focus on my plight immediately. On the phone to Mutti, I said: "Tell Haleh not to forget to make my usual contribution to the tsunami victims." I was sure Mutti would repeat this unusual message to Shaul, who would understand the reference.

The next day, Hajj Agha asked me please not to use code words such as "tsunami" over the telephone. I went into a long spiel about the contribution I had made to the Indonesian tsunami victims. He clearly wasn't taken in. "Please don't use foreign words and don't speak in code," he said.

A Walking Corpse

I genuinely did not want Mutti to visit me in Evin. I thought the sight of me—my face thin and sagging, hollows under my eyes—would kill her. I was a walking corpse; even size-zero pants hung loosely on me. In any case, Ja'fari had told me to tell my mother to stop coming to the prison gate with fruit, medication, and clothing. Food and medication from home was not allowed, he insisted. I also concluded that the Intelligence Ministry understood very well that if a photograph of my mother was published abroad—bent over her cane, barely able to see, slowly making her way and carrying a bag of fruit to Evin's grim gate—it would cause a sensation.

Yet I was desperate to see Mutti, to make sure she was all right. I asked Hajj Agha whether I could go home for a weekend. This was not an unusual request. In past years, I recalled, imprisoned journalists Akbar Ganji and Emadeddin Baghi had been allowed weekends home. In the 1990s, Tehran's former mayor Gholam Hossein

Karbaschi had been briefly let out of Evin to attend his daughter's wedding. (In the bizarre ways of the Islamic Republic, Mohseni-Eje'i, the infamous judge who had presided over Karbaschi's trial and had unjustly sentenced him to a long prison term, attended the wedding, too.)

Ja'fari noted that these three men had been tried and sentenced before they were allowed home visits, but Hajj Agha agreed to ask permission for a home visit from his superiors if I could guarantee none of the neighbors would find out. I could give him no such assurance. Mother's apartment building was small, the neighbors all knew one another and noticed comings and goings in the building, and a caretaker was on duty at all times. Hajj Agha suggested an alternative. "We have a number of safe houses around Evin," he said. "We can move you and your mother to a safe house, where you can live together and keep each other company." The idea of living in a "safe" house belonging to the Intelligence Ministry made my skin crawl. I imagined hidden cameras, listening devices, Intelligence Ministry minions monitoring our every move. "I absolutely refuse," I told him. "My mother would never agree."

By the end of July and my third month in prison, I had resigned myself to the reality that there would be no family visits. I learned much later that the International Committee of the Red Cross (ICRC) had asked for and had been refused a visit. Relations between the Iranian government and the ICRC were strained, and the Intelligence Ministry may have not wished me to learn of the extensive coverage I was receiving in the American and European press. I had hoped at least for a visit from the Swiss ambassador, who was supposed to look after American citizens in Iran, but that didn't take place, either.

The "Interview"

On my very first day at Evin, Hajj Agha had hinted that my release would be expedited if I gave "an interview" explaining what I knew of the American agenda for regime change in Iran. He cited the example of Ramin Jahanbegloo, the philosopher and scholar who had spent four months in Evin on fabricated charges of acting against the interests of the state and who "at his own suggestion" had given an interview to the Iranian Student News Agency (ISNA) on the very day he was released from Evin. "Three weeks later, we allowed him to go to India and resume his work," Hajj Agha pointed out. He returned to the "interview" idea on several occasions. Now, four weeks later, during an interrogation, he informed me that the "interview" would take place on the following Thursday.

I had always loathed seeing political prisoners paraded on television to parrot what they had been told to say. I hated seeing decent men and women struggling to retain their dignity in such undignified circumstances. And I knew that under the Islamic Republic taped interviews were spliced and tailored to suit the regime's propaganda purposes.

Nevertheless, Hajj Agha was insistent on my doing an "interview," and I believed I had nothing to hide: I could only repeat on film what I had been telling Hajj Agha and Ja'fari for the past six months. Hajj Agha made clear which subjects he wanted me to talk about. In addition to a brief biography and a description of my working career, he instructed me to describe the way foundations in America and Europe operate, the reasons they gave fellowships to Iranians, the networking that takes place at conferences and meetings organized by these institutions, and the "revolving door" that allowed individuals in America to shuttle back and forth between government service and work at foundations and think tanks. Hajj Agha obviously had his own agenda. But I believed I could cover all these subjects truthfully and without violating my own sense of integrity.

When it came to the Soros Foundations, one of Hajj Agha's favorite topics and about which I knew nothing, I told him I could only repeat what he and Ja'fari had told me, making clear the information came from them. Last, Hajj Agha said that I could mention that I missed my family and hoped to be reunited with them soon. I would not actually be interviewed, he noted. There would be no questions. I was to simply talk before the camera for about an hour.

The preparation for the "interview" had its farcical side. Ja'fari suggested I wear something more colorful than my black robe and scarf, and use a bit of makeup. I had to laugh—inside. That same evening the guards brought me a pile of documents on the Soros Foundations, its Open Society Institute and on George Soros himself—material evidently downloaded from the Web and translated into Persian by the Intelligence Ministry—so that I could "bone up" on these subjects before the filming session.

On Thursday morning, Hajj Khanum appeared with my purse, which I had not seen since it was taken from me the day I entered Evin. She also handed me lipstick and a powder case. "These belong to the girls," she said. "The gentlemen want you to wear makeup." I used my own face powder and lipstick. I also retrieved my watch from my purse and determined not to give it back after the interview. I put on my black robe and scarf. I had washed them so often the cloth was faded and threadbare. Ja'fari was waiting by the iron door for me. He told Hajj Khanum not to accompany us. But, as if protective of me, she ignored him. Blindfolded again, I followed the two of them down what seemed like three flights of stairs into a large room.

It was full of men, some sitting, some standing. A few rose to their feet when I walked in. I could feel the tension in the air. I noticed a bearded, disheveled man sitting behind a desk. A young man with sleek black hair, tight jeans, and a T-shirt was manning one of the two cameras. I was told to sit on a sofa facing him, next to a potted plant. A vase of flowers sat on a coffee table in front of the sofa. My days were spent in solitary confinement in a bare cell, but I was to be shown to the world in a comfortable, living room–like setting. Ja'fari sat on a chair across from the sofa, but out of the view of the cameras.

I was amazed at how calm I felt. I had brought a few notes with me and had divided my intended remarks into four sections: my background and my work in Iran before the revolution; my work in the

United States, including teaching at Princeton and employment at the Wilson Center; the activities of think tanks and foundations in America and Europe; and what I had been told by my interrogators regarding the Soros Foundations and velvet revolutions.

After a voice test, the cameras began to roll. I had no sooner started—"I am Haleh Esfandiari. I was born in Iran. I am a sixty-seven-year-old grandmother living in the United States"—than the disheveled man stopped the cameras and went over to whisper in Ja'fari's ear. Ja'fari scribbled a note to me: Be sure to mention the Soros Foundations and the women's movement in Iran, he said. The cameras rolled once more, and I began to speak again, covering each of my four broad topics. Twenty-five minutes into the taping, with the cameras stopped again, the man came over and sat on a chair next to the sofa. He obviously was not getting what he wanted. He wanted velvet revolutions, intellectual networks, and American plots. He told me to talk more about "the conferences, especially the conference organized by UCLA."

The Intelligence Ministry was obsessed with a conference organized by faculty members at UCLA and the Greek government that met twice a year in Athens. Hundreds of scholars from America, Europe, Asia, and the Middle East, including Israel, attended. The Intelligence Ministry was convinced that scholars coming from Iran were recruited and indoctrinated in some fashion at this very conference.

Hoping to prolong the break in the taping, I tried to tease the bearded man now sitting uncomfortably close to me. "In the Islamic Republic, you shouldn't be looking at me, and I shouldn't be looking at you," I said. He wasn't amused and growled back, "We have no problem looking at you." The taping continued.

At one point, I saw Ja'fari frantically gesturing and pointing at my scarf, and I pulled my scarf forward. He continued to gesture, and I realized he wanted me to push the scarf back, not pull it forward. I laughed out loud. Here I was, accused of endangering state security, yet my interrogator wanted to make sure that I looked "modern" and, like the young women on Tehran's streets, casual in the way I wore my Islamic dress. During the rest of the session, Ja'fari continued to remind me, fingers jabbing at his own hairline, to keep my scarf well back on my head.

I finally noticed Ja'fari pointing to his watch, and eagerly brought my remarks to an end. My voice broke when I began to say I hoped to rejoin my family soon. We had to do another take of these last sentences. With the taping over, tea was served; but after an hour of this charade I felt drained and exhausted and was impatient to leave. I signaled to Ja'fari and we walked out. Back in the ward, I wanted to shower. I had done my best under the circumstances; I had implicated no one; I had spoken no untruths. But I felt soiled and tainted by the whole affair.

Still, I thought, my family and friends would see how I looked and what these people had done to me. At one point in the interview, I deliberately said, "In the five months I have been here . . . ," hoping my family would deduce when the taping session had taken place. I also expected Shaul would realize that the language I used was frequently not my own. For example, a new term, *shabakeh-sazi*, had been coined for "networking" and had become fashionable in intellectual circles in Iran; but I had not heard it before or ever used it myself. Shaul knew I was not in the habit of talking of "discourses" or of "velvet revolutions." I hoped he and others would know this was the vocabulary of my interrogators. I also expected that friends and those familiar with the ways of the Islamic Republic and police states would know that the "interview" was staged and coerced.

Hajj Agha had led me to believe I would be released once the "interview" was done. But four days passed and nothing happened. I concluded I had been deceived; I felt like a moron. I berated myself for having trusted Hajj Agha. I paced my cell in anger and frustration. I banged my cell door behind me when returning from the bathroom or the rooftop terrace. The guards, sensing my anger, kept well away from me.

Hajj Agha disappeared for a week after the taping. Ja'fari told me he was on a trip, but I thought he was ashamed for having lied to me. When he finally returned to the interrogation room Hajj Agha said the interview "was not what the gentlemen expected." Nevertheless, he claimed, "I am doing my best to get you released, but the Americans don't make it easy for you. They didn't allow any visits to the families of the Irbil five." The "Irbil five" referred to five Iranian officials who had been arrested in Irbil, Iraq, by the American military forces in January. They had been held incommunicado for more than five months; neither Iranian officials nor their families had been given access to them. I was dismayed that my case was being linked to them. I was a private citizen. The Irbil five were Iranian officials in a war zone. Still, I thought: *No family visits allowed by the Americans? Why is the United States acting like the Islamic Republic?*

Several weeks later, Hajj Agha informed me the "interview" had been broadcast on July 18 and 19, alongside tapes of Kian Tajbakhsh and Ramin Jahanbegloo. Tajbakhsh was still at Evin. Jahanbegloo had been released from Evin a year before, after spending four months in solitary confinement. I assumed he had been taped when in prison, but I had no sense of how the three "interviews" had been put together or in what form they had been broadcast.

A few days after the broadcast, Hajj Agha came to Evin fuming. Jahanbegloo, now at a research center in India, had given an interview to the Spanish newspaper *El País* and had described the broadcast as a page out of Stalinist Russia and George Orwell's *1984*. I listened quietly as he continued his tirade: he had vouched for Jahanbegloo the previous year when he was in Evin; he persuaded his superiors to release him and let him go abroad; now look how ungrateful he turned out to be. Hajj Agha failed to say that Jahanbegloo had to put up his in-laws' apartment and his mother's house as security before he was let go and that these properties could be expropriated if he was summoned and failed to show up. I felt no interest in what Jahanbegloo had said or done, but I felt crushed that Hajj Agha said nothing about my release.

In the Name of Democracy

Only much later did I learn how the interviews with me, Tajbakhsh, and Jahanbegloo had been cobbled into a program, *In the Name of Democracy*, that was put together by the Ministry of Intelligence and broadcast in two parts and with much fanfare on Iran's national television network on July 18 and 19.

The program focused on the "velvet revolutions" in Ukraine, Georgia, and other former Soviet Republics. It showed footage of opposition groups planning demonstrations, organizing for elections, and toppling regimes, with Americans always hovering in the background, presumably assisting the opposition or orchestrating the revolutions.

The camera switched from such footage to me or Tajbakhsh or Jahanbegloo talking about our work with American think tanks and the democracy promotion programs some of them sponsored. The clumsy aim of the broadcast was to suggest a link between think tank activity and the revolutions in East Europe and in the former Soviet republics. The Intelligence Ministry even spliced two disparate sentences of mine to make it appear that I was conceding that I had taken part in creating networks whose purpose was to bring about fundamental change in the Iranian system of government.

In the Name of Democracy was universally condemned abroad as a reprehensible example of coerced "confession." The Wilson Center denounced the broadcast as "scripted, contrived, and completely without merit." Shaul and the Wilson Center also moved quickly to discredit the conclusions the Intelligence Ministry wished to be drawn from program. Lee Hamilton called the program "shameful." Shaul went on the BBC to stress that I was using vocabulary not my own and to point to the dishonest manipulation and splicing of my words. In a *Washington Post* op-ed, my daughter, Haleh, described the program as "a KGB-style television 'confession' . . . a typical secret-police job of deception, vicious in intent yet clumsily contrived."

But it was the response to the broadcasts in Iran that fascinated me. Iranian national television aired snippets of the program two days before the broadcast, promising sensational revelations. During the broadcast itself, two analysts—mouthpieces of the Intelligence Ministry—provided commentary, referring to me, Tajbakhsh, and Jahanbegloo as "spies." Afterward, publications close to the Intelligence Ministry ran sensational headlines about what the program supposedly revealed about foreign plotting against Iran. But there were also indications that the regime itself was conflicted about the program, how it should be presented, and its results. On the eve of the broadcast, a spokesperson for the Ministry of Islamic Culture stressed that Tajbakhsh and I would be appearing as "experts," and not in relation to whatever accusations had been made against us. Several courageous reformist publications ridiculed it as hype and as obvious propaganda. Even *Kayhan*, in a post-broadcast commentary, criticized the program as badly executed and confusing in its message to the mass of viewers. The program clearly didn't create the impression the security agencies intended. It was supposed to vindicate my arrest and long incarceration; but it persuaded no one, and its utter failure helps explain my subsequent release.

✤ News of the Outside World

In early August Haji Agha offered me a TV for my cell. I said no. Even at home I rarely watched anything except the news. I also saw the offer of a television as a bad sign. On more than one occasion, Hajj Agha had threatened to extend my detention order for another four months. The offer of a TV suggested that they were settling me in for a long stay.

I told Hajj Agha I preferred newspapers, to which I had so far been denied access. Three newspapers were generally available to inmates of ward 209, but *Kayhan* had been reduced to the organ of the Intelligence Ministry and specialized in lies and character assassination. *Ettela'at* and *Iran* published with an eye to the censors. Nevertheless,

Ettela'at tended to be factual and unideological, and *Iran* specialized in economic news. Hajj Agha agreed to allow me access to these two papers, and I began to learn something of what was going on in the outside world.

I had asked Ja'fari whether I could get *Time* and *Newsweek*, knowing, of course, that he would refuse, but I wanted to probe all the possibilities. "No way. You will read what they write about you," he said. "Tear out the pages about me," I replied. "The censors tear out the pictures of skimpily dressed women." He paid no attention to me, but he had at least revealed that the foreign press was writing about me. Still, I experienced no great lift of spirits at these bits of information. I assumed that by now Shaul and Hamilton had left no stone unturned, yet I was still in prison. I concluded that only the intervention of a very senior and powerful Iranian official could get me released, and I saw no sign that the deus ex machina I had prayed for was going to appear for me.

One morning in early August Twiggy came to my cell and told me to put on my chador. "A man is coming to install a television." I was furious. This was my prison, a hellhole. I didn't want them to make it homey; I didn't want my interrogators to boast to my mother and the world that I was comfortable and had what I needed; and I hated the idea that they were preparing to extend my incarceration at Evin.

My request for access to the BBC and CNN only elicited a laugh, as I knew it would. In a country where satellite dishes are officially banned (although every home has a concealed or a shockingly not-so-concealed satellite dish), one can't expect CNN in prison. I used to turn on the TV to the twenty-four-hour Persian-language news channel, which also gave news in English for a few minutes three times each day, put on my blindfold, and listen as I exercised. My eyesight had grown worse in prison, without my usual medication, and I woke up each morning with excruciating pain. I wanted to avoid too much light or additional strain on my eyes.

During the next two or three weeks, I learned a lot about Iranian provinces and new ski resorts in Iran. I heard numerous discussions of economic issues and of developments abroad. Most foreign news broadcasts began with a couple of anti-Semitic cartoons, showing, for example, a "Jew" with a long, crooked nose being dragged through the mud. On the anniversary of Israel's 2006 war with Lebanon, I heard the speech and an interview given by the Iranian ally and Hizbollah leader Hassan Nasrallah numerous times. He was full of praise for the Iranian regime and its support for the anti-Israeli cause. But about me, the twenty-four-hour news service was silent.

One day I saw clips of French president Nicolas Sarkozy being received by President Bush at the Bush family compound in Kennebunkport, Maine. The clips were like a stab to my heart—for personal reasons. The previous summer, we had spent a week in Kennebunkport with Haleh; my son-in-law, John; and our grandchildren. They had rented a house and had invited us to join them. We were supposed to go again this summer. Even if the rest of the family went, I would not be there. My strength ebbed away. I looked around at the four bare walls of my cell. This was my reality. I went to a corner of the room and sat down, my head in my hands. I wondered if I would ever see my family again or be able to watch the children grow up. I berated myself for having allowed the TV in my room; I berated myself for ever having turned it on.

❧ A Surprise Visit

One morning, as I was washing my clothes on the small terrace, Hajj Khanum walked in. "Your mother is here," she said. My feelings swung from disbelief to alarm and back again. I couldn't believe that after all this time they had granted my mother a visit. The thought even crossed my mind that they had decided to execute me and were letting Mutti see me one last time. During the previous afternoon's interrogation, Ja'fari hadn't said a word about a visit. I put on my chador and blindfold and with a heavy heart followed Hajj Khanum down the stairs. We walked out the same door through which I had entered the prison building three months earlier. Once we stepped into the courtyard of Evin, I removed my blindfold.

For the first time in twelve weeks, I stood in the open air. Hajj Khanum and I got in the back of a rickety Peykan. The driver and another man sat in the front seat. My eyes hungrily took in everything. This was perhaps the last day of my life, I thought. I also feared the whole thing might be a ruse, and that I wasn't being taken to see Mutti at all. What if they are moving me to one of their safe houses? I thought. What if they take me to a deserted place outside the city, beat me to death, and dump my body in a ditch? Such "accidents" happened in the Islamic Republic.

The car stopped in front of a large building still in the Evin compound. After Hajj Khanum signed a batch of papers, we went down a long flight of stairs and entered a hall the size of a theater. All over the room, inmates sat at small tables talking to family members. A man came and whispered in Hajj Khanum's ear. "Let's go upstairs again," she said. "No visit?" I asked, heart sinking. "No," she said. "They decided your mother cannot manage the stairs."

We went into a spare, smaller room, where a woman sat behind a desk. Suddenly the door opened and Mother came in. She was bent over, holding her cane with one hand and hanging on to Nahid, my cousin Farhad's wife, with the other. She was wearing a black robe and black scarf. She looked worn out and emaciated, her bright blue eyes tired and anxious. It broke my heart to see her this way. I took her in my arms, fighting back tears. I wanted to stay strong for her. We held on to each other. I then led her to one of the chairs arranged against the wall, not letting go of her hands. I spoke in German. I tried to comfort Mutti by telling her I was doing well. I said I had fruit, books, newspapers, and a TV. I begged her to take care of herself, to receive people, to go out and not stay at home so much. I even urged her to get her hair done.

Mutti explained how the visit had come about after several requests for a family visit had been denied by Matin-Rassekh. "Her mother can see her on television," he had told my cousin Farhad.

But Rassekh had called Farhad that very morning and told him Mutti could visit—today. He never explained the sudden reversal. Mutti went on to say that Shirin Ebadi was acting as my lawyer but had been denied any access to Evin whatsoever. I was not surprised. I knew how much they hated her. Mutti had written a letter to the supreme leader, Ayatollah Khamenei, pleading for my release. A friend in Tehran had seen to the delivery of the letter, and Mutti knew the leader had read it. She said the trio of Shaul, Haleh, and Hayedeh were doing all they could to have me set free. She couldn't give me any details.

I both heard and did not hear what she was telling me. I felt numb and tired. For three months, I had tried to shut out all thoughts of home and family. I had lived in the world of ward 209, with its female guards dreaming of rash-free skin and flatter tummies, interrogators endlessly repeating the same questions, and the doctor with the ridiculous hairpiece. Now all the memories I had tried to block came rushing back.

Besides, I did not want Mutti to see me this way. I had not seen myself in a mirror until the day of the TV "interview." Occasionally, I caught a blurred, indistinct reflection of my face in the metal water fountain on the small terrace. But for the "interview" I had been able to look into the mirror of my powder case. I did not like what I saw: a haggard, wrinkled face, sunken eyes, uncoiffed hair, a dark blue-and-white chador and an ill-fitting black robe, threadbare from daily washing, hanging loosely on my emaciated frame. I could see in the eyes of Nahid and Mutti how shocked they were at my appearance, and I saw tears swell in Nahid's eyes.

When it was time to go, we kissed and I held Mutti's wrinkled face between my hands, then bent down and put my forehead to her palms. We said good-bye. I asked Mutti to promise not to come again. I knew the long car ride, the traffic, and the heat were hard on her. I thought this was the last time I would see her.

I walked out of the building with Hajj Khanum in tow. We didn't exchange a word. We drove to the main building. Once again I put on my hated blindfold and climbed the stairs back to ward 209. Sour

Face, with her usual contemptuous look, was on duty. I asked Hajj Khanum if I could shower. I knew all eyes were on me, and I didn't want the guards to see me crying. In the shower, I let go of myself and cried copiously. I cried for what I had done to my mother. Instead of the calm, happy old age she deserved, she was experiencing a living hell. I felt hatred in my heart for the men who had injected this torment into our lives. Had I the power, I would have called down the wrath of God on them.

9.

THE RELEASE

By the end of July, I was in despair. I waited for good news on important religious holidays, when the leader customarily issued pardons, but the birthday of the Prophet and of Imam Ali passed and nothing happened (I should have known I was hoping in vain, as pardons are issued only after trial and sentencing). Even my guards had stopped talking of my release. I saw less and less of Ja'fari and Hajj Agha. I certainly didn't miss them or Hajj Agha's repeated "We are doing our best to get you released," but to be forgotten was as bad as to be lied to.

All the other female prisoners in ward 209 had left, and the ward was virtually empty. This meant I had greater use of the outdoor terraces, and I sat outside as long as I could, even though the weather was hot and dry. I stuck to my rigorous schedule. I rose at six each morning, gathered up the six blankets that made up my bed and the chador that served as my bed sheet, had breakfast, and exercised most of the day. But despite all the hours of pacing and stretching, flesh was hanging from my arms and legs. My hair was thinner and duller. My cheeks were sunken. When I looked in the mirror of my powder case I was startled by the wasted face I saw.

I prayed I would be let out in time for the anniversary of my father's death. I knew Mutti would want to go to the cemetery and, after Modarress's betrayal, she had no one to take her. I mentioned this to Hajj Agha. His only response was "*Khoda rahmatash koneh.*" May his soul rest in peace. My mother, I thought to myself, was hardly in a mood to let Father rest in peace. Before my arrest I had seen her standing before a picture of my father in the apartment and mumbling to him: "Helli is your daughter. Do something for her!"

I decided to go on a hunger strike. They would then either free me or let me die. I understood the gravity of my decision, but the thought of spending years in prison was unbearable to me. It gave me a sense of relief to have determined on a course of action. In one of my books I copied out these lines from Shakespeare's seventy-first sonnet, for Shaul, hoping, somehow, he would see them if I was gone:

No longer mourn for me when I am dead
Than you shall hear the surly sudden bell
Give warning to the world that I am fled
From this vile world, with vilest worms to dwell:
Nay, if you read this line, remember not
The hand that writ it; for I love you so
That I in your sweet thoughts would be forgot
If thinking on me then should make you woe.

The Letter

On the afternoon of August 2, Ja'fari summoned me for another interrogation. As usual, he walked a few steps ahead, reminding me of the turns, of a stairway here, a low ceiling there. We waited for a group of male prisoners to pass. Beneath my blindfold I could make out a line of men in standard prison jumpsuits, blindfolded like me, shuffling past, each man holding on to the shirt of the man in front.

Ja'fari led me to the room where I had already spent so many hours. A small worn-out rug and prayer stone indicated that someone had used the room for noon prayers. I hung my chador on a wooden peg and sat facing the wall. How much I hated doing that!

Hajj Agha came in, sent Ja'fari to get me some hot water, and asked me how I was. I told him how unwell I felt. I had a flare-up of arthritis, my fingers were swollen, and my hands were hurting. While still facing the wall, I stretched my hand behind me to show him my swollen fingers. My eyes were weaker due to the lack of eye drops and the lights that were on in my cell twenty-four hours a day. "Why am I still in jail?" I asked him. "You know very well there is nothing more I can tell you."

He listened patiently and then very deliberately said: "Mr. Hamilton wrote a letter. An answer to this letter has been sent. They are waiting for a reply to this answer."

He was maddeningly vague. He did not say to whom Hamilton had written a letter. He did not say who had answered his letter and was now waiting for a reply. He did not reveal what either of the two letters said. But from his tone, I knew something significant was under way. Hajj Agha continued: "The answer to Mr. Hamilton's letter went to the Iranian Mission to the United Nations. It has been sitting there for some time. It hasn't been picked up." He clearly wanted me to comprehend the gravity of this negligence.

For the first time during my entire ordeal, I felt as if the Wilson Center had abandoned me. A letter about me had been sitting in New York and hadn't been picked up! How could they be so indifferent, uncaring? In my agitation, I knocked over my glass of water. It fell to the floor and shattered. "Water brings light," Hajj Agha said, citing an Iranian proverb, meaning that spilled water is a good omen.

For a moment, I wondered if the business about a letter was a lie to make me believe no one on the outside cared about me. I probed for more information. "Why doesn't Mr. Khazaee fax the letter to Mr. Hamilton?" I asked.

Mohammad Khazaee was Iran's UN ambassador. Oddly enough, he was a graduate of George Mason University, where Shaul taught.

Before taking up his present post, he had served as Iran's representative to the World Bank, then as deputy minister of economy in Tehran. He was reputed to be close to President Ahmadinejad and to Iran's supreme leader. His predecessor, Javad Zarif, had tried to help, but his intervention on my behalf had fallen on deaf ears. I did not know if Khazaee would act simply as a messenger, relaying messages back and forth, or if he would throw his weight behind a resolution of my case. Still, I knew there was now a channel of communication between Hamilton and the supreme leader's office, and that gave me hope. The letter exchange could be the key to my release.

Hajj Agha said the letter was highly confidential and for Hamilton's eyes only. It could not be faxed or read to him over the telephone. He had to pick it up in person.

"Well, what do you want *me* to do?" I asked. He suggested I tell my mother to pass a message to Shaul: Hamilton must go to New York and take delivery of the letter. "This is important," he said.

I did not think Mutti would understand the complications of this letter exchange in Persian. I told Hajj Agha I would have to talk to her in German. He agreed and added, "The sooner you are released, the sooner we can get back to our normal lives," as if I had been detaining *them* all this time.

Rashti was on duty when Ja'fari took me back to the ward. He told her I could call my mother and speak in a foreign language. The significance of this break in protocol registered instantly; even Rashti sensed something was afoot. We went straight to one of the phones outside the ward. Mutti was excited to hear me speak to her in German. I could hear her frantically taking notes as I spoke and I imagined the huge capital letters she would have to use due to her rapidly failing eyesight. She would then read her notes to my sister, Hayedeh, in German, and Hayedeh would translate the message for Shaul. I put the phone down. Rashti looked at me with a silent question in her eyes: "Any hope?"

"Maybe we have a *goshayesh*—an opening," I said.

I was asked to call Mutti again the next night, on August 3. She had spoken to Shaul, and learned something of the background to the letter exchange. Hamilton had written to Ayatollah Khamenei at the end of June. A month later, near the end of July, Hamilton received a call from Ambassador Khazaee in New York. A letter had been received from the office of the leader for Hamilton, Khazaee said, but he had to pick it up in person. Hamilton, about to go out of town on a speaking tour, said he would drop everything and come to New York. But he was told there was no urgency. It was a puzzling reply, given the weight Tehran now attached to the letter. Clearly, there had been a miscommunication. Hamilton may not have understood that Khazaee was engaging in Persian *ta'aroff*—excessive courtesy—and was leaving it to Hamilton to say he would come immediately. Shaul had now told Hamilton that the letter could be important, and Hamilton planned to go to New York; but it was already Friday; the mission was closed Saturday and Sunday and Khazaee was engaged all day Monday. Hamilton was scheduled to go to New York on the following Tuesday, August 7.

Sunny Face summoned Ja'fari for me—he and Hajj Agha wanted to know as soon as I heard from Mutti—and ten minutes later we stood face-to-face at the iron door of the women's block of ward 209, I in my robe and scarf but without a blindfold or chador, he in his checkered shirt and sandals. I told him Hamilton was going to New York on August 7 to get the letter from the leader. He corrected me: a letter, he said, not from the *rahbar* but from the *rahbari*, meaning not from the leader but from the leader's office. He and Hajj Agha carefully adhered to this form of words in subsequent exchanges with me. It clearly was important to them.

I thought about what this parsing of language meant. The leader, I assumed, was considered too important to get involved in such mundane matters as my detainment. Besides, this precise formulation offered deniability. Hamilton's letter had persuaded Khamenei to take steps to end my ordeal. It came from an American of standing in Washington. It was a personal appeal. My incarceration had dragged on, and the adverse publicity was damaging Iran's international standing. Khamenei probably decided it was time he stepped in to bring the case to an end. However, if anything went wrong, if there was an uproar in Iran and the decision had to be reversed, the supreme leader would be protected. He would not have been directly involved.

I was to call Mutti on August 7 to find out what happened during Hamilton's meeting with Khazaee in New York. It seemed so far away. Haleh, John, and the children would already be in Kennebunkport. They were staying for two weeks, and I dreamed of getting out soon enough to join them, to walk with them by the sea, and to take the children for breakfast at the pancake place near the house where they were staying. I had a fantasy of walking into the house unannounced and surprising them all.

The next four days were the longest of my stay in Evin. My mood oscillated wildly between hope and despair. At one moment I pictured myself on a plane heading for home; in the next moment, I saw myself pacing my cell week after week and month after month, in timeless, Sisyphian futility. In the morning I imagined Hajj Agha handing me my Iranian passport and telling me I was free to go; in the afternoon I pictured him apologizing yet again that another *gereh*, or hitch, had developed and he could not set me free. I had trained myself in Evin to avoid such thoughts and mood swings, and not to hope in order not to despair. What, I now asked myself, had happened to my iron discipline?

On the seventh, I impatiently counted the hours before calling Mutti. We spoke in German. She had heard from Shaul. Hamilton, she said, had been to New York. He had met with the ambassador, read the letter in Khazaee's office, and replied orally. The meeting was positive and they were all very hopeful, she said.

To me, this all sounded very vague and not the clear break in my case I had desperately begun to believe in. I experienced a sharp letdown. I had maintained my fortitude in front of my guards and interrogators, but I was feeling physically unwell and increasingly fearful I wouldn't be able to hang on much longer. I broke a rule never to cause Mutti anxiety about my health. I needed to convey to her and to Shaul my sense of urgency. I also wasn't sure how much longer I would be allowed to speak to Mutti in German. I told her the ugly growth on my arm had become enlarged and I feared it could be a tumor. My arthritis had grown worse and my eyesight was weaker. I also managed to tell her in coded language that I had lost twenty pounds—one-fifth of my body weight. We hung up.

This time Twiggy located Ja'fari and I told him what Mutti had said about the New York meeting. He, Hajj Agha, and their superiors at the Intelligence Ministry now knew Hamilton's mission to New York had been accomplished.

✤ The Delay

For the next several days, I did not see Hajj Agha or Ja'fari—surely not a good sign. On the phone, Mutti too sounded exhausted and in poor health. The bits of news I picked up were not encouraging. In *Ettela'at* I read two brief references to me. The head of the Supreme National Security Council, Ali Larijani, told reporters he expected my case to be brought to conclusion soon and that "we don't want to keep her," or words to that effect. But I no longer believed anything Iranian government officials said. Separately, the spokesperson for the judiciary told the press that I still had some written work to do before my files could be completed. The information he gave out was incorrect. I had no written work to finish. Besides, if the Intelligence Ministry was about to hand my case over to the judiciary, this could mean formal charges, a trial, and a guilty verdict. Given the accusations against me, a sentence could mean anything from twenty years to penalty of death.

There was worse news. Pacing in my cell while listening to television news in mid-August, I heard that the Bush administration was about to designate Iran's Revolutionary Guards a terrorist organization. Whatever the reasons for this decision, I knew Kian Tajbakhsh and I would pay a price. The regime would see our release as giving the appearance of softening under American pressure. For the first time, I felt like a disposable chess piece in a contest between Iran and the United States. Iran wanted to use me as a bargaining chip; the United States, engaged in an undeclared war with Iran and focused on its global interests, would not stop to consider the impact of its decisions on the fate of a single individual.

Athlete announced she was taking a few days off and came to the door of my cell to say good-bye. "I hope you won't be here when I get back," she said. I asked Hajj Khanum whether she too was going on a holiday. "Not as long as you are here," she said. "Then, I shall be keeping you company for a long time," I said. I was feeling desperate. Nothing was moving. Matin-Rassekh might renew my detention order for another four months or, at best, issue an order transferring me from ward 209 to the general ward for women prisoners. I would be out of the clutches of the Intelligence Ministry but, oddly enough, I did not welcome the prospect of becoming an "ordinary" prisoner or being lost in the general prison population. I would have to share a cell with other inmates, and I would be allowed to bathe and call my mother only once a week. Here I at least had privacy, and I had imposed on the deadening dullness of ward 209 a rhythm and order that allowed me to survive.

On August 18 or 19, Hajj Agha showed up without Ja'fari. He met me, in my blindfold, by the iron door of the ward and led me to one of the interrogation rooms next to the dispensary. He said he wanted to review the Wilson Center's relationship with the Soros Foundation, using the singular form, as he always did, and the Open Society Institute; he also asked, as he had on many occasions before, how well I knew the OSI associate director, Anthony Richter. He was reviewing material we had covered many times before, but he said he wanted to make sure that I hadn't left out anything.

I was facing the wall; but behind me I could hear the rustling of paper as he leafed through my file, going over the responses I had given to earlier questions. In a matter-of-fact tone, he proclaimed, yet again, that I had been an unwitting pawn in the hands of the Wilson

Center, and that the center and other think tanks were engaged in a plan to overthrow the Islamic Republic. I had heard the same tired accusations countless times. I felt so weary, I did not even bother to refute them.

Hajj Agha was by turns conciliatory and threatening. First he said, "We are satisfied that you did not know," as if wrapping things up. Then he claimed: "The Islamic Republic is merciful, and we are giving you one last chance to tell what you have kept from us." I insisted I had nothing to add. The session did not last long. As we got up to leave, my heart sank at the fact that he had said nothing about the exchange of letters between Hamilton and the leader's office. He had not mentioned Larijani's comment—"We don't want to keep her." He had not mentioned the Bush administration's designation of the Revolutionary Guards as a terrorist organization. Most important, he made no mention of my possible release. He led me back to the ward. All I had seen under the blindfold were his hairy hands. Once again, I felt a powerful urge to look up, to have him look me in the face. But that was not possible.

❧ "You Must Be Joking"

Two or three days later, I was doing my afternoon exercises in my cell, standing as close as possible to the door and its peephole to catch the bit of cool air from the air conditioner in the hallway. I had decided not to think about the letter. Two weeks had passed since Hamilton had been to New York, and there was still no movement in my case. *Don't raise your hopes*, I told myself. *You're here to stay.* Hajj Khanum came in and told me to prepare for interrogation. The interruption annoyed me. At the door of our block, Ja'fari gave me his elongated, polysyllabic *salaaaam*.

"*Che ajab?*" I asked. Why the visit? "Hajj Agha wants to see you," he said.

I sat in the interrogation room, facing the wall. Hajj Agha walked in. "*Salaam*," he said. "How are you?" I went through a long litany of my physical ills. "I am sick," I said. "But what is the point of complaining about my health to you?"

"I have *good news* for you," he said. "You can go home."

I sat bolt upright in my chair. I felt giddy with anticipation. "*Shookhi mi konid*," I said. You must be joking. "No," he replied. "I am serious. You can go home—right now." In my excitement I half rose in my chair and could hear Hajj Agha swiftly turning his back to me. I laughed. "Don't worry," I said, "I know I am not supposed to see you." I inquired about bail. Hajj Agha said only, "Don't worry. All the conditions to allow you to go home have been met." I asked to call my mother to tell her I am coming home. "She is already here, waiting for you," Hajj Agha replied. It finally sunk in: this was for real; it was not a ruse or cruel trick. The narrow, suffocating interrogation room seemed suddenly larger; instead of pressing down on me, the walls seemed to be moving back; the ceiling seemed to be rising. Finally, I had room to breathe.

Hajj Agha was getting ready to leave: "I will call you at home," he said.

"Will I get to see you outside prison?" I asked. I wanted so much to look into his face, to see if I could detect any sign of remorse in his eyes. He repeated the words he had used during my first week in prison: "*Sharmandeh*." To my shame. In other words, I am sorry, no. He left. I too got up and was about to walk out of the interrogation room when I heard Ja'fari's loud "*Kojaaa?*", the *a* elongated as always. "Where do you think you're going?" I realized that in my excitement I was walking out without my chador and blindfold. I put them on.

I would have run back to the ward had I not feared crashing into a wall or another blindfolded inmate. Hajj Khanum answered the buzzer at the door. "*Azad shodam*," I told her. I am free. For four months, I had prayed for this moment, and I could not leave ward 209, Evin Prison—and Iran—fast enough. I quickly went about my business, asking for two large garbage bags, which Twiggy brought from the back room. I removed my scarf and robe and threw them in the bags. I gathered every item of clothing in my cell; they went into the garbage bag, too, to be thrown away. Twiggy, thoroughly excited, had brought my handbag and a pair of trousers, a T-shirt, a robe, and a scarf I had set aside for the day I was freed. I dressed, determined to walk out wearing nothing bearing the mark or odor of Evin. Having lost twenty pounds, I had to hold up the trousers with a safety pin. I chose a blue scarf rather than the black scarf I had worn every day since my incarceration. I even used some face powder on my cheeks.

Hajj Khanum walked back in: "Where are your discharge papers?" A jolt of panic shot through my body. No one had given me any papers. Sour Face, who had been glaring at me, looked gleeful: "You cannot leave without an official discharge; and it has to be in writing," she said. Hajj Khanum pushed her aside and went out to make a phone call. I put Tajbakhsh's books in a pile and mine in a plastic bag. Twiggy brought my clean underwear from the clothesline on the terrace. These went straight into the garbage bag, too. I wanted nothing that belonged to the prison to touch my body again. I wanted to erase all Evin's traces; I wanted to be clean again. I set aside only a couple of T-shirts and pants that I had never worn in prison and a few personal items to take home with me.

Hajj Khanum returned. Everything was in order, she said, but I had to sign a receipt, confirming the return of my handbag with its contents and money intact. I also had to fill out a questionnaire regarding prison conditions: the cell, the food, the medical attention, the general hygiene, and how I had been treated. I gave the prison guards a glowing evaluation, then I embraced each guard in turn, even Sour Face. I asked Hajj Khanum to say good-bye to Athlete, Rashti, and Sunny Face for me. With her finger, Hajj Khanum traced the name of Imam Ali on my forehead, as she had done when I went for my TV interview and sometimes even when I went for interrogation. It was a form of blessing, a prayer for protection.

Twiggy took charge of my bags. For the first time since entering Evin, I walked out of the ward without a chador or blindfold. As we moved toward the exit, I saw a group of incoming prisoners:

they stood blindfolded and facing the wall, anxious and disoriented—grown men and women reduced, like children, to helplessness.

We stepped out into the hot sun of the prison courtyard. Twiggy and I got into a white car that was waiting for us; Ja'fari followed in a new Peugeot. We stopped at the building where I had met my mother two weeks earlier. Inside, a crowd of prisoners were waiting to be discharged. Twiggy, suddenly authoritative, went to the top of the line and handed over my discharge papers. There were other papers to be signed; I was fingerprinted again. We were soon done with the formalities. I walked with Twiggy across the cobblestones toward the great iron gates of Evin.

I walked out of the gates that I had entered nearly four months earlier. It was only late afternoon, but I felt I was stepping out of darkness into sunlight. The hulking prison, with its gray walls and barbed wire, its cells and interrogation rooms, which had been my prison and my home for 105 days, was now behind me.

Outside the gate, a television camera crew was waiting. A reporter stuck a microphone in my face. "How do you feel?" I thought it a most stupid question. Any released inmate feels the same. "I feel wonderful," I said. I thanked the people who made my freedom possible, without mentioning any names. The reporter persisted: How did the prison authorities treat me? What was solitary confinement like? How was the food? I was impatient to go, but wanted to handle this last ritual with composure and dignity. I told the reporter I had dealt only with the prison guards, and they were helpful and courteous. Solitary confinement was hardly pleasant. The prison food was good. *Jay-e shoma khali*, I was tempted to add, a Persian expression meaning, Your place was empty beside us, or Wish you were there. When he asked me once again whether I was happy to be out, I replied, "Yes. But I will be much happier if you let me rejoin my family."

I had seen Mutti a little way off, cane in hand, holding on to Nahid and waiting for me. I ran toward her and took her in my arms. She let go of Nahid and held on to my arm. I kissed her and Nahid. I turned back to embrace and say good-bye to Twiggy and waved good-bye to Ja'fari. He stood alone by his Peugeot, the usual smirk on his face, as if to say, "This is not good-bye; you're not yet free from our clutches; I will be seeing you again soon."

In the car, Mutti, Farhad, and I began to piece together the events preceding my release. A few days earlier Farhad had phoned the investigative magistrate to request another visit for Mother, since she was very concerned about my health. The magistrate, Matin-Rassekh, insisted he could discuss my health only with my mother, but when she called he was curt and cutting. She mentioned my deteriorating health. He said there was nothing wrong with me. She reminded him that she hadn't heard from me for four days. He snapped, "That is not very long." She asked when I would be set free; he replied, "Whenever her work is finished"; and when she pointed that out they had held me in prison for more than three months already, he replied, "*Hamineh ke hast*," a rude expression in Persian that means, That is the way it is. In effect, he was telling my mother that there was nothing she could do about it.

But on the morning of my release, Matin-Rassekh called my mother himself. She couldn't understand what he was saying and quickly summoned Farhad, who called the prosecutor back. Matin-Rassekh was now all sweetness and light. Mother and Farhad should come to the prosecutor's office right away with the deed to my mother's apartment, he said. "She can take her daughter home by five this afternoon." Mutti and Farhad hurried to Matin-Rassekh's office with the deed. He had set bail at 300 million tomans, or around $375,000, more than ten times the bail set by the first magistrate I had seen and before Matin-Rassekh took charge of my case. Mother put up her apartment in lien for this amount. After signing the papers and before leaving the office, Mutti, in her usual courteous way, walked back to Matin-Rassekh's desk and thanked him for releasing me. I wondered if he was ashamed to look my mother in the face. Then I realized shame was not a sentiment a man like Matin-Rassekh often experienced.

Paradise Regained

We walked into Mother's beautiful apartment. It was spotless, and full of sweets and flowers. I walked from room to room, taking in her paintings, her Augarten china, her carpets. I sat in each of the armchairs, I ran my fingers over the kitchen countertops, luxuriating in the feeling of the familiar, of the ordinary. I telephoned Shaul and Haleh, and Hayedeh called before I could call her. I also spoke to Lee Hamilton. I told each of them how elated I was to be out of Evin Prison, but that I didn't know if and when I could leave for home. I urged them to continue working for my departure. I was certain our phone was still tapped, so even at this moment when I wanted to say, and ask, much more, I had to choose my words carefully.

I spent a long time in the shower. I had to cleanse myself of Evin and its smell. I wanted to wash away the loneliness and anxiety. After the bath, I changed into fresh clothes. For the first time in 105 days, I wore an ironed pair of pants and an ironed T-shirt. It was a sensational feeling. I drank tea from a real china cup served on a silver tray. I wiped my mouth with a cloth napkin, not a piece of paper. Friends and family had heard of my release and began calling. Soon the telephone rang constantly. Flowers arrived—so many that the apartment reminded me of the Karaj botanical garden in the spring.

The doorbell rang, and to my dismay, I saw on the closed-circuit TV Ja'fari downstairs. He had called earlier. "Don't worry, I won't come upstairs. I just want to bring you your medicine," he said. For some inexplicable reason, he insisted on delivering the medicine prescribed by the prison doctors, which I had never used at Evin. I dressed in a white robe and put a white scarf over my head and went downstairs. If they snatch me and shove me into a car, I thought, neighbors will see me more easily in the dark. Ja'fari was in a hurry to go home to his family. "I've never seen you smile so much as you did this afternoon," he said. Ja'fari made my skin crawl even when he tried to be friendly. The smirk seemed permanently etched into his face, and I couldn't erase from my memory the pleasure he had taken in tormenting me. He reached into the trunk of his car and handed me a bag of medications and left. The bag went straight into the garbage bin.

Friends came by and Mother asked me if she could invite a few to stay for dinner. I agreed. Mother laid out a beautiful table, with a fine tablecloth and her best china. She had ordered an excellent meal of rice and leg of lamb from a neighborhood restaurant. For the first time in three months, I broke with my meatless diet and ate a bite of succulent lamb.

That night I slept in a real bed, between real sheets, in a real nightgown. I laid down my head on a real pillow. It felt like paradise.

The Tsunami

On the day after my release, a friend handed me a CD that her daughter had put together. "This will interest you," she said. It was a collection of the many hundreds of news stories about me that had appeared during my incarceration. The CD included links to Web sites that had been dedicated to me and had campaigned for my release. That night I slipped the CD into a borrowed laptop and encountered, with growing astonishment, the huge media coverage and public interest my case had generated. There were letters from prominent scholars and intellectuals to Iran's leaders, public statements by politicians calling for my release, petitions on my behalf signed by thousands of people, and interventions by human-rights organizations, women's groups, and NGOs. From Baghdad to Brazil, from Paris to Pakistan and Tokyo, people had written about me and acted on my behalf.

In prison, I was unaware of any of this. I had never been allowed to telephone Shaul, and my mother never mentioned this sort of news on the phone since we knew our brief calls were monitored. In moments of despair, I even thought I had been forgotten. But I had not been. The tsunami Shaul had promised had occurred, and many had contributed to it. Shaul, Haleh, Hayedeh, and the Wilson Center staff later helped me piece together the larger picture. This press coverage and international attention, I realized, were important parts of the story behind my release.

Just before my incarceration, Shaul had concluded that silence and quiet diplomacy were doing us little good. Four months had passed, and I was still stuck in Iran. He had arranged to meet with Lee Hamilton and Wilson Center deputy directory Mike Van Dusen on May 8 to urge that we go public and discuss the best way of doing so. As it happened, I was arrested early on the morning of May 8, and by the time Shaul and the Wilson Center people met, I was already in Evin Prison.

Later that morning, Lee Hamilton had issued a statement expressing his dismay. He had addressed a hastily summoned press conference and had firmly rejected any suggestion I was engaged in illegal activities. "Iran is trying to turn a scholar into a spy," he said. My arrest was widely reported that day, and press interest and coverage of my ordeal remained strong for almost the entire 105 days of my incarceration. The story of a sixty-seven-year-old grandmother held in solitary confinement in a notorious prison simply for having organized conferences on Iranian and Middle Eastern issues was in itself compelling. The Iranian government fueled press attention by the extraordinary allegations it made against me. As Shaul put it to me, "Every time we thought the story was dying, the Iranian government did or said something outrageous to reignite interest in your case."

Within a week of my incarceration, the spokesperson for the judiciary, Ali Reza Jamshidi, announced that I was being investigated for "crimes against national security." Two weeks later, he said I was accused by the Intelligence Ministry of espionage, activities against national security, and propaganda against the Islamic Republic. The Intelligence Ministry accused me of "seeking to topple the Islamic regime" and claimed my interrogation had allowed them to uncover "networks" and expose "subversives." These accusations, if formalized as charges in an indictment, carried the death sentence. On May 12 *Kayhan* published its vicious attacks on me, and then, eight days later, on Shaul, accusing us both of being Zionist spies, and agents of Israel and the CIA. In July, national Iranian television aired the program *In the Name of Democracy*. Each of these events generated a spate of press reports.

My incarceration also evoked memories of the seizure of the American embassy in Tehran in 1979, when American diplomats were taken hostage; journalists were quick to draw parallels. Robin Wright, the *Washington Post* diplomatic correspondent, wrote that "the United States has not faced such tension over Americans held in Iran since the 1979–1981 hostage crisis, when 52 Americans were held for 444 days." Other journalists and commentators speculated that the Iranians intended to swap me for the "Irbil five." In March, a naval patrol of Iran's Revolutionary Guards had arrested fifteen British sailors and marines in the Persian Gulf, claiming they were in Iranian territorial waters. The sailors, unofficially accused of trespassing and pressured to make "confessions," were released twelve days later; but the incident was useful for keeping my ordeal in the spotlight. Shaul cited the British affair in a number of interviews to insist that if Iran could show consideration for British sailors by releasing them, it could show the same consideration for its own countrymen.

Shaul, Haleh, and the Wilson Center also actively refuted the allegations Iranian officials made against me, either directly or by implication and innuendo. They spoke to the press whenever Iran's judiciary or security services issued statements about me; they undermined the conclusions that the Ministry of Intelligence wished to draw from the *In the Name of Democracy* broadcast. Shaul pointedly addressed each of the falsehoods in the *Kayhan* article.

Shaul was particularly anxious to prevent a show trial and to discredit such a trial even before it had begun. He could not think of a major political trial under the Islamic Republic in which the accused was found innocent. Rather, a trial was synonymous with a finding of guilt. Judging by the manipulation of my remarks in the television "interview," he feared they would produce a "confession" in court. In a June 27 op-ed in the *New York Times*, he warned that a trial based on false confessions seemed imminent. "No one, in Iran or elsewhere, believes these coerced statements," he wrote. "They only make the regime look inhumane."

My lawyer, Shirin Ebadi, generated considerable press coverage as well. When Shaul first spoke to her by telephone, she had stressed the impossible obstacles the Iranian judiciary placed before lawyers in political cases. "Don't think we can do anything, but we can make noise," she told him. The judicial authorities and intelligence services loathed her; she was outspoken and unafraid, yet since she was a Nobel laureate, they did not dare arrest or silence her.

Shirin was right about the judicial system; it allowed the accused very little recourse to a fair hearing or even legal representation. Matin-Rassekh refused to allow Shirin to meet with me in Evin Prison, refused to allow her to see the file on my case, and refused even to specify the charges against me. Essentially, he barred her from representing or defending me. He also refused to meet with her, and when she was finally able to speak with him by telephone on July 4, he told her in effect that "Haleh Esfandiari does not need a lawyer." But, true to her word, Shirin did make a lot of noise. She announced to the press that I was being denied my legal rights and challenged the accusations against me. On visits to Europe and the United States, she used press conferences and speeches to publicize my case. The media tracked the ongoing story.

My arrest and incarceration earned Iran universally bad press. The *New York Times*, the *Washington Post*, the *Los Angeles Times*, and the *Chicago Tribune* published editorials strongly critical of Iran. Newspapers in Paris, Madrid, and Brazil joined the fray. In the *New York Times*, Thomas Friedman wrote,"This Iranian regime is afraid of its shadow. How do I know? It recently arrested a 67-year-old grandmother, whom it accused of trying to bring down the regime by organizing academic conferences!" Robin Wright wrote an eye-catching profile of me for the *Washington Post*'s Style section. *Glamour* magazine featured my daughter Haleh in a column, "A Daughter's Nightmare." The *Today Show* interviewed her. I never thought

I would be mentioned in the pages of the French fashion magazine *Elle*. Yet I was.

This made holding me increasingly costly for the Iranian government, and it raised doubts in the minds of some officials about the Intelligence Ministry's attempt to construct, on my slight frame, a case of subversion and espionage.

Shaul at times detected these doubts. For example, when listing the accusations against me on May 21 (espionage, actions against the security of the state), the judiciary spokesperson seemed to distance the judiciary from these accusations by describing the Ministry of Intelligence as the "complainant" in the case and implying these were still accusations, not formal charges. As late as August 6, the judiciary's spokesperson said no criminal charges or indictment had yet been brought against me.

Even the Intelligence Ministry seemed at times to be of two minds about me. In June, a ministry official told the press that Tajbakhsh and I "have accepted that they have carried out some activities, but they say their aim was to help," officially suggesting that we were unwitting rather than active participants seeking to topple the Islamic regime.

In prison, I had dismissed the remark of National Security Adviser Larijani that "we don't want to keep her" as mere talk. Shaul, carefully monitoring each official statement, saw signs that some elements in the regime were beginning to back off. Factions in the government seemed to be debating what to do with me. Larijani, in Europe as Iran's chief nuclear negotiator, found to his annoyance that he repeatedly had to answer questions about me when speaking to the press.

Moreover, while the Intelligence Ministry expected some American and international disapproval when they arrested me—Hajj Agha told me as much—they were unprepared for the deluge of prominent international figures who interceded on my behalf, producing an international effort that spanned Europe, the Middle East, and Asia.

Javier Solana, the EU foreign minister, referred to my incarceration on at least two occasions with the Iranians. As part of the EU dialogue with Iran on human-rights issues, the European ambassadors in Tehran formally raised my case and that of several other dual nationals with the Iranian Foreign Ministry twice, in written demarches presented in late June and early August. The Austrian ambassador in Tehran, Michael Postl, was particularly persistent in pursuing my case with the supreme leader's foreign policy adviser.

Strobe Talbott, president of the Brookings Institution and former deputy secretary of state, spoke about me to Japanese prime minister Shinzo Abe when he met with him in Tokyo in May, and Abe's foreign minister spoke to his Iranian counterpart. Martin Indyk, head of the Saban Center at Brookings and a former assistant secretary of state for Near East affairs, raised my case with the foreign minister of Oman.

The *New York Times* Paris bureau chief Elaine Sciolino found herself sitting next to Sidney Blumenthal, a prominent journalist and writer and a former aide to President Bill Clinton, on a flight to Paris. She told him about me and he, in turn, spoke to French foreign minister Bernard Kouchner and urged him to speak to the Iranians. The Iraqi deputy prime minister Barham Salih spoke about me to Iranian officials on a visit to Iran during the late summer. Another friend arranged for an approach to the Turkish foreign minister Abdullah Gul. My friend Barbara Slavin, then of *USA Today*, repeatedly pressed high-level contacts in Iran to do something to get me released. Bush administration deputy undersecretary of state Nicholas Burns raised my case with the Indian foreign minister, who spoke to his Iranian counterpart.

In the end, diplomats from as many as twenty governments around the globe spoke to the Iranian Foreign Ministry. It is reasonable to assume that the supreme leader was informed of at least some of these interventions.

Lee Hamilton also reached out directly to Iranian officials. In February, he wrote a letter to Iranian president Mahmoud Ahmadinejad, urging his intervention in the case, but received no reply or acknowledgment. In May he wrote to the speaker of the Iranian parliament, Gholam Ali Haddad-Adel, and to former president Ali Akbar Hashemi-Rafsanjani. Again, he heard nothing. It was only after he wrote to the Iranian leader, setting in motion his August 7 trip to New York, that there was concrete movement in my case.

❧ An International Civil Society

On the day of my arrest, my Iraqi friend Zainab Al-Suwaij, the president of the American Islamic Congress, told her husband, "I have to do something for Haleh." Two days later, she and her colleagues at the AIC launched the Free Haleh Web site. The Web site rapidly became a principal source for news about me and efforts on my behalf, registering thousands of hits each week. It also started a petition drive calling for my immediate release, which eventually collected nearly 11,500 signatures, from all across the world and especially from Muslim countries, including Iran.

Free Haleh was the most prominent volunteer effort on my behalf, but it was only one of many such initiatives. Through the Internet, an international civil society had come into being, ready to be mobilized in cases like mine. Some of my former students at Princeton got together, located their colleagues all over the world, and signed a letter to the Iranian leader, calling for my release and pointing out that they had learned to love Iran, the Persian language, and Iranian literature in my classes. Middle East scholars, joined by other prominent intellectuals, addressed a letter calling for my release to Khamenei that was published in the *New York Review of Books* in June.

Iraqi and Arab women for whom I had organized workshops signed petitions and contacted their own governments on my behalf. A Syrian friend accosted an astonished Mohammad Javad Larijani, Ali Larijani's brother and a prominent Iranian official himself, at the Davos World Economic Forum. Why, she demanded, was I in jail? At the initiative of Haleh's father-in-law, John Warden Sr., the New York Bar Association produced a detailed legal brief describing the ways in which the Iranian government had violated the Iranian constitution, its own laws, and Iran's international commitments in incarcerating me and denying me legal representation.

The Nobel Women's Initiative, which brings together women winners of Nobel prizes, also wrote to the Iranian government; my close friend Mahnaz Afkhami from the Women's Learning Partnership circulated petitions calling for my release to the thousands of women on her organization's mailing list, as did Nayereh Towhidi, who was involved with several women's and scholarly associations. Amnesty International and Human Rights Watch issued statements; they were among the more than twenty-five nongovernmental organizations to do so. A rabbi in Brazil learned about my case through the efforts of my cousin Goli and urged all 3,000 people on his e-mail list to sign a petition initiated by the Women of Washington, an organization she helped run. I learned that prayers were said for me in synagogues and churches in many places in America. Clare Wolfowitz was instrumental in having a video made of my story in readiness for circulation on the Web. Professors Juan Cole from the University of Michigan and Chibli Mallat from Saint-Joseph University in Beirut and the University of Utah turned down invitations to go to conferences in Iran as long as I was in prison.

Members of Congress also got involved in my case. The two Democratic presidential candidates, Senators Barack Obama and Hillary Rodham Clinton, issued statements calling for my freedom. Senators Barbara Mikulski and Benjamin L. Cardin and Representative Chris Van Hollen of our home state of Maryland sponsored resolutions in the Senate and House that were unanimously approved. All sixteen women members of the Senate, led by Hillary Clinton, wrote a letter to UN secretary general Ban Ki-moon urging him to intervene with the Iranians to secure my freedom.

There were dissenting opinions as well. The Iranian community in the United States was highly supportive, but as always in the tangled politics of an exile community, there are those who oppose any effort to build bridges. Shaul received phone calls—but only two—

from Iranians who actually seemed to relish my arrest. "I am happy your wife is in jail," one anonymous caller told him. Particularly hurtful was a *New York Times* op-ed by an older, former student of mine published while I was still in Evin Prison. Under the title of "Prisoner of Her Desires," the author, an advocate of punitive sanctions and military threats against Iran, used my arrest as a prop to argue his own case, suggesting that I had received my just deserts for having naively advocated dialogue with the Iranians. But these were the exceptions.

It is impossible to judge with certainty the effect of this international effort on my behalf, but it is difficult to believe that it did not have an impact. The public outcry surely strengthened the hand of moderates in the regime, who saw no profit in holding me, against the hard-liners who wished to make an example of me. The Intelligence Ministry sought to persuade a mass audience that it had a strong case in claiming American schemes for a "velvet revolution" in Iran. But even its allies in the press judged its propaganda efforts a flop.

At the very least, the international effort on my behalf hastened my release. But perhaps far more important, if the Intelligence Ministry was toying with the idea of a show trial, international attention and condemnation of Iran's behavior made sure such a trial—and its possibly fatal outcome—never took place.

10.

FREEDOM

In the days after my release, I gloried in my freedom and took pleasure in small things: sleeping in a clean bed with ironed sheets, being able to turn off a bedside lamp and sleep in soothing darkness, looking into a mirror again, wearing my own slippers instead of plastic prison slippers. I did not have to see, first thing in the morning, a toilet that was a filthy hole in the ground. I took immense joy in wearing ironed clothes, sipping coffee while chatting with my mother at the breakfast table, putting on perfume. I no longer had to wait with pleading eyes for Ja'fari to hand me his cell phone to make a thirty-second call to my mother. I could talk to Shaul, Hayedeh, Haleh, and anyone else I wished with no one standing by to monitor my conversation. If I wanted fresh air, all I had to do was step out on the balcony of the apartment. I did not have to negotiate for an extra five or ten minutes outdoors. I felt I was giving in to wild abandon.

Three days after my release I joined an extended family gathering for a lunch organized by a cousin. I had gone to the hairdresser, and although my clothes were two sizes too large due to my weight loss, I felt coiffed and neat as

I basked in the affection and concern of my close-knit family. Was I physically mistreated? Did I need a doctor? Was I sleeping well? Was I eating enough? All the cousins remarked on my weight loss, and everyone wanted to feed me. My eyes ran over a buffet laden with food: a huge tray of chicken and meat kabob; an assortment of stews; salads; and trays of rice with cherries and saffron, with lima beans and dill, with almonds, pistachios, and red slivers of orange peel. Only four days ago, I was forcing myself to eat bread and cheese, sitting alone at a child's desk in a prison cell.

Meeting with My Lawyers

The next logical step was to meet with my lawyer, Shirin Ebadi, who had officially been representing me since my arrest in May, although the Intelligence Ministry had successfully prevented any contact between us. Early one morning I took a cab to her apartment on a street off Yusefabad Shomali Avenue in northwest Tehran. From the cab window, I saw her familiar figure at the apartment door. Barely five feet tall, compactly built, she stood with her feet planted firmly on the ground, as if to say, "Here I stand; you're going to have to deal with me." She had used her Nobel Prize money to set up the Center for the Defense of Human Rights, and along with two other lawyers who also worked pro bono, she represented political prisoners like me. Practical and pragmatic, she insisted only that the Iranian government adhere to its own laws, constitution, and international undertakings.

I ran to meet her and we embraced. I wanted to shower her with gratitude. But she was all business. As we paced on the sidewalk, since we both knew her office was bugged, she queried me about the conditions of my incarceration, my prison cell, methods of interrogation, questions I had been asked, papers I had signed, how Matin-Rassekh had dealt with me—all the details important for a human-rights lawyer. Later, at her center, I signed powers of attorney for Shirin and her two partners. She would continue to represent me. The Intelligence Ministry, which had not yet closed my case, could still summon me to trial, and the lien on my mother's apartment remained in their hands.

That evening Ja'fari called. He had been telephoning me regularly since my release five days earlier, ostensibly to chat but in fact to keep tabs on me. He asked whether I had met with Shirin or signed any papers. He was obviously spying on me. I had met with Shirin, I told him, and signed papers appointing her my attorney. It was an act of defiance on my part, and I meant for Ja'fari to know that.

❧ On the Streets

I was out of Evin but I was still in limbo. I worried lest hard-liners in the Intelligence Ministry succeed in reversing the decision to release me or in preventing me from leaving the country. The danger was real. *Kayhan* spoke for the faction in the security services that was unhappy that I was free and that the opportunity to make an example of me was slipping away. I tried to maintain a low profile and stay indoors as much as possible. I gave no interviews. I avoided being too much on the streets because I feared being run down in a fatal traffic "accident" or being kidnapped, or disappearing in some other unexpected way.

But I still needed to get a new national identity card, and I decided to resume my habit of daily walks, either with cousins or friends. It was summer, and I thought I could hide behind a pair of large sunglasses. But I was surprised to find, whenever I took a cab from the taxi stand at the corner of our street, that the owner knew me, as did several of his drivers. They had seen me on Iranian TV or heard of me on the BBC, Radio Israel, the Voice of America, or the American-run Radio Farda, broadcasts that Iranians listened to for the accurate news they could not get from Iranian radio and television. While I sat in the backseat, the drivers would talk: how much weight I had lost, they would say; and how concerned they had been for my mother; and why doesn't she leave Iran? What brought me back to this "cursed land"? The antipathy to the government they displayed surprised me. Had those "beasts" tortured me? One asked me matter-of-factly whether the allegations that I was a spy and a Zionist agent were true. "If there was a shred of truth in these allegations, they would have barbecued me," I told him. None of the drivers wanted to accept my money. "You are our guest," they insisted, and we would have a long back-and-forth before they allowed me to pay the fare.

The cobbler on my mother's street leaped to his feet the first time I walked by his shoe stand. "Hajj Khanum," he said, addressing me with an honorific. "We were so worried for you. I can't afford to give you flowers, but I prayed for you."

When I entered a fruit shop in my mother's neighborhood, the greengrocer was so astonished to see me he dropped the tomatoes he was weighing and sent them rolling across the floor. Recovering, he cried out to his shop assistant, "See what Khanum Esfandiari needs. Give her the good fruit from the back." (Iranian grocers traditionally hide their choicest fruit in the back of the store, reserving it for their best customers.) A woman in a black chador gave me a big smile and said, "We are so happy you are out. May God burn them in hell."

"Inshallah," added the greengrocer. God willing.

At a government registry office where I had some business, the woman clerk behind the desk took one look at me and said in a whisper, "Haleh Esfandiari! Welcome. We are so proud of you." A man came over with his cell phone and asked permission to take a picture with me.

Four girls headed for the student dormitory on the corner of Mother's street recognized me one afternoon as I was going to the supermarket. One of them stopped to hug me. "You are a role model for us," she said, and added, "You are so thin; I could feel all your bones." It was a moving moment for me. All the propaganda of the Islamic Republic had not convinced these young women that I was a villain; instead, they were on my side. They understood what I had gone through; they realized that under interrogation, I had not chosen the easy way out. I felt vindicated, able to walk with my head held high.

Many of these people had seen me on *In the Name of Democracy*. My numerous encounters with strangers on the street suggested that the footage of the Ukrainian and Georgian "velvet revolutions" had exactly the opposite effect than the one the government had intended. More than one person came up to me to say that the protests, demonstrations, and fair elections they observed, and the "velvet revolutions" themselves, hadn't seemed such a bad thing after all. One man approached me and said, "Hajj Khanum, if you ran as a candidate for president you would be elected." As I later told Ja'fari, "You only succeeded in making me the cow with a white forehead," a Persian expression meaning, You made me stand out, turned me into a celebrity.

Ja'fari's Frantic Phone Call

Ja'fari called again on the evening of Thursday, August 30, almost a week after my release from Evin. My heart fell when I heard his elongated *salaaaam*, but this turned out to be the call I was praying for. "The *aghayun* [the gentlemen] have decided you can leave the country," he said. He wanted to know if my paperwork at the passport office was complete. I had filed all the necessary application forms and supporting documents with the passport office in January, I told him. "The only thing that stands between me and my passport is a clearance from the Intelligence Ministry." He didn't appreciate my sarcasm. "Meet me first thing Saturday morning at the passport office," he said. He sounded like a man in a hurry.

Hajj Agha also called. "You will get your passport Saturday morning. You should leave Saturday night," he said. Having kept me in the country for eight months, these men were suddenly forcing me out. I could only guess why: now that the decision to send me home had been made, they feared attacks from a hard-line newspaper like

Kayhan for letting me go. President Ahmadinejad was going to New York at the end of September for the opening of the United Nations General Assembly, and the government didn't want him to be hounded by questions about me and Tajbakhsh.

Mother and I spent an anxious weekend at home. I was still on pins and needles lest something go wrong. I slept fitfully Thursday and Friday night. On Saturday morning, I woke up very early to make it for my eight o'clock appointment at the passport office. At seven, the telephone rang. It was Ja'fari. He sounded frantic. "*Kojayin?*" he said. Where are you? "*Parvandeh nist!*" There is no file! My file had probably "disappeared" because agents of the Intelligence Ministry had themselves removed it to stop me from securing a passport and leaving the country clandestinely. The ministry's left hand did not know what its right hand was doing.

I grabbed my folder of important papers and rushed to the passport office. Ja'fari and passport chief Torabi were waiting for me. I gave Torabi my papers and two hours later he handed me my passport, setting some kind of a record for rapid passport delivery. Both he and Ja'fari suggested I leave that evening. But I needed an Austrian visa and the embassy was closed, since it was Saturday; the next Austrian Airlines flight was not until Monday, anyway.

The next morning, Mutti went herself to the Austrian embassy in my stead to pick up my visa. We were worried that something untoward would happen to me in the last thirty-six hours; Ja'fari's and Hajj Agha's own haste to see me go was hardly reassuring. Both Mutti and I were straddling two emotional worlds at the same time: elation that my ordeal was over, and gnawing anxiety that it was not.

I had decided to spend a few days in Vienna before returning to America. I needed time alone with Shaul, away from the media spotlight. Shaul and I had married in Vienna and I had close friends there from my university days. I wanted to sit in a Viennese café with Hayedeh and stroll the city's streets. My dearest Viennese friend, Ute Sassadek, had already moved to her country house, leaving her apartment to Shaul and me.

One Last Interview

On the Tuesday afternoon that Hajj Agha showed up at Evin Prison to tell me I was free to go, he "requested" that I do one more interview that they could film. He assured me that it would take the form of a friendly chat, with me appearing as a *karshenas*, an expert. He praised the interviewer, Morteza Haydari, as knowledgeable and "the Larry King of Iran." I did not think it wise to refuse, and I knew I could stick to banalities and refuse to answer anything that smacked of propaganda, à la *In the Name of Democracy*.

On the night of my departure, at seven in the evening, Ja'fari picked me up at my mother's apartment for the drive to the TV studio. I purposely decked myself out in my best "Islamic" dress. I wore a white robe and a light beige scarf; I put on makeup. "You look chic," Ja'fari said. I sat next to him on the front seat, only barely able to disguise my feeling of revulsion. We made small talk as we made our way to Seda va Sima, the studios of the Voice and Vision of the Islamic Republic of Iran.

Inside, Iran's Larry King, lacking suspenders or tie, was waiting for me. The bearded, disheveled man present at the *In the Name of Democracy* interview was also there. Haydari tried to impress me. He told me he had interviewed many famous people, including the Nicaraguan president and Sandinista leader Daniel Ortega.

The cameras started rolling and Haydari began to discuss United States policy in Iraq and Afghanistan, Palestine and Lebanon and the Middle East. I realized he liked to talk and to impress his interviewees and audience. I gave brief answers to his paragraph-long questions and encouraged him to comment at length on the issues he was raising. The disheveled minder appeared displeased again. He had wanted talk of soft revolutions, the conspiracies of the American government and U.S. think tanks, and the villainies of George Soros. But Iran's Larry King was focused on other issues. In half an hour or less, the interview was over. I said good-bye to Haydari, thankful he had done most of the talking, and flashed a smile at the bearded man.

He glared back; I thought he could have strangled both me and my interviewer.

As far as I know, the interview was never broadcast. The Intelligence Ministry had made a last stab at getting me to endorse their conspiratorial worldview, and it hadn't succeeded.

✥ A Present from "the Boys"

Ja'fari drove me home. Before saying good-bye he reached into the trunk of his car. He had a farewell present for me from the *bacheh-ha*, "the boys," meaning his Intelligence Ministry colleagues. He handed me a large, beautiful inlaid box. There was something heavy in it. "What is it?" I asked. "You will see," he replied, and drove off.

Back in the apartment Mutti and I opened the box. Inside was a handsome, leather-bound volume of the poetry of Hafez, Iran's great fourteenth-century poet. Iranians memorize his verses, and they open his book at random at important turning points in life to receive guidance on critical decisions. Hafez happened to be my favorite poet. In Evin I would recite to myself those of his poems my grandmother had taught me or that I had memorized in my youth.

I examined this curious gift, turning over and over in my mind its intended meaning. It was truly bizarre. The Intelligence Ministry was sending a message: "No hard feelings. Let's be friends.

"Never mind that we kept you away from your family, your work, your friends, and your home for eight months. Never mind that you nearly died of fright the night of the robbery and your mother nearly died of fright the night we raided her apartment. Never mind that we violated your privacy and filmed you in bed in your nightgown. Forget the months of senseless, grueling interrogations. We kept you in solitary confinement for 105 days in Evin Prison, but don't give that another thought. No hard feelings. So what if we took your mother's home as bail before we let you go? It's the way we play the game. We will never close your case; we will leave the threat of indictment and trial hanging over you forever. We won't lift the bail on your mother's apartment. But we are sending you home, and giving you Hafez as a good-bye present to show you how much we care for you, and to say, once again, 'No hard feelings.' "

Farewell to Mutti

It was already ten at night, just hours before my departure for the airport and my flight. Mutti sat with me in my room as I threw my few pieces of clothing into a suitcase. I took a last look around my room. I wanted to imprint every detail on my mind: the pink-striped easy chairs, the inlaid wood-carved table Father had brought back with him from one of his trips to Pakistan, the sofa and cushions covered with Persian kilims, the paintings and family pictures on the wall.

I knew there would be no return in the foreseeable future for me—not as long as these people were in power. I knew I could never visit Mother in Iran again. She would not hear of it; she would rather stay alone and suffer the separation than have me or Hayedeh risk a visit. Nor would Mutti leave Iran to live with one of us. My father exercised the greater pull on her. She wanted to be buried at his side. I apologized, needlessly, for having put her through this crisis. She wiped away my tears. We both had to be strong, she said.

It was time to leave.

Three friends came for me at around two in the morning. Mutti held up the Quran and I passed under it. From a jug, she splashed water on the hallway floor to ensure I had a safe journey. I kissed her one last time and hurried down the staircase. Outside on the street, I looked up; the open window framed her small face; she leaned out to take one last look at me. We waved, blew kisses, whispered good-bye. The street was dark and quiet in that early-morning hour and the August air cool, not frigid like the last time.

We didn't take the fastest route, avoiding the highway I had taken eight months earlier. We drove through the city streets. I was quiet and pensive. This might be the last time I would see the city where I was born, and which I had always loved. I took in the streetlights, the buildings, all the familiar and unfamiliar landmarks. We passed by Tehran University and the Azadi Tower; I caught a glimpse of the new Milad Tower, which, when finished, would be Tehran's tallest building. Near the airport, I saw families, some with children, picnicking along the pavement and on the grass along the street while waiting for their passengers to arrive from abroad: Iranians eating, chatting, being together, following age-old traditions, even though it was two in the morning. Inside the airport building, there were large crowds, pushing, standing on tiptoes, bouquets in hand waiting for arriving relatives.

We went, as arranged, to a special lounge, where you pay a little extra for expedited customs and passport procedures. In my last telephone conversation with Hajj Agha, I had insisted Ja'fari be at the airport; I didn't want some last-minute hitch or some rogue operators barring my departure, hauling me off to prison again. "Another sleepless night because of you," Ja'fari said, as if I were to blame for the conundrum they were now in a hurry to end. As we waited, I only half heard Ja'fari's attempt at small talk until the call to board the aircraft came over the loudspeaker.

I embraced my friends, walked through the metal detector, held up my hands for body inspection, and headed down a hall leading to a long corridor to the plane. Ja'fari could not accompany me farther. He walked rather alongside me on the other side of a glass wall that separated passengers from non-passengers for the full length of the hall. For about a hundred paces we walked like this, in lockstep, as if still bound together, with only the glass wall between us. Finally, my path took a sharp turn left; Ja'fari remained standing there. I was rid of him at last.

I took my seat and called Mutti on my cell phone. I told her I had boarded and would call her from Vienna. I would not really feel safe until the aircraft had taken off, crossed the Iranian border. But there was an unexpected delay. The hostess and the ground crew kept on going up and down the aisle and counting the passengers: once, twice, three times, five times. The pilot announced that there was a missing passenger; we would have to disembark if he or she were not found. We sat on the tarmac for another thirty minutes. Finally, they solved the mystery: a small child who had been assigned a seat had been in his mother's arms. The hostess secured the plane door and I heard it click shut. This time, the sound of a door closing signaled my return to my family, my friends, and my freedom.

EPILOGUE

In September 2008, almost exactly a year after I had returned home, I received a formal-looking envelope from the Iranian Mission to the United Nations in New York. Inside was an invitation from the ambassador to a reception for President Ahmadinejad, who was going to be in the city for the opening session of the UN General Assembly. The irony was overwhelming. The very government that a year earlier had branded me a spy, an agent of Mossad and the CIA, an enabler of "soft revolution," and a threat to national security was inviting me to appear in the same room with the Iranian president and perhaps to engage with him in idle chatter as he circulated among his guests. But I should not have been surprised. Iran's leaders are heedless of the damage they do to their own citizens and the havoc they inflict on the lives of individuals and families. They assume everyone else is as indifferent to basic human decency as they. They pretend to forget what they did to me—and the worse torment they inflicted on countless others. But I cannot forget.

. . .

On my way home from Iran after my release, I spent four days in Vienna, alone with Shaul and Hayedeh. After eight months of suppressing my feelings, calculating every word and weighing every move, I needed time to unwind. By the time we returned to Washington, I was ready to face the world. I held a press conference and gave many television, radio, and newspaper and magazine interviews.

I knew the best therapy for me was work and a return to my normal routine. I arrived home on a Thursday; I was back at work on Monday morning. I had to prove to myself and my family and friends that I was the same Haleh, and that Evin had not broken my spirit or my will. Besides, I had been jailed, accused, and hounded by the Iranian Intelligence Ministry because of my Wilson Center activities. I wanted to send a message to Ja'fari, Hajj Agha, and their bosses that they could not cow me. I would continue doing exactly what I had been doing in the past.

Ja'fari telephoned me almost immediately after my arrival in Vienna and then again, about a week later, in Washington. He inquired insistently after my health. In Evin, he and Hajj Agha had been indifferent to my physical well-being. Now that I was out of their hands, they were alarmed lest I experience a relapse or tell the world of the physical damage solitary confinement had done to me. Ja'fari was aware I was giving interviews and had written an account of my incarceration for the *Washington Post* and had coauthored an essay for the *Chronicle of Higher Education*. He was worried as to what I might say. After these early phone calls and a couple of e-mails, however, I never heard from him again.

In those early weeks, I remained physically frail and psychologically fragile. The slightest noise would make me jump; a stranger at the door caused me panic. "You're home; you're safe. They cannot touch you here," Shaul would say. But I could not shake off the feeling that my interrogators were still at my heels; their eight-month intrusion into my life still haunted me.

I began to heal. I recovered the weight I had lost. I threw myself into my work and returned to a full schedule in the Middle East Program. I went back to my daily routine at my gym, exercising not in the manic Evin way, but in the old way—measured, tempered, and alongside friends. I took strength from the embrace of my family and the warm welcome of my Wilson Center colleagues.

I was overwhelmed by the support I received. Cards, flowers, and chocolates arrived from friends and from people I did not know. I received a poem one of our oldest friends had written for me while I was in Evin, "I Have a Friend There Too." A colleague at the Wilson Center sent me Maya Angelou's "Phenomenal Woman." As in Tehran, I was stopped in supermarkets, malls, and cafés, on the Metro, and on the streets by strangers who recognized me. They came up to say they were happy to see me back and that they had prayed for me. The words "welcome home" took on a new meaning for me. And everyone was concerned about Mutti. Even today, the first question I am asked if I am recognized or introduced to someone new is "How is your mother doing?"

Mother is doing well. At ninety-five, she is, as ever, a woman of indomitable spirit. Since Hayedeh and I could not risk returning to Iran, we both traveled to the Persian Gulf sheikhdom of Abu Dhabi in November 2008, and Mutti met us there. The trip, though short, was still difficult for her. Iranians all, we had to meet on foreign soil; but for three days we took pleasure in one another and in our reunion. She worries, of course. True to form, the Islamic Republic has not brought closure to my case; nor has it lifted the lien on Mutti's apartment, leaving both hanging like a sword of Damocles over my head.

I still have nightmares about Evin. I sometimes wake up not knowing where I am. The birds chirping at five in the morning outside our Potomac home bewilder me; I think I am hearing the birds chirping at dawn outside Evin Prison. The scars of prison never really heal. I have discovered that the confidence one once had in the basic stability of things never returns; once experienced, the fear of power-bloated men who think they can do with you what they will is never fully erased.

But I have grown wiser and more appreciative not only of the material comforts I unthinkingly enjoy every day—a leisurely cup of coffee, a moment in the sunlight, the reassuring touch of Shaul's hand on mine—but of the freedom with which I am blessed.

I have come to value with every fiber in my body the freedom to speak, think, read, and associate with others; I appreciate as never before the idea of government subject to the rule of law. Autocrats and dictators may bring order and stability; but in the end, not answerable to the will of the people or anyone else, they grow reckless, trampling on human freedom and individual rights, wrecking their societies and their countries.

In every talk I have given since my return, I have reminded my audience of these common truths; and I have emphasized the need for all of us to speak out against governments and rulers who consider themselves above the law, who prey on their unprotected citizens. I was fortunate that my imprisonment captured worldwide attention; I owe my freedom to those who took up my cause. But what of others? We need to find more effective ways to be heard and to mobilize international opinion for the many thousands of prisoners of conscience around the world who are imprisoned, terrorized, tortured, and raped, yet have no one to speak for them.

I have lost none of my devotion to Iran, even though I never had much affection for its current government. I continue to believe—or hope—that I will someday return to an Iran whose government is subject to the rule of law and whose leaders respect the rights of their citizens and treat them with decency.

I continue to believe that the governments of Iran and the United States should sit at the same table and talk to each other. Thirty years of estrangement have yielded nothing of value, and I believe that change is more likely to come to an Iran that is engaged with the rest of the world rather than isolated from it.

When I returned home in September 2007, my reunion with my daughter, Haleh, and my grandchildren, Ariana and Karenna, was particularly emotional for me. All three met me on the front lawn of our house in Potomac. Haleh had managed to keep them thinking about me, but to shield them from the story of my imprisonment. At the age of four and six, they wouldn't understand why their grandmother was in jail. After I embraced them both and sat them on my knees, my youngest grandchild, Karenna, said, addressing me in her usual way, "Mamma Joon, don't you ever go away for such a long time again."

"No," I whispered to her. "I won't."

ACKNOWLEDGMENTS

I would not have been released from Evin Prison and allowed to leave Iran had it not been for the efforts of my husband, Shaul Bakhash; my daughter, Haleh Bakhash; my mother, Fanny Esfandiari; and my sister, Hayedeh Oviedo. For eight months they worked ceaselessly to gain my freedom. They were supported by tens of thousands of people from across the world: friends, colleagues, politicians, journalists, intellectuals, and ordinary citizens who added their voices to the campaign to free me.

I was fortunate to work at the Woodrow Wilson International Center for Scholars, where we all are one family. I am grateful to Lee Hamilton and Mike Van Dusen, the unsung hero of this saga who worked behind the scenes to push hard for my release. I also thank Sam Wells, Cynthia Aronson, Blair Ruble, Philippa Strum, Robert Hathaway, Christian Ostermann, Geoffrey Dabelko, Andrew Selee, Paulo Sotero, and the directors of other programs and projects at the center, and my colleagues and staff at the Wilson Center who for four months worked tirelessly to assure my return. Wilson Center board chairman, Joseph Gildenhorn, tapped every connection he could in the United States and abroad to facilitate my release.

I feel a special debt to my colleague and friend Robert

Litwak, who made sure every scrap of paper that was needed from the Wilson Center found its way to Shaul and to me in Tehran. My former assistant, Azucena Rodriguez, worked unremittingly to provide all the information about the Middle East Program that my interrogators demanded, and maintained the Middle East Program while I was gone. My previous assistants at the center, Jillian Frumkin and Julia Bennett, helped identify work we had done many years earlier. William Green Miller spoke on my behalf with Ambassadors Javad Zarif and Mohammad Khazaee at the Iranian Mission to the United Nations.

Sharon McCarter, the head of outreach and communications at the Wilson Center, headed an extraordinary team to keep the American and international press up to date on my ordeal. In this, she was ably assisted by Erin Mosely, Vicki Dodson, and others. My sister, Hayedeh, handled the European press. My former colleague Ben Rhodes was helpful in more ways than I can count, and my colleague and friend David Hawxhurst assisted me in putting together the photographs for the book.

I cannot adequately thank the advisory group that was formed to help the Wilson Center in its efforts to free me. Cheryl Benard put out the Free Haleh bumper sticker, circulated a petition at the summer 2007 Vienna conference of Women Leaders Networking for Peace and Security in the Middle East, and raised my case with several influential people. Melanne Verveer, from Vital Voices Global Partnership, committed her organization to my support. Henri Barkey represented us in a meeting with Kofi Annan in Geneva. Tara Sonnenshine was persistent in coming up with ideas for new initiatives. Clare Wolfowitz worked with a team consisting of filmmakers Jeff Kaufman, John Langley, Tyne Daly, Autumn Mason, and Nick Kirgo to produce a TV video on me and my work.

Friends outside the center put into motion a highly effective machinery to publicize my case. Zainab Al-Suwaij, the executive director of the American Islamic Congress, and her colleague Nasser Weddady set up the Free Haleh Web site and collected more than ten thousand signatures, including signatures from courageous residents in Iran.

I am indebted to my former students at Princeton, who signed a letter to Iranian leader Ayatollah Khamenei. Cherry, Erin, Parinaz, and Jonathan formed the core group, located their former classmates all over the world, and hand-carried the letter to the Iranian Mission to the United Nations in New York. My thanks also go to my friends and colleagues in Princeton—Andras Hamori, Leon Carl Brown, and Hossein Moddaressi—and to Shaul's colleagues at George Mason University for their efforts and advice.

I owe special thanks to my lawyer, Nobel laureate Shirin Ebadi, who mobilized other women who had won the Nobel Peace Prize to speak for me, wrote to the UN secretary-general, and publicized my case in numerous interviews with the international press. My good friend and relative Mahnaz Afkhami, the president of Women's Learning Partnership, and Nayereh Tohidi mobilized women's groups. On every possible occasion, Swanee Hunt, Carla Kopell, and Alma Gildenhorn reminded people of my incarceration.

My Arab women friends set up support groups and worked for my freedom in various Arab capitals. My special thanks go to Hind Kawabat, Rola Dashti, Fatima Sbaity Kassem, and the businesswomen I met in conferences in the Middle East. Amal Kashef al-Qita and several other Iraqi women lent their voices to the call for my freedom.

I am also grateful for the friendship, efforts, and concern of the members of my reading group: Jacqui, Clare, Gisella, Rachel, Susan, and Joan. As a gesture of solidarity, they agreed not to meet in my absence.

Ali Banu Azizi and Hormoz Hekmat were instrumental in drawing up, circulating, and securing signatures for the petition issued by the Middle East Studies Association. Robert Silvers, the editor who led the effort of the *New York Review of Books*, published the petition and encouraged several prominent intellectuals to sign it. Karim Sajjadpour was a source of sound advice and unfailing support. I will never forget the grace of Juan Cole and Chibli Mallat, who refused to attend academic conferences in Iran as long as I remained in prison.

At the initiative of John Warden Sr., the New York Bar Association issued a detailed brief on my case.

Many close friends steadfastly stood by us at this difficult time. Farrokh and Guity, and Shahrzad and Reza were Shaul's closest confidantes, and provided unstinting support and homes where he could unwind and share his thoughts. Reza helped Shaul monitor the international and Iranian press and devise strategies for dealing with the attacks on me by Iranian media and Iranian officials. Farideh shared her personal experiences with Shaul and helped him analyze government statements about me.

Strobe Talbott, Martin Indyk, Barham Salih, Nicholas Burns, and Susie Nemazi and her husband, Sir Peter Westmacott, interceded on my behalf with foreign diplomats and statesmen, as did Secretary of State Madeleine Albright. Michael Postl and Peter Launsky-Tieffenthal of the Austrian Foreign Ministry went out of their way to be of assistance. Bonnie McElveen-Hunter, the chairman of the board of the American Red Cross, sought permission for the International Red Cross to visit me. Senators Barack Obama and Hillary Clinton issued statements calling for my release, and Senator Clinton also mobilized other women in the Senate to urge UN Secretary-General Ban Ki-moon to intercede on my behalf. Senators Barbara Mikulsky and Ben Cardin and Congressman Chris Van Hollen of Maryland sponsored the Senate and House resolutions that called for my release. Alan Makovsky did the staff work on the House resolution.

My special thanks to Joe Reeder, Robert Destro, Marshall Breger, and their colleagues for suggesting and helping shape the letter addressed to the Iran's supreme leader that played a decisive role in my eventual release.

Barbara Slavin, Elaine Sciolino, Elizabeth Farnsworth, and Ute Sassadek were journalists who not only wrote about me but also used their contacts to urge my release. Ute and Heidi Schmidt were instrumental in involving Austrian president Heinz Fischer in my case. I am grateful to numerous other journalists from America to Pakistan and Brazil to Spain who wrote about me and helped keep my case alive.

I also owe thanks to my brother, Siamak, and my cousins, Gilan and Goli, Mina, Nahid, Vahid, and Sohrab for their steadfast support; to Lili, the believer in the family who didn't stop praying for me; and to my son-in-law, John Warden; and my brother-in-law, Patrick Oviedo, whose lives were put on hold for eight months because their wives were so busy trying to get me out.

Then there are the wonderful friends and relatives in Iran who for eight months provided me and my mother with comfort and courage. They know that I am indebted to each one of them and why I refrain from mentioning their names.

A blanket thanks to the many leaders of human-rights organizations who spoke on my behalf, circulated petitions, and sponsored a vigil in New York. I wish especially to thank Elise Auerbach of Amnesty International and Hadi Ghaemi of Human Rights Watch and all those attended the New York vigil, as well as those across the country and around the world who remembered me in their prayers in churches, synagogues, and mosques. My daughter's law school classmate, Corinne Richardson, went around New York City getting people to sign the Free Haleh petition—even people she came across in a shoe store. I know of many similar instances of volunteer work and am thankful to the perfect strangers who took up my cause. *Glamour* magazine editor Cindi Leive took up my cause. Christiane Amanpour featured me in a special broadcast on CNN.

I owe special thanks to my neighbors in Potomac, Maryland, who showed discretion and care when they were approached by the press, and who welcomed me home on my return. I feel fortunate to live among them.

I thank the organizations that honored me with awards and recognition after my release. I have tried to answer every card and phone call I received, but am sure I missed many. I know that I am back with my family because of their prayers and support.

Barbara Slavin, Michael Ross, Aaron David Miller, Shahrzad and Reza Ghotbi, and Jack Censer read the manuscript and gave me the benefit of their insights and advice.

My literary agent, Scott Moyers, not only ably represented me but has been a friend, offering sound advice at every stage as this book was written and took shape. Lee Boudreaux, my editor at Ecco, offered excellent editorial advice and helped me pare down a long manuscript, resulting in a leaner, sparer book. Abigail Holstein shepherded the book through the press. I also owe thanks to Ecco's publisher, Dan Halpern, and to Michael McKenzie, Rachel Bressler, Mary Austin Speaker, Allison Saltzman, David Koral, and Mary Ann Petyak, who were involved in the copyediting, design, production, and promotion of this book.

This has not been an easy memoir to write, and I am not sure I could have finished it without the encouragement of my daughter and my husband. Shaul kept me company night after night until the late hours while I was writing and reliving these frightening experiences. He discussed every phase of the book with me, and sat through my agony, anger, and tears. His extraordinary patience and love pushed me past the final lines of the book.